MY
SEARCH
FOR THE
MESSIAH

MY SEARCH FOR THE MESSIAH

Studies and Wanderings in Israel and America

MARK JAY MIRSKY

MACMILLAN PUBLISHING CO., INC.

NEW YORK

Portions of this book first appeared in *The Village Voice* under the following titles: "Our Greatest Sage —Elegy for Harry Wolfson" (January 13, 1976, page 39), "To Show the World How Crazy We Are" (May 30, 1974, page 10), "Why Did I Go to Israel" (May 9, 1974, page 13). Reprinted by permission of *The Village Voice*. Copyright © The Village Voice, Inc., 1974-5.

Macmillan Publishing Co., Inc.
866 Third Avenue, New York, N.Y. 10022
Collier Macmillan Canada, Ltd.

Library of Congress Cataloging in Publication Data

Mirsky, Mark.
   My search for the Messiah.
    1. Judaism—United States—Addresses, essays, lectures. 2. Israel—Social life and customs. 3. Mirsky, Mark—Religion and ethics. I. Title.
BM205.M55   296'.092'4 [B]   76-54910
ISBN 0-02-585120-9

FIRST PRINTING 1977

Printed in the United States of America

I would like to express my thanks to Rabbi Stephen C. Lerner for his help in editing this manuscript, and to its three mothers, Regina Ryan, Betty Anne Clarke, and Amanda Vaill. Many of the other debts of gratitude are acknowledged in the text itself, but special mention has to be made of Nahum N. Glatzer's *In Time and Eternity*, a handbook of Rabbinic references which is an invaluable primer. Ben Zion Gold, who continues to unravel difficult knots in the Jewish tradition for me, gave me a copy at Harvard and for eighteen years now it has remained a well-thumbed companion.

Contents

x Contents

1
Opening Questions

On the High Seas

VVVVV

SOME TIME AGO, while boarding a vessel that chugs between the Canaries, I encountered four creatures of myth. In the jargon of the age, they were archetypes—perfect stand-ins for the typical Jewish parents, uncles, aunts of my generation —or, more accurately, of the one just after mine. Two couples, about age fifty, were arguing vociferously with the ship's stewards, at the bottom of the gangplank, making the kind of righteous noise about being let on immediately, *regardless* of the *ridiculous* rules, that I recognized as not only native Jewish-English but the particular nuance of my adopted city, New York. Without specifically revealing my kinship as a Hebrew, I commiserated with them in such a way that later that evening, as I was strolling into the third-class lounge to which the steward, eyeing my mop of hair, had assigned me without even asking to see my ticket, I received a tap on the shoulder from that white-jacketed eminence, who informed me that some people requested my presence in the first-class dining room. I followed dutifully and was greeted by these four, who wanted to know if I had eaten, pressed drinks on me, and behaved, in general, as if I were a family prodigal from Westchester or Long Island.

"You're Jewish, right?" one of the men asked, winking. I nodded, and since they were pressing bread-and-butter Judaism on me, the milk of human kindness, charity to a stranger, I thought I would reciprocate with a flask of my own. They (an engineer and a businessman, a woman psychologist and a housewife) were a bit surprised to learn that I was closer to them in age than they had expected, and what's more, that I was not only a professor at City College but interested in their "Jewishness." It was that itch in me to go beyond the pleasant, slightly smug smile of recognition between cousins, to define the relationship, to discover how "Jewish" they were and what they meant by this, or if indeed they had thought about it at all. Were we just related by blood or did we have a common imagination?

I told them I wrote books about the Boston Jewish world. Without further ado they began to spill out horror tales of vulgar suburban synagogues, bad experiences in Hebrew schools and with preparation for bar mitzvahs. They were intelligent people, educated and earnest, and I shook my head sympathetically at their accounts of venal boards of directors who came to their front door to sign them up for the local congregation armed with Dun and Bradstreet profiles and of the hysterical audience of Westchester Jews come to shout down an Israeli leftist at a Methodist church where he had been scheduled to speak, to the outrage of his fellow tribesmen, on the night after the holiday of Yom Kippur.

Then slowly, watching the bewilderment that registered on their faces, I began to speak of the Judaism I knew, to unroll the flying carpet of the past on which I hope you will join me in the pages ahead. One of the men resented the narrative I spun, its implications, and I can understand the pain it must have caused him. His children, following his lead, were disaffected, but they had gone the step further that he could not go; they did not identify as Jews. All through the conversation, which went on and on for hours, he kept repeating that despite the fact that he did not believe in God, did not care for any kind of religious involvement, knew nothing of the Jewish past, he *was* Jewish. And I agreed. He was. His anger, his rebellion, they were of that mysterious *geshmack*, taste, that *is* Jewish. Just the tone of his voice at the bottom of the gangplank marked him as the querulous, ever argumentative Jew. But his children? Could they inherit much more than a tone of voice? He was angry. He hadn't asked this young man to the table to be lectured, and I saw him moiling with the question. The mystical talk that fascinated the others upset him. He accused me of being an idealist, which he "used to be," but wait and see, "life would teach me better." Finally, he got up and left.

But my tales of the craziness, the dreams, the unbelievable folly of our ancestors in their attempts to grasp the Unknown held the others. They were excited by the idea that only a few hundred years ago most rabbis, in accordance with talmudic law, were not allowed to take compensation, that according to Talmud you could not introduce a law that most of the community could not obey, that many of the radical ideas their children were toying with had been tried before within the Jewish fold. It was a history that was simply unknown to them. Yet how could one answer the question of survival as a Jew, the survival of Judaism, without knowing our history?

This is an incomplete book, probably incoherent in places, full of missing pieces. At times I must beg, as I did that night, that my listeners turn to more competent authorities for answers to specific questions. I write to provoke questions. Many, because they have no sense of the tradition of inquiry, don't know where to begin to ask. And "Ask, ask!" is a much older Jewish injunction than "Eat, eat!"

It began as a journal of a trip to Israel. When I showed that journal to friends, something more than just my narrative excited them. Like the passengers on the boat, they asked questions about Judaism, *my* Judaism. Personal revelations about my difficulties with Jewish education, girl friends, began to mix with more technical material. To explain myself I had to initiate them into the work of such philosophers as Harry Wolfson, the rabbinical storytelling of Rabbi Soloveitchik, the scholarship of Gershom Scholem. I was surprised at how acute their attention was. Perhaps there was a middle class not so entirely asleep in the comfortable suburbs of America, between the sentimental tags of *Fiddler on the Roof* and the world of purely technical scholarship. My auditors didn't want anecdotal portraits, Rabbi Soloveitchik fighting with the butchers of Boston over how kosher the meat was, but information. What was the concept of kosher about? What does it mean, clean and unclean? The story and the law were bound up with one another, as in the Talmud, and the end of telling both was to teach, to learn.

I wanted to learn too. I threw out the title of this book, *My Search for the Messiah*, in an early conversation about the manuscript. I was surprised when it was taken seriously. Yet as I look at what was implicit in the Israeli journal and became explicit as I sifted Wolfson, Soloveitchik, and Scholem, I realized I was hiding from what I was up to in a joke.

Yes, I am searching for the Messiah. The joke is that this overheated postadolescent, this junior Don Quixote, Mark Mirsky, should set out through the vast geographies of Jewish learning to seek the Bride, the Shekinah, the Presence of God. My half of the search is absurd. Not the search itself, though. The Spanish knight made the mistake of leaving his volumes behind. We Jews remain half in the study, half in the world. By the end of this book I hope to have revealed the radical Jewish conception of the Messiah. The historical Messiah is reserved for some distant day. We Jews, pragmatic dreamers, have had several historical Messiahs like Jesus—Bar Kochba, Sabbatai Zevi—but they faded away in our consciousness. For there is another Messiah in the Jewish tradition, or rather a foretaste of the Messiah, which we refuse to attach to any name or person, but which, like our conception of the Holy One, Blessed Be He, remains faceless, mystical. It lies within each of us. Those two contemporary prophets, Marx and Freud, between them split this Messiah two ways, into justice and eroticism, and forgot the third, the mystery of death; but anyone who feels, who reads, who broods over the abyss, who is "religious," may encounter, as I did, with a blazing face, the Presence of the Messiah. And where did I encounter that?

In writing this book.

"Do you dismiss us with a broken reed?" the students of the sages would complain at a facile answer to a difficult question.

I'll tell you a story. In graduate school, a professor of mine lured me down to Tijuana to see the fabulous wickedness of that border town, which glowed much more lurid in the late fifties, with its restricted mores, than it does now. After we had toured the bars with naked women dancing on the counters above us, he left me in the parking lot beside my motorcycle with the fatherly advice to use a prophylactic. A Mexican cab driver materialized like Satan out of the darkness within seconds and began to proposition me. What did I want? Virgins? Children? Dogs? Three women? Four? Lust, like fever, made me tremble so much I could hardly stand.

Suddenly my grandfather, Israel Mirsky, who died when I was four and a half years old, stood in the parking lot. He waved his head slowly back and forth, warning me, pointed to the seat of my motorcycle, and stood there until I had gotten on, started the machine, and ridden away.

The story doesn't end here. Shaken, I rode up to San Diego, where my cousin had invited me to stay on a boat. I climbed into my bunk at three in the morning, ready to go to sleep, when a sweet voice sounded from across the cabin. The young woman—a friend of my cousin, a stranger to me—and I be-

came acquainted that night and though I didn't see my grandfather, I laughed at the gifts of a Jewish ghost.

Reading the Talmud, the Zohar, Jewish history, I have again
and again encountered my grandfathers. They are not so
solemn. Their laughter surprises me. They are searching too.
When I hear them speaking to me I feel an uncanny presence,
something more than just the re-creation of a moment lost in
history. I feel the Messiah. Or, if you want to use the technical
language of the Spanish mystics, which has been the lingua
franca of Jewish mysticism for centuries now, I felt the
Shekinah, the Female Presence of the Holy One, Blessed
Be He.*

Let me return for a moment to the boat, rocking on the
Atlantic. That man's walking away from the table, hurt, angry,
feeling excluded, still upsets me. In his stubborn, pragmatic
refusal, he was closer to me than the others at the table. When
my grandfather appeared to me, as ghost or hallucination,
it was, I know, to keep the tradition, family, tribe, safe. I too
feel the responsibility to the tradition. I am an imperfect vessel
of it, but my own flaws make me sympathetic to the anger
of others. There must be a way to include that man, to include
the assimilated Jewish world, the best of it, to whom middle-
class homilies have no meaning, in the tradition, its questions,
its dreams; to make the inheritance of our grandfathers part
of the life of Jews in America. Gentile or Jew, whoever you
are, despite the shrillness, the mockery, the bravura, this is my
intention. Several times after I have spoken about Judaism,
or my sense of it, strangers have come up to me and revealed

---

* The Zohar is the title of a collection of mystical commentaries on the
Bible which were probably written in thirteenth-century Spain. Gershom
Scholem has detailed how the medieval Kabbalistic mind transformed
the talmudic reference to the presence of God, the Shekinah, into a
conception of a female spirit. The Shekinah of the Kabbalists accom-
panies the male Jew, is embodied in the Jewish woman, and brings
them both into a foretaste of Paradise and the Messiah. How? Making
love takes them into sexual union with an aspect of the Holy One,
Blessed Be He.

their own deep affection for what had been consigned in their lives to the toy chest of childhood. And seeing that it might not be only a childish dream, but could be born again, now, we have both fought back silent tears. Dream, says the twelfth-century Jewish sage Maimonides, is one-sixtieth of prophecy.

Sailing Off

WHY IS IT IMPORTANT in this century of progress, light, the United Nations, and emancipation to speak of a narrow, parochial clan, to assert kinship in a people who insistently and arrogantly declare in their prayers, "Thank you for making us different among the *other* nations?" Goyiim—in Yiddish the Hebrew is tinged with scorn and disgust; the other ones, *nations*, the unwashed, uninitiated. Those of you who speak my precious English, the language of the Jews' blessed, golden exile in America, languish with tears over the fate of the land's aborigines. My former girl friend, a Connecticut hillbilly with roots in West Virginia, strung herself in Hopi beads and amulets. All over the continent, the white American dashes about for tribes to belong to, weep over—Indians, blacks, Puerto Ricans—sensing that American culture is too vast to contain any anchor. As well claim a heritage in the waves of the Pacific. Yet how often, staring at me with the marks of my own Hebrew colors daubed in my speech and writing, they turn away puzzled. Why are you interested in Jews, Judaism? Aren't you one of us?

They are right. This Jewish business isn't just flirtation with anthropology, civil rights, playing Robin Hood to the poor and oppressed. There is something sneaky and dark in it all. Mixing up religion, race, literary tradition, and an exclusive men's club with a few token ladies. And it's obsessive, a disease. Man, according to Unamuno, is only a diseased animal, his sickness "the main element of progress." We Jews are ill. Everyone else has sorted out what they are, and we are still running around with an old Babylonian hodgepodge. We break into the tombs of our ancestors and get sick from plagues that were extinguished in Egypt five thousand years ago.

And if there are any Jews listening, listen! Your Jewish ideal and mine are not the same. I don't care how hip it is—a drunken folk singer, pie-eyed with pot, strumming on his guitar. I have seen him advertised in a dozen temples as the answer to disaffected youth. No! The middle-of-the-road rabbi who breathes clichés, the closet conservative who quietly extinguishes the flame of enthusiasm in his intellectual mausoleum, the gentle undertaker crying to us from the pulpit to bury ourselves in our parents' pieties (who after all pay his salary). Nightmare! Almost as bad is official Judaism's answer to the problem of adventure—Israel! All of us who have smarted from the nasty, selfish, and arrogant one-upmanship of the cousins from Tel Aviv (you Americans are half Jews, Diaspora Jews. We're on the front line—the firing line. You can only be Jewish in Israel and so, how about a check? You owe me—I don't owe you) know how bankrupt it is just to point vaguely in the direction of the Israeli state, saying, "That's the answer." In fact, an end to institutional answers, radical, rabbinical, patriotic.

All right, Judaism can't be all things to all people, but I insist that every Jew has the right to construct his own ark, set sail, trim his vessel as he sees the mountain rising in the distance. Fleets of us going in every direction, hallooing, helpless, mountain, mountain, have you seen a mountain?

In this century no dry land is in sight. Sometimes frankly I'm so tired of the whole Jewish rigamarole, I'd like to junk it. Forget it. Just be an average American. After too many hours in the synagogue or rabbinical company, I bolt for the door, out the window, jump into the waves, anything. I get claustrophobia. It's a fact that I've never since the age of eighteen had a Jewish girl friend.

What have I to do with that vast bourgeoisie sleeping every Saturday morning in the temples and synagogues of America? My family? Walking past a synagogue on Manhattan's lower East Side, I jerk my head toward the entrance. Should I be in there? Even if it bores me stiff? Why?

For the sake of my grandfather. For the sake of what's slumbering in the service. For the sake of the Name. Finally you have to load the whole family into the ark, the cows, chickens, camels, the lot. It's no good sailing to Jerusalem or the Seven Heavens yourself. You have to get all those obnoxious businessmen, bubble-gum children, rabbinical bores on board too. As a Jew one believes that the whole people, tribe, *mishpochah*, has to go along on the trip. Is it a religion or a travel agency? Either you're all going or no one is going? God has made it clear. And finally the other nations too. *Vey!* No one takes off until the whole world is ready. The Messiah. Wait for the Messiah. You're responsible for everyone's arrangements. Too much! Man overboard!

So how come I'm still holding on?

Let go of the ship that bore my father and grandfather before me? Perhaps, when we are no longer sailing toward death. . . .

Again and again as the mysteries of science are revealed in terms that sound like ancient riddles—the double helix, the black hole, the shattering and reassembly of the universe—I feel the strength of my attachment to a tradition that ties me to a past. The English have abandoned their tribal deities. Not so we Hebrews. Ours is as old as our language, old as the breath, wind blowing off the planet, blowing in our mouths, ears.

God? Where does God come in?

It's all mixed up together. You can't stop it. The puzzles that started driving me crazy when I was nine, ten: Where did I come from? Where am I going? The only help for it is in the books, the histories of this family argument, the parables, puzzles, riddles by which we Jews have preserved our poor heads from the wind howling inside them. To dress their sails to that wind, the Jews have constructed the vast apparatus of the Halakhah (Hebrew "law" from *halakh*, to go, to follow), the Ten Commandments, the 613 commandments of the Five Books of Moses, the codes of the priests, scribes, post-biblical assemblies, rabbinical academies, commentators, etc. To understand the hold of the law on the Jewish imagination, you have to live through the generations of Agada—stories—which they wove around the skeleton of the commandments. The law became the mystical partner to man, acquired flesh and blood. According to the rabbis, the 613 commandments correspond to the 613 parts of the body, 248 members, 365 veins.

To obey the law, hinted the mystics among the rabbis, would restore not only the parts of one's own body, but bring about the healing of the mysterious first man, Adam Kadmon, Adam of the East, an Adam who existed before the biblical Adam of the Garden of Eden, "a cosmic being which contains the whole world in itself and whose station is superior even to that of Metraton, the first of the angels."* Behave, cry the rabbis, and the whole world will be reformed, restored. Our persistent romantic fantasy as Jews is that by behaving better we may turn the very planet about, make it tack to another wind, sail, yea, even against death.

The effort that Judaism makes is to rib an ark that will

* Gershom Scholem, *Major Trends in Jewish Mysticism* (New York: Schocken Books, 1961), p. 279.

carry us, Jew, Gentile, inhabitants of the globe, into another world.

That is why halakhah is so important to understanding Judaism. The quarrel as to what the law is (and if it has not been frozen by orthodoxy during the last few hundred years so that it has become a nightmare, not a dream) waxes violent because the sense of acting within the law, within a body of law, is what the experience of Judaism is all about.

Law, death, and the Messiah.

At Harvard, my roommate was a real thorough-going rationalist. He believed in a world without God. I spent several afternoons and evenings walking around the landscape of his universe with him. Such a bleak place, my mouth was dry just from speaking of it. I couldn't live there. So empty, hopeless. The belief in an Unknown that takes an interest loads me down with liabilities and responsibilities, but I can't endure to live otherwise.

Of course in Hebrew school efforts were made by some to convince us that Judaism was the most rational of religions. This dust didn't last long on anyone's palate except those who were intent in taking like as a long snooze. Anyone with any intelligence or imagination soon spit it out. American Jews are still in the grip of that delusion, that their religion as derived from Maimonides (not the Maimonides of the Messianic demand but the Maimonides of the Greek philosophers) is the most rational religion that can be, and this obsession with rationalism accounts for the mighty tide of assimilation.

No, the Jew is not rational.

Is it possible then to be a Jew *and* an intellectual in the twentieth century? Not a scholar (that's easy), but a member of that general community that sees man as a creature of self-scrutiny, subject to the twists of myth, psychology, biology, believing in some form of evolutionary theory that extends his ancestry beyond the biblical storytelling, determined at least in part by chemical combinations billions of years old?

The answer is not obvious to me. The irrational allegiance of Judaism turns one away from easy agreements about our common humanity. We are not all the same. Leaving apart racial differences, the staggering fact that one person is a woman and another a man makes for difficulties so profound that only in death can we dream of perfect reconciliation. Only with the Messiah. Is it that messianic itch that one finds so strange in Maimonides? The twelfth-century master rationalist who in his *Guide of the Perplexed* recasts Judaism in the spirit of Aristotelian philosophy cannot but reach past the Prime Mover, the mechanisms of his Greek teacher, and as a tenet of faith, cry out for something tangible: "I believe with perfect faith in the coming of the Messiah, and, though he tarry, I will wait daily for his coming."

Finally we, the Jews, want magic. Even if we don't get it in our lifetime. The Messiah isn't here. We aren't happy.

Judaism stresses disappointments, differences. There is the itch to argue, to distinguish, to bend one's neck only before the whirlwind.

Perhaps the information is false, but in the historic genes of the Jews is stored the memory of a voice that spoke loud enough to turn its inheritors very stubborn about surrendering the compact to which it promised to speak again. "You shall be unto me a kingdom of priests, and a holy nation," the Jews are exhorted in Exodus, and again, in Leviticus: "Sanctify yourself therefore, and be ye holy, for I am holy." Keeping the commandments, thereby keeping oneself apart from other peoples, yet also obeying the injunction: "And if a stranger* sojourn with thee in your land, you shall not do him wrong. The stranger that sojourneth with you shall be unto you as the home born among you, and thou shalt love him as thyself: for ye were strangers in the land of Egypt" (Lev. 19: 33, 34).

To keep a sense of distinction and yet preserve a common

* The "stranger" some rabbis assume to mean only the proselytes among the Jews, but I think the word can bear a wider application.

justice to the other nations of the world as they come among us and we among them, this is the paradox of Judaism; to love the stranger as oneself and yet to keep holy, apart. "All the distress that Israel shares with the world, that is real distress. The distress that Israel shares alone, that is not distress." These are the hard words of a talmudic sage.

I asked, at the beginning of the chapter, why remain Jewish, apart, different? Holy?

Is it to preserve a tradition? Something in me keeps referring to the collective wisdom of the Jewish past. I want to know what Rabbi Hillel and Rabbi Shammai* in the first century thought about women, even if at first glance it seems hopelessly outdated. One ought to know what the tradition is. What did its wisdom do? To give up my history is to surrender knowledge of myself.

Will we Jews survive? Should we survive? Do our fellow citizens want us to survive? The answers are as complex as a few pages of Talmud.

"The distress that Israel shares alone."

What makes us different is what gives us identity—more often suffering than joy. So the Jew often looks as if he is a stubborn masochist. One could get lost here in endless discussions of the difference between Christian suffering and Jewish, or fashionable clichés about the Jew as outsider, perpetual wanderer, secret seeker after holocaust. The fact is that Jews don't look for suffering or their villains, Hitler, Haman, the satans of the world. It's just that these other pretenders to the crown of messianism, the inquisitors of earthly perfection,

* Famous antagonists; in myth, Hillel was a liberal, Shammai, a conservative. Modern scholarship has shown that, in fact, they represented different economic groups whose interests helped shape the law. Hillel credited intention; Shammai, the deed.

always find us obnoxious. Jews attract trouble because they are a stumbling block in the imagination of such dreamers who have a single vision of the world with themselves at the center. And because Jews have suffered so much, the tradition has become adept at extracting something—music, wisdom, love, philosophy—out of that terrible waste product, suffering. Jews *want*, on the contrary, impossible joy. We carry about with us in our genes, I believe, even to the second and third generation, like Freud and Marx, the expectation of hearing the Messiah. Anything that confirms us in this belief is a source of comfort. It is possible, strangely, to believe in the Messiah without God: in other words, that an age of harmony is coming, whether economics or psychiatry will usher it in. There is a moment in the tradition when the Holy One, Blessed Be He, *Himself* is pessimistic about the capacity of man to believe in God. "Had they but abandoned me," He says, "and keep faith with my Torah."*

A world perfected under law, Torah, man-made—what other people make a perfect social justice the sine qua non of their existence? The attraction of communism to so many Jews is nothing but the stirring of ancient dreams. Only it is a bitter thing, this messianism. Once you have tasted of it, you have little patience with the Am-Ha-Oretz, that person whom the Talmud calls "the man of the earth." The man who is always in the majority, even among the Jews, the man with his nose in the dust, who eats of it, sleeps in it, and will not join you to dream of the impossible. No matter how much I protest my love for humanity, I must, like Thoreau, admit that humanity disgusts me. It's too practical. Add to this the fact that I cling to the notion that the Messiah is arriving in my immediate family, and you can see what a suspect creature the Jew is as an intellectual. I can smirk reading Freud, Marx, seeing all this pushed under, turned into something fancy.

* Yerushalmi Hagigah 76 c, interpreting Jer. 16:11

So I should become an ordinary intellectual? Please. If, as all creatures in love with abstraction do, I suspect that it is all an abstraction, why should I give up the most pleasing abstraction of all? Especially as it has been handed down to me through thousands of years.

Of course we have to pay for this arrogance with guilt. Possessing the oldest living tradition of messianism, Judaism is laced with powerful draughts of pessimism to prevent impossible constipation; no dreams, prophecies, miracles, only the event itself will do, not even the Messiah but the messianic age.* And until then, one is guilty. What did I do to undo it that it didn't come about? Now, go about medicine, economics, the theory of relativity, etc., but with a sense that something more is required.

Again, you will protest, there is nothing unusual here. Plenty of non-Jewish intellectuals feel this way. I can reply, first, from the Talmud: "A pious Gentile is equal to the High Priest." Judaism is not restricted to the family. Actions make certain people, Job, for instance, into Jews. Second, there is not yet a people, race, tribe that have made this uneasiness their distinguishing characteristic for generations. So that when a Jew feels this uneasiness, he feels close to the roots of his tribe.

If Marx had been more Jewish, he would have said, Everything I'm telling you is wrong and must come right, will not come right, until man becomes like the Messiah. And Freud would have admitted, Everything I uncover cannot be resolved until man becomes another creature. Both qualifying their tale, their science fiction, with the disclaimer that something mysterious and unknown would have to touch man if he was significantly to alter his behavior. And in not bowing their necks before the whirlwind, they committed an arrogance which their followers must pay bitterly for. Now, that is the good taste of Jewish doctrine; for in drinking deep of

---

* The Messiah will come one day after he's no longer needed, says the Talmud.

that utter wormy pessimism,* you can speak of illusion knowing you will never confuse it with what is under your nose
—dust.

Between Ur and Aram, the Jew wanders. Between Babylonian despair—out of that ancient charnel house, the Meso-
patamian city, groaning with dead, "the bodies floating on the
river," as the epic of Gilgamesh laments—and the night vision
of the nomad, Laban's magic. (According to the Zohar,
Laban, Jacob's uncle and father-in-law, was a wizard.) City
and desert, these are the compass points for messianic dreams.
Abraham flees like so many Jewish heroes out of Necropolis
to the wide open spaces.

Yet the pull of the towns is strong. The sorcerer's magic
turns into social ethics. The minute they get into contact with
God, they start bargaining: how many righteous men to
protect a city, thirty, twenty, ten? You think these are fairy
tales? Yes! Tradesmen's tales that have transformed the world.
Messianic dreams. As a Jew, one's worst enemies are other
Jews, those who have forgotten half of their origin, one of
the compass points. It's not easy in the company of assimilated
Hebrews to believe in the Messiah. I'd rather proselytize the
Gentiles. And when you come to the professional messianists:
Chassidim, the California Kabbalists, the 100 percent *glatt*
kosher crowd, there is no market for Babylonian vinegar. The
dead are piling up but they are off in the clouds with Laban's
mumbo jumbo.

Fortunately for me, my father's tent was pitched between
the two places. He was an agnostic in love with talmudic
learning. Rashi, the wittiest of medieval commentators, and
Spinoza, the heretic, the excommunicated Jewish philosopher
of Amsterdam, were just two sides of the same Hebrew coin.
If he was more of a skeptic than I was, perhaps it was because
during his childhood in Poland he had imbibed too heavy a
draught of Eastern European faith. It was too much, at least

* See the tale of Rabbi Huna's sour grapes, p. 24, for an explanation of
this imagery.

for America. Yet through his eyes I understood some of the dreams of Orthodoxy in the generations of my grandfathers.

One of the reasons the vast sleeping majority of Jews in America are so confused today is that they have no direct knowledge of their traditions. In the welter of publicity and nostalgia for Chassidism, most Americans are unaware that the mainstream of intellectual Jewish life in the past, its paradoxical embracing of mysticism and practical law, was somewhere else entirely. The Lithuanian yeshivas and German or American universities produced minds like Harry Wolfson, Joseph Soloveitchik, Chaim Weizmann in Europe and in this country, a host of intellectuals, doctors, lawyers, scientists, professors, who felt nonetheless real joy in Judaism.

This tradition, with a few exceptions, has come to a dead end. The majority of *thinking* Jews in America are puzzled. Is it possible to join a modern community of Jews who share a common sense of law, ritual, sentiment?

Now wisdom is with the people. You have to take them all on board. The Talmud won't recognize the imposition of a law that the community can't obey. The majority of Jews in America can't live under the strictures of sixteenth-century Orthodoxy or return with the Chassidim to an eighteenth-century past. The children of the educated among that majority reject the sentimental ragtags of popular Jewish culture as a valid basis for retaining a Jewish identity. Like the generations after the return from exile in Babylon, young Jews have mingled with the peoples of the land. It is this community that I belong to. I believe that there are traditions in Judaism that speak to us.

Was I abusing the multitude? How could I? I love them too much. Come, let us awaken them. To what? To what an uneasy life we have.

Be specific! To what?

The frenzies of practical Kaballa? Lurianic possession, sleeping with angels, wife-swapping under the aegis of the false Messiah, Sabbatai Zevi, ritual murder with Jacob Frank, conversion to Islam, Catholicism for the sake of anathema, deliberate abrogation of the law? Ha! Despite the accusation the short-story writer Cynthia Ozick, that *frumma* sweetheart (extra kosher), hurled at me after fifteen minutes of my conversation on the above subjects ("You are a demonist!"), I don't desire that all the wildest times of Jewish history resurrect themselves. I do ask that part of the craziness come back into our houses of study. To reengage the majority of American Jews, their children, in the question of what is and isn't legal, what the law in this century requires for us as a community to bring about the messianic age, demands a breadth of vision and poetry that none of our teachers has yet demonstrated. Perhaps the founding of the state of Israel, enthusiasm for western science, and the experiment with that universalist Jewish heresy, Marxism, has absorbed the energies of our most creative spirits. Only scholars have kept alive the tradition. Soon, I dream, the radical implications of these traditions will be acted out again and Judaism will begin to step into its vital and dangerous responsibilities among the nations. We, as a tribe, will outstrip the Swedes, the Danes, the Chinese as innovators in modern man's social behavior. The individual Jew will mingle holiness with righteousness in such a way that something more than the pinched face of moral arrogance will distinguish our features. Then, at last, we can disappear among the nations, all of whom will bend down and take on the yoke of Another Kingdom.

It's for this possibility that I remain a Jew, that the characters in my fiction speak almost wholly within the tradition of inherited Hebrew stories, for I will not surrender my own spark of the Messiah. I want to catch it and pass it on within my life, work, generation unto generation.

Home in Dorchester

vvvvv

Like most American Jews I came from a family whose orthodoxy was fading away as we grew up in the United States of the forties and fifties. It was impossible to keep kosher on long rides to relatives or when visiting in other parts of Boston or surrounding towns. At home meat and milk dishes were separated, and there was never any ham or shellfish in the refrigerator. We bought our meat from a butcher with the yellow Star of David on his window and generally obeyed the rules.

At our summer house, under the influence of Irish carpenters, Swedish house painters, who were always bartering their services for my father's legal fees, strange meats and dishes were introduced. Bleeding sirloin steaks, lobster, clam chowder, these accompanied the year-round repairs as the wives of my father's clients chipped in to prepare meals for us and the continual work crews. Slowly, as the population of the Jewish streets dispersed, our sense of orthodoxy even at home in Dorchester, where the kosher butcher still reigned, diminished. Meats were just much cheaper at the A & P. On my trips home from Harvard, I noticed that the dishes in the house for meat and milk were mingled, silverware for *flaisheh* and *milcheh*, the Yiddish equivalents for those categories, the hallmark of an observant household, were all mixed up. At ten years old I would have looked with horror at the silverware pattern for *flaisheh* lodged in the drawer of the *milcheh* knives, forks, and spoons.

Does this seem trivial to those of you outside the Orthodox circle? Yet without a strong intellectual anchor, the ark of Judaism floated out of our house as it did in so many because the cables that bound one to it were one by one let loose. What distinguished us from our neighbors, Gentiles, on the streets beyond the synagogues? Less and less.

Friends, other American Jews, often come up to me slightly embarrassed, knowing that I identify with Judaism. It meant something to their parents. It was a secret like Yiddish, a language they dimly remember or relearn a few catchwords of from TV comics. Did I lose something? they seem to ask. How can I answer? Lecherous, half educated, my Hebrew pathetic, my Yiddish hardly existent—a few swear words and phrases my parents used once too often—I am no teacher, no paradigm. Why then do I find myself turning the pages (in translation) of the Talmud? The Zohar? Running after Israel, avaricious of information, discussion, obsessed with Jews. And why do I insist always in the first few minutes of conversation on a bus or train with strangers on letting it be known, You are talking to a Jew. What is this terrifying feeling of clan that makes me want to leap up on the Greyhound bus to Boston and tear up the aisle in the midst of gentile faces to pump the arms of two white-bearded Chassidim with whom I have little in common—just to say, Me too! Me too!

Is it my grandfather I am worshiping? I think so. I understand that snake gliding out of Faulkner's bestiary, the grandfather; it is some spirit of history, not tied to land, woods, therefore more difficult to encounter—its forests are books, words, the ancient wisdom comes slithering suddenly in the rattle of a Babylonian voice.

Take for instance the tale of Rabbi Huna's four hundred casks of wine that turned sour. The other sages of the Talmud couldn't understand how the Almighty could punish such a pious man without reason. They begged him to examine his actions—couldn't he discover a sin?

"Am I suspected of a sin?" he shouted at them.

"Do you suspect the Almighty of punishing you without one?" they retorted.

"Okay," boasted Huna, "whoever has heard anything bad about me, let him say it."

"Oh," said the rabbis, "we hear you don't give your tenant, the gardener, his share of the vine tendrils."

"Who has any?" objected Huna. "He stole them all."

" 'Steal from a thief, get a taste of the theft,' " quoted the rabbis. Rebuked, Rabbi Huna agreed to give a share of the vine tendrils to his tenant.

What was the outcome? The book, Berakhot, states: "Some say that the vinegar became wine again. Others [it adds drily], that vinegar went up to the cost of wine."

This is talmudic humor, and the essence of its philosophy (in my commentary, my father's, my grandfather's) is pessimism, vinegar, sour waiting for the Messiah. Christians who are waiting for the Jews to convert don't understand that dry reedy laughter, awful hopes, awful disappointment, a vigorous realism that is holding in check insane dreams. During a dangerous public debate on the Coming of the Messiah forced on the leading rabbis of Spain and Italy in 1413 by a Jewish heretic, the pope, Benedict XIII, interjected: "You Jews, you say terrible things. What sensible man would say that the Messiah was, to be sure, born, but that he lived in the Garden of Eden for a long time, and that he has now been living for fourteen hundred years?"

Rabbi Astruct jumped up and said, "Sir, since you believe

so many improbable things about your Messiah, let us believe this one about our Messiah."

Was this tradition held secret from me? The American Hebrew school often seemed a conspiracy against it. Like Franz Kafka I may whine, "My education has done me great harm." The good humor of the Talmud never echoed in the incessant Hebrew grammar drilled in my ears. The prayers were just rote memory exercises. Even the biblical narrative only came to me in tortured bits and pieces, half coherent as better students limped through its translation into English, a task hopelessly beyond me. The Messiah lay dead as Dracula under the basement floor of the Beth El Hebrew school. As the afternoon sun sank in the window frames to the shouts of happier kids outside still playing handball, the monster rose, sucking my blood, leaving a pale corpse senseless to the questions hurled at it. One year I sat so conspicuously mute, a clay man, that even the presence of my father on the board of directors did not suffice to promote me and I was kept back. "That ignoramous, the grocery man, his son is at the head of the class—your boy can't even get promoted!" my father raged at my mother. Her side of the family was held responsible for this degeneration of the Mirsky intelligence. The shame made what was unpleasant into a tale of horror. I hated Hebrew school as the Israelites hated the bondage of Egypt. My fiction keeps returning to the trauma. Describing the grocer's son, elevated into a rabbi's child, I am his sad double, the inept Harvey Blatz,

"Idiot! Blockhead!" No half crazy, old woman for his Hebrew teacher, hitting him on the head with the five books of Moses, shouting as she kicked him, "Pay attention!" He was never made fun of in front of the class. . . . "Look at the stupid one. Look! Look! Stop mumbling, stand up, show yourself off, *pisherkeh.* You make in your pants yet?"

He never had to dig his pen deep into the oak top of the desk, carving his heart into it, cutting the channels of an imaginary river that would carry him off into another country where he might understand the language.

A book sailed down the aisle and smacked Harvey Blatz silly. If the son of the Rabbi stared through the windows of the yeshivah rather than at the text before him, his teachers smiled and looked to another student. The Lux boy could start up from his dream and answer the question. Hebrew was a second tongue to him. He had learned it at home in songs and riddles. It was not a sack of incomprehensible words hurled to learn by rote. A smack of the ruler ready to catch him at the first mistake. Hebrew vowels swarmed around Harvey's head, bees, the consonants, a fire of thorns. He was beset on all sides.

I was mercifully released from this after I staged my first show of defiance to my mother's and father's educational plans, a refusal to go on to Hebrew high school. My parents insisted on loading me down with lessons, Hebrew school, Latin school, music school, so as not to lose the least glimmer of talent in their offspring. Now Judaism centered for me in the marriage arrangements of Dorchester, Mattapan, Roxbury. At fourteen, fifteen, sixteen, the virgins of Blue Hill and Brookline Avenue, and Newton Highlands were bound as tight as Chinese *maidles'* feet, into their bras and girdles. Not only was chastity absolute but the conversation, that platonic dish, didn't taste of much. My tongue wagged in place of other tools, but it only got me deep into hot water. I was not a desirable commodity among the Jewish girls. Desperation made me scratch my face. My revenge was to play Franken-stein at all the grim parties that fifteen- and sixteen-year-olds arrange for themselves. In the damp, pine-paneled playrooms that parents laboring in the cellar holes of suburban split-levels had transformed into "recreation areas" for their children, I stamped my foot, a self-conscious monster confounded in the midst of Jewish princesses. What a "pain" I must have been to those girls emulating the chatter of their mothers, interested in the small talk of dresses, houses, automobiles, whatever the dating manuals said constituted the language of an "attractive personality." (I too fine-combed those softback wisdom books between the stacks of more salacious material at the corner drugstore, desperate for instruction.) I cut, uninvited, into their delicate cackle with undigested passages of Descartes, Spinoza, Jean-Paul Sartre, Nietzsche, Franz Kafka.

"Do you believe in God?" I thundered, interrupting two lovely, untouchable fifteen-year-olds who were discussing the relative merits of Filene's or Jordan Marsh for lingerie. They began to back cautiously toward a corner, entreating the president of the Jewish sorority who had invited us for help, trying to latch on to one of the other boys in my club (the Consuls of Blue Hill Avenue) suntanned Danny Blum or the effervescent joke-teller, Eddy Cohen. "I'll prove he doesn't exist!" I was shouting, as horror bloomed on their faces and they threatened to call the mother of the hostess while I advanced to the proof, a demand for a bolt of lightning on the spot, my finger poking upward at the fluorescent bulb of the ceiling. "Have you read *Nausea*?" Then a quick plot summary of a man with a pistol in his pocket forcing a prostitute to open her legs and experience shame. Such book reviews and chitchat did not endear me to the marriage-bound upward-striving daughters of the *nouveau riche*. Especially as I tore at the outbursts of my face, adolescent acne, locked into the basement toilets between bouts of this intellectual "existential" Grand Guignol.

From such mirrors, deep in Brookline, Newton, Belmont, I fled out to anti-Semitic Wellesley, where a friend, non-Jewish, happened to be president of the high school senior class. With his introductions, I discovered another world, girls who had read philosophy, literature, were curious about my passion for "existentialism," Freud, Marx, *vey iz mir*! Ecstasy. Even though a few angry fathers pulled phones out of the wall on me as I chattered from my room in Dorchester to their daughters on the elegant country estates of Wellesley and Weston, even though I felt myself as curious a figure at their debutante parties (in territory where a Jew could not buy real estate) as the UN delegate from the Spice Isles might a generation later, still the revelation that young women were interested in ideas was so heady that I ignored all the embarrassments put in my way. I, like so many of my contemporaries, found myself outside the narrow ghetto streets with their cramped sleepy alleyways, breathing the air of the wide world. Anything was possible. All those American dreams we thumbed over in *Life*, those blonde girls on ice skates in baby blue and pink. *Shicksah*. What a tender word. For the guilt of white protestant America that was to wash many a black boy under in a harem of American thighs was ours for a few short years. All those girls revolting against father, family, seeking exotic connections.

Only all the while, glutted with Harvard, rubbing noses and bellies with the daughters of famous American families, now I was haunted by voices out of Dorchester. Even as I fell hopelessly in love with a Scotch-Canadian girl in Cambridge, the pull of Jewish loyalties began to tug at me. I had no identity outside of my roots in the Jewish past. The Jewish present, however, seemed vulgar, shallow, silly. When in the sociologist David Reisman's course or the analyst Erik Erikson's, the question Who are you? was asked, I could not help but look back as they did, particularly Erikson, to childhood. And the back and forth over the puzzle that has occupied me in all my writing began. It is dangerous for a writer of fiction to understand himself too well. (Magic speaks in silence and I believe in insoluble puzzles.) The lines of my first story came out of my mouth as I left the front door of the rabbi at Harvard, Ben Zion Gold, a puzzle in which anger at Judaism and a constant obsession with it, that could only be love, contended. The rabbi had found me in a hospital bed at Stillman Infirmary during my sophomore year. All because, on some qualm, I had listed Jewish rather than agnostic when I registered at Harvard.

Not that any love was lost between me and my fellow Jews at Harvard. I had walked away from them a week after my freshman registration when they questioned that tall, blunt-nosed friend of mine from Wellesley High who for a lark had gone along with me for a Jewish mixer at Hillel House. I stamped out at his elbow, indignant. "So his name is Kelly?" I shouted back over my shoulder in the face of a fat Bronx *fellah* whose chicken-soup breath disgusted me. "So what?" I exited, shaking my fist.

Now I ranted at the rabbi, secure in my invalid status. I mocked when he quoted Alfred North Whitehead, a particular favorite of mine, corrected a mistake he made, contradicted, and crowed over his head like an idiot. With the patience of a Mormon missionary he kept after me, loading me with books in English on biblical scholarship, giving me a collection of Yiddish stories in translation, slowly making known to me that fabulous world of the Jewish past which Hebrew school had shut me out of. Now many of my childhood lessons were clearer to me as I stumbled through Eastern Europe, Talmud, Jewish mysticism; the anecdotes and joking banter which my father dropped into at the table, in the car, the odd moment.

I was in touch with magic, and a bitter spring began to well up. The Boston papers had recently reported a rash of anti-Semitic slogans scrawled on the sides of local synagogues. "So," I wrote in my head that night, half in love with Judaism, still stinging with the pain of earlier rejections, Hebrew school flunkout, washout of the Jewish princess circuit, "It was Epstein, the butcher's boy, who had painted the swastika on the wall of the Beth El Hebrew School. Oy."

Synagogues

—————————
VVVVV

OH, THE ROTTING SPICEBOXES of my childhood, synagogues—
dusty Edens where sweet fruit hung on the gnarled trunks
of the elders, and we children played under the trees without
knowing good or evil. Here I wandered in the press of old
men, a sea of black-and-white Bedouin stripes, silk shrouds,
gold and silver threads, velvet caps, high beaver hats: my
grandfather in striped pants and frock coat bending to me
and lifting me out of the seats where the other toddlers were
squeezed in among *zaides* whose pockets leaked honey, clusters
of lollipops, sour balls in cellophane, chewy Tootsie Rolls, as
if the old oily walnut paneling wept rock candy. After the
service there was sure to be heaps of sponge cake, yellow
with eggs and sugar, crisp bows of cookies, herring, bottles of
orange soda, ginger ale, the mysterious feast, the *kiddush*;
and I am elevated in these magical proceedings by my father,
who unwrapped shiny wooden boxes on black leather thongs
from a rich embroidered cherry plush bag and strapped himself up like a horse in an occult harness; am given into the
arms of the patriarch of our family, Grandpa Israel Mirsky,

shammus of the Fowler Street Schul who swung me into the light of the whole synagogue, waved me before the women in the balcony, my mother, over the polished mahogany banister and set me down so close to the mysterious ark, the great parchment scrolls, silver hangings; the awful wail of the cantor in his milky satin crown, a mighty puff on top, I could hear the angels brushing their wings back and forth across the altar, and I sang out, all voice and no words, my four-year-old soul swimming up clumsily in the rush to catch hold of a gleaming feather.

With the holy calls of Fowler Street in my ears, the coughing, hawking, the yammer under the prayers and melody, gaveling of the noisy women's section to attention, sudden surge of the whole crowded room into the prayers so that all the crystals in the chandelier under the dome shook and tingled soprano notes into "Hear, O Israel!" how, beloved auditors, can I invoke a childhood you never had? I am at a loss before many Jewish friends to explain the grip of the synagogue on me because their experience of it is so arid. The most poignant description of parched infancy I have read is by Claude Lévi-Strauss:

My only contact with religion dated back to my childhood when, already a non-believer, I lived during the First World War with my grandfather, who was Rabbi of Versailles. The house was attached to the synagogue by a long inner passage, along which it was difficult to venture without a feeling of anguish, and which in itself formed an impassible frontier between the profane world and that other which was lacking precisely in the human warmth that was a necessary precondition to its being experienced as sacred. Except when services were in progress, the synagogue remained empty and its temporary occupation was never sustained or fervent enough to remedy the state of desolation which seemed natural to it and in which the services were only an incongruous interruption. Worship within the family circle was no less arid. Apart from my grandfather's silent prayer at the beginning of each meal, we children had no means of knowing that we were living under the aegis of a superior order, but for the fact that a scroll of printed paper fixed to the dining room wall proclaimed the motto, "Chew your food well for the good of your digestion."

It is in the Brazilian jungles that the great anthropologist finds a compatible congregation, worthy of admiration:

Not that religion was treated with greater reverence among the Bororo: on the contrary, it was taken for granted. In the men's house, ritualistic gestures were performed with the same casualness as all others, as if they were utilitarian actions intended to achieve a particular result and did not require that respectful attitude which even the non-believer feels compelled to adopt on entering a place of worship. On a particular afternoon there would be singing in the men's house in preparation for the evening's public ritual. In one corner, boys would be snoring or chatting, two or three men would be humming and shaking rattles, but if one of them wanted to light a cigarette, or if it were his turn to dip into the maize gruel, he would hand the instrument to a neighbour who carried on, or sometimes he would continue with one hand, while scratching himself with the other. When a dancer paraded up and down to allow his latest creation to be admired, everybody would stop and comment upon it: the service might seem to be forgotten until in some other corner the incantation was resumed at the point where it had been interrupted.

Claude Lévi-Strauss! Come to the men's house on the corner of Fourteenth Street and Second Avenue, the Cantor's Synagogue, you can watch them passing the daily racing sheet around, shouting advice in Yiddish back and forth, scratching their behinds and picking their noses to your heart's satisfaction while the reader struggles to make the prayer heard above the din. In any of the *schuls*, the men's houses, of Dorchester when I grew up, you would have been struck by "the apparently incompatible activities." Bookies circulating in the back benches, business deals, marriage making, politics—an old story. Doesn't Sholom Aleichem draw the same portrait for us in "Dreyfus in Kasrilivke," when the outraged Russian postmaster cries out to a mob of jostling, noisy Hebrews besieging his office for the latest news of their coreligionist, "The post office wasn't a place for carryings-on. It wasn't the synagogue." There was a vitality in these old *schuls*, now mostly abandoned, a lack of pretense in them that came from a common assumption of faith. Boredom, rudeness, shuffling in and out were a mark of a culture so completely rooted in prayer that it allowed itself laughter, noise, craziness.

The synagogue has not taken root in American Jewish life since the generation that brought it over in the context of Eastern European habits. As our grandfathers died out, so did the warmth of their prayer halls. You can point to a host of expensive buildings in the American suburbs, but like the synagogue of Lévi-Strauss's childhood in Versailles, the atmosphere is deadly. It is a funeral parlor, a wedding chapel, its chaplains schooled in euphemisms. The rabbi, a much abused figure in the traditional synagogue since there were at least ten or fifteen Jews who had also been through the yeshiva and knew as much law or more, has taken unto himself the trappings of priesthood, a holier-than-thou aura, a sacrosanct smell in his robes; at best, he descends to raise funds, organize youth activities, orchestrate the sisterhood and brotherhood, showering prepared worn-out homilies. The prayer books of the Conservative and Reform synagogues reflect this dangerous distortion of rabbinical duties and prerogatives. The new editions turn the Hebrew text into bland, tasteless English, and one mouths the pap of *Reader's Digest* Judaism. When the whole congregation is required to mumble this aloud, it's enough to turn any intelligent believer out the door forever.

Why is the synagogue so empty? Is it the architecture of America? The destruction of town and city living arrangements that put it once at the focal point, crossroads, of daily life has weakened its present structure. It is not in walking distance. Nor is the urban neighborhood it was born in alive anymore. When morning and evening light marked the beginning and end of the farmer's or tradesman's day, common attendance at prayers was more natural. Scattered labor sites, homes, an eight-hour working schedule have played havoc with Jewish ritual.

Its inner architecture has crumbled too. Although synagogues existed before the destruction of the Second Temple, it was this cataclysmic event that dispersed the awe of the central shrine among the houses of study. Academic discussion and worship were now sanctified wherever ten Jews could be assembled for services. At one blow was annulled the authority that the weight of kingly, prophetic, and rabbinic power had centered in Jerusalem, and an extraordinary effort had to be exerted with the Temple in ruins to keep Judaism from flying apart. Its survival to this day testifies to the success of the Jewish intellectuals, their ability to create a state without visible trappings, the permanent underground that carried on without imposing altars, shrines, relics, in houses of study all over the world.

In order to understand the hold of the synagogue on Jews through the centuries, you have to feel the tension of its congregation, the contempt of temporal powers toward the Jew and his powerless position, the contempt of the Jew for the state, which was always caught through its exercise of power in obvious hypocrisies. The synagogue became a mystical bastion, a fortress of history. Man's ability to inhabit abstractions in preference to reality is undeniable. Jews gathered at their commons to lick their wounds, sneer, and study the book of promises.

In Cordoba, I went with a girl friend, the daughter of Catholic-Jewish parents, from the massive cathedral to the tiny box where Moses Maimonides had prayed, its walls covered with algebraic script, an intricate filigree of Hebrew letters, looking like a secret handwriting, literal Kaballah by which the Spanish worshipers o'erlept the insignificant dimensions of their narrow hall and built Heaven upon Heaven.

. . . When a man expounds something new in the Torah, his utterance ascends before the Holy One, Blessed Be He, and He takes it up and kisses it and crowns it with seventy crowns of graven and inscribed letters. When a new idea is formulated in the field of the esoteric wisdom, it ascends and rests on the head of the "Zaddik, the life of the universe," and then it flies off and traverses seventy thousand worlds until it ascends to the "Ancient of Days." And inasmuch as all the words of the "Ancient of Days" are words of wisdom comprising sublime and hidden mysteries, that hidden word of wisdom that was discovered here is joined to the words of the "Ancient of Days," and becomes an integral part of them. . . . The "Ancient of Days" savors that word of wisdom and finds satisfaction therein above all else. He takes that word and crowns it with three hundred and seventy thousand crowns, and it flies up and down until it is made into a sky. And so each word of wisdom is made into a sky which presents itself fully formed before the "Ancient of Days," who calls them "new heavens," that is, heavens created out of the mystic ideas of the sublime wisdom. . . .

When the Torah was delivered to Moses, there appeared myriads of heavenly angels ready to consume him with their fiery breath, but the Holy One, Blessed Be He, He covers and protects that word, and also shelters the author of that word so that the angels should not become aware of him and so be filled with jealousy, until that word is transformed into a new heaven and a new earth.*

My guide, raised by nuns, was at home in the vaulting empire of the great churches, Cordoba, Seville, but I slunk out of them, uncomfortable, and in the synagogue of Maimonides I began to recite the Shma Yisroel, the Jewish credo, aloud, despite my embarrassment.

So much blood—those medieval pogroms, the Spanish Inquisition—had hallowed this place. All through Europe: Amsterdam, Copenhagen, Paris, even their gloomy, unlovely synagogues are steeped in the horror of the holocaust, worshipers torn from their pews and railings. And so the shadow of this

* The Zohar.

ought to fall on the American halls, but it doesn't. The price of the firstborn, that sacrifice which God did not forbear to ask of our ancestor, Abraham, though at the last moment He withdrew His demand; blood on the lintels in Egypt, that smear by which the angel passed over the sheep of his congregation and slew instead the sons of their haughty persecutors—that stain, sadness, is not on the lintels of our suburban temples.

Ah me, is it tragedy you want, Maishe Mirsky? Must we spill blood to make this synagogue you speak of holy?

"Look from heaven and see how we have become a scorn and a derision among the nations: we are accounted as sheep brought to the slaughter, to be slain and destroyed, to be smitten and reproached." That is the morning prayer. Are we to say it or not? There I can join you. I want a house to cry in, laugh, carry on; not to show off, dump the kids, get swimming lessons, and Israeli bonds, see my neighbor's sons and daughters have an unholy fuss made over them one Saturday in their lives.

Let's come to my own bar mitzvah, a disgrace. My father invited half of Dorchester, Mattapan, Roxbury, forty thousand Jews, since he was representing them in the Massachusetts legislature: a banquet so big no one even had a table to sit down at, all the *draff* of ward politics showed up to shout, cavil, send up clouds of smoke among my confused relatives who were wandering in this throng trying to find me to press their envelopes or a gift package into my hands while I, I had my hand slapped by a nasty waitress at the buffet who had no way of recognizing the bar mitzvah boy when he reached for a second piece of the catered noodle pudding.

That slap! I'll never forget. My cheeks are red and I storm out to the street and cry. Ugly! It's so ugly!

Yet how pleasant had the preparations for the ceremony been. My father, a former Hebrew teacher, wisely distrusting the aptitude of his former colleagues at the Beth Hillel Hebrew School, had begun to sit down with me for an hour in the morning several months before my scheduled recitation and teach, slowly and patiently, the chant for the chapter of Isaiah that was my portion to read on the Saturday closest to my birthday, "Comfort thee, Comfort thee, my people." He explained the text and added to instruction in the song of the Haftorah commentary on the text that led me into inner music, melancholy and angry Isaiah bringing to a broken, unhappy nation a message of new hope. In the hot beach house, his white shoulders broken out in red splotches from the sun, my father, seeing that I had an unsuspected skill at mimicry and could memorize the verses easily, sing them back with passion, began to smile on me. (It was rare; all through my childhood, measuring the distance I was lagging behind his own precocious record, he looked at me with unconcealed grief.) Stories, anecdotes, that vast store of talmudic learning that had been lodged in this Eastern European boy before he leapt from Poland to Boston, Harvard College, Harvard Law, began to drop easily from his lips as we paused between the repetition of the opening prayers. He spoke of his own bar mitzvah with admiration, the simplicity of it. His father (or grandfather) had taken him to the synagogue one day, a Thursday, not even a Saturday. He had said the prayers, sung a portion of the Bible, and that was it. No fuss, no banquet, just the moment when a boy could be recognized as a man, counted as a member of the ten that make a congregation.

So why was I abandoned to a crowd of strangers and relatives at a public feast, while my father shook hands somewhere off in the horde of ward heelers?

These fathers of ours—not only mine, Kafka's, Mandelstam's—a current of anger at Judaism, the synagogue, runs through the biography of all our assimilated parents. They introduce us to the tradition, but there is a distaste that they do not admit in their introductions. "It was indeed," says Kafka, writing to his father,

so far as I could see, a mere nothing, a joke—not even a joke. Four days a year you went to the synagogue, where you were, to say the least, closer to the indifferent than to those who took it seriously, patiently went through the prayers as a formality, sometimes amazed me by being able to show me in the prayer book the passage that was being said at the moment, and for the rest, so long as I was present in the synagogue (and this was the main thing) I was allowed to hang about wherever I liked. And so I yawned and dozed through the many hours. . . . I was not fundamentally disturbed in my boredom, unless it was by the bar mitzvah but that demanded no more than some ridiculous memorizing, in other words, it led to nothing but some ridiculous passing of an examination, by little, not very significant incidents, as when you were called to the Torah and passed, in what to my way of feeling was a purely social event. . . . I have received a certain retrospective confirmation of this view of your Judaism from your attitude in recent years, when it seemed to you that I was taking more interest in Jewish matters. . . . Through my intervention Judaism became abhorrent to you, Jewish writings, unreadable, they "nauseated" you. This may have meant you insisted that only that Judaism which you had shown me in my childhood was the right one, and beyond it there was nothing.

"As a little bit of musk fills an entire house, so the least influence of Judaism overflows all of one's life. Oh, what a strong smell that is!" cries the Russian poet Osip Mandelstam. How grim is his portrait of the family religion. "Once or twice in my life I was taken to a synagogue as if to a concert. There was a long wait to get in—one practically had to buy tickets from scalpers—and all that I saw and heard there caused me to return home in a heavy stupor."

Mandelstam feels the poetry of the synagogue, its music. "The Jewish ship, with its sonorous alto choirs, and the astonishing voices of its children, lays on all sail, split as it is by some ancient storm into male and female halves." But finally, like Kafka, it is a social, not a religious, institution that he senses: "And all of a sudden two top-hatted gentlemen, splendidly dressed and glossy with wealth, with the refined movements of men of the world, touch the heavy book, step out of the circle and on behalf of everyone, with the authorization and commission of everyone, perform some honorary ritual, the principal thing in the ceremony. Who is that? Baron Ginzburg. And that? Varshavskij."

And measured in social scale, in these assimilated worlds—St. Petersburg, Prague, Boston—Judaism is sediment. Ironic, almost cruel, Osip Mandelstam details the place of Judaism in his family hierarchy through their bookcase.

There was nothing haphazard in the way that strange little library had been deposited like a geological bed, over several decades . . . a cross section of the strata showed the history of the spiritual efforts of the entire family. . . .

I always remember the lower shelf as chaotic: the books were not standing upright side by side but lay like ruins: a Russian history of the Jews written in the clumsy, shy language of a Russian-speaking Talmudist. This was the Judaic chaos thrown into the dust. This was the level to which my Hebrew primer, which I never mastered, quickly fell. In a fit of national contrition they went as far as hiring a real Jewish teacher for me. He came from his Torgovaja Street and taught without taking off his cap, which made me feel awkward. His correct Russian sounded false. The Hebrew primer was illustrated with pictures which showed one and the same little boy, wearing a visored cap and with a melancholy adult face, in all sorts of situations—with a cat, a book, a pail, a watering can. I saw nothing of myself in that boy and with all my being revolted against the book and the subject. There was one striking thing in that teacher, although it sounded unnatural: the feeling of national Jewish pride. He talked about Jews as the French governess talked about Hugo and Napoleon. But I knew that he hid his pride when he went out into the street, and therefore did not believe him.

Above these Jewish ruins there began the orderly arrangement of books: those were the Germans—Schiller, Goethe, Kerner and Shakespeare in German—in the old Leipzig and Tubingen editions, chubby little butterballs in stamped claret-colored bindings with a fine print calculated for the sharp vision of youth and with soft engravings done in a rather classical style: women with their hair down wring their hands, the lamp is always shown as an oil lamp, the horsemen have high foreheads, and the vignettes are clusters of grapes. All this was my father fighting his way as an autodidact into the German world out of the Talmudic wilds.

The works of Alfred North Whitehead, of Winston Churchill, Durant's *Story of Philosophy*—in the wake of my bar mitzvah, these were the texts my father would instruct me in, admitting to a polite agnosticism. I was attending the Boston Public Latin School, and turning the wheel over to me for our morning dash downtown, he read aloud beside me. Now and then in that skeptical conversation of his, replete with Spinoza, Santayana, elegant Harvard gilt, a phrase of Talmud would come up like a gleaming nugget out of a buried vein, the corrosive wit of Babylonian erudition. It sprang from his lips without forethought on the floor of the Massachusetts legislature, in the law courts. An assistant district attorney whom he had twitted about a second-rate legal background goes through the swinging doors of the courtroom with him, arms full of heavy legal volumes. "See, you're not the only one around here who reads, Mirsky!"

My father sighs. "The rabbis say, 'Though the ass may be laden with books, it's not necessarily wise.'"

That tongue, which will cost Wilfred Mirsky his judgeship, wags cocky, cruel, contradicting itself, a rich confusion of New England ethics and the codes of his childhood, Polish yeshivas. He is father and grandfather to me, conferring, at once, respect and disdain upon Judaism and synagogues.

So when I embark on a search for the holiness I felt in my grandfather's *schul*, it is with an ironic wrinkle in my cheek. Can I become again the soul who was borne upward on the heart-shattering sweetness of the Russian cantor's voice? Can I find the assurance that I had, tugging at the cotton fringes on my grandfather's shawl, that he spoke aloud to God? A friend, a contemporary at Harvard, now a book editor, asks me to take him to synagogues. We go to the old Sephardic temple on Central Park West, Rabbi David de Sola Pool's, where the service is beautiful but staid, distant. One visits it like a museum, touched by faint historical associations, a nod

to one's genealogy, really like the memory of a Jewish ancestor in a Yankee bloodline, a pleasant memento of ancient
feeling.

I shake off my sadness and propose that we visit the prayer
hall of the Bobover Chassidim. I don't want to take him to the
Lubavicher, the usual watering hole for Jews curious about
Chassidim. The assembly of the Lubavicher has left me cold, a
big room filled with too many sharp-looking characters, while
the Lubavicher himself, Rabbi Shneersohn, frowns down on the
whole, half bored, it seems to me: professional proselytizers
hanging on the skirts of the crowd, unfolding brochures of
literature about the movement like insurance salesmen, button-
holing the uninitiated.

The courtyards of the Bobover are pure Eastern Europe,
dirt worn down to the bones of its stones, a sagging broken-
down hall that smells of all the spices in Yiddish Araby, herring, beer, pickle brine, schnapps, snuff: thick with fur hats,
embroidered frock coats. On my first visit there in company
with Seymour Simckes, a rabbi's son, a writer fluent in Hebrew
and Yiddish, I cling to his arm as we push through the mob
of eighteenth-century costumes, afraid that they'll stone me
because I'm wearing a black bowler, the only hat I possess,
a joke that my father laughingly conferred on me as a real
Bostonian's chapeau, the Irishman's favorite, and every eye is
on me. I'm telling you, the Bobover aren't shy about staring
at strangers, especially long-haired young men who come
tramping in out of the twentieth century. From three-year-olds
to the octogenarians, they are drinking in an eyeball full of
this zany who comes among a respectable congregation, clad
in white kneesocks, black britches, swallow-tailed coats, and
gorgeous golden, silver filigree frocks, with his absurd jacket,
tie, pants and—what? They point to my bowler. What's this?
Haman's hat? Fortunately I duck in and out of sight for the
men are pressed right up to the rafters and standing it seems
on each other's shoulders, the windowsills, scraping the ceiling. "It's kind of crowded," I gasp to Seymour.

"The Chassidim say it's like life. You rub up against one another." I'm getting to know my neighbor, it's true, as the whole room sways back and forth and the chant, the dance step of the body to it, is pressed in upon you from all sides.

Only a Chassid in an elegant coat, knickers, a handsome mink *shtreimel* is staring unbelieving into my face, glaring. I can't help but look back when he shouts, "Mirsky?"

"Goodman?" I can't believe it. "Phil Goodman?" The kid I went through six grades of elementary school with, tied B plus for fifth or sixth spot at the head of the class every time. Phil who dug up nineteenth-century pornography long buried in his cellar on Hiawatha Road in our adolescence and shared out the secrets of randy English lords and ladies until his uncle, an editor of the Yiddish press, confiscated the books in the name of scholarship. Phil?

Hugging, shaking, smiles. Explanation? "The whole world comes to Bobov," he quotes on the way home. He is teaching at the school for the Bobover children while taking his degree as a conservative rabbi at the Jewish Theological Seminary.

For the first time, Chassidim in the flesh appeals to me. It is the closest I have come to that world I have heard about from my father's cousins, the rebbe whose appearance in Pinsk set off an orgy of feeling, a parade of followers shouting down the main street, singing, rejoicing, banging on drums, pots. "If that rebbe was alive today," our cousin Isaac cried, "I would pay him ten thousand just to come into my factory." My father made the wry face of the *misnagid* at the dining-room table (this is the other side of the family, not the Mirskys, his tart eye signaled) as Isaac leaped up in enthusiasm. "A hundred women would crowd around when the rebbe sat, fighting for the chance to be the first to sit in that seat. For" —his elbows came together like wings—"it was believed that if the heat left from the bottom of the rebbe rose up into you, it would make you fertile!"

I can feel that piety, belief, good humor in the prayer hall of the Bobover. Philip promises to be my guide for a *shiur*, the lecture contained in a feast and dance session after the Sabbath service. The rabbi, though briefly glimpsed, attracts me. The dignity in his bearing is obvious, but there is ease too, and an instant sense of authority. I love the children clambering up and down over the laps of the elders, shrieking in high spirits, the sense of females hiding behind the wall where the rabbi sits, peering through holes in it at us, veiled, nakedness, curiosity, bubbling on the other side. There's something to this.

I return a week later, taking the editor with me. We eat first with the Goodmans. Philip's wife wears the Orthodox wig. (This custom always puzzles me. Where are the Cossacks? According to the Zohar, devils are bald.) Not cutting the corners of the beard, but hiding the hair of the head, what mockery of the biblical injunction to respect God's intentions as to our natural state! Give me those wild Moroccan, Iraqi beauties who flaunt their locks on the beach at Tel Aviv. There's the concupiscent spirit of my lady ancestors, Rachel, Rebecca, terrors whose behinds drove the patriarchs crazy. Still, there's such a warm feeling in the kitchen as we mumble after Phil through the prayers, talk to his wife, that I can forgive the plump *maidle* her wig.

We start for the synagogue of the Bobover. Though it's after dark, the surrounding streets deserted, there are Chassidim in the shadows as we approach the bare earth of the driveway that leads into the Brooklyn backyard where the hall slumps, hidden from the gaze of the casual sightseer. We are early and it seems somewhat bare, meager; the tables are set with pitchers of beer. "They love beer in Bobov," Rabbi Goodman explains. Slowly the room fills, faces that I have seen only in my imagination of the Twelve Tribes, snowy beards that look like hoarfrost of the generations coming in from Sinai, the courts of King David, Solomon, and the circle of the Baal Shem Tov's princes. Rabbi Halberstam, the Bobover, arrives, and now the hall, humming, begins to shine with an unearthly light. It really is the countenance of a biblical sage, a nose like an

Assyrian hawk, the classical broken beak of the Semite, slender and strong, under it a beard sharp as a dagger and the eyes gleaming with laughter. This is the face of Abraham, renewed among us. He speaks in Yiddish beginning the meal, and although I can understand little of it, the strength of the discourse radiates from the gestures of his limbs, the expression of his mouth, lines through his cheeks. He doesn't recite or recall a lesson. He calls out into the room. Swept up by an idea, he half rises from his seat, bangs on the table, pulls at his cheek. I can feel the argument as Phil whispers the bones of it in translation and it moves me. Now the singing begins and the sour, closed faces opposite us, those unhappy frozen Jewish noses, lips, which curl in scorn against the world, suddenly split open, the husks of nuts, such joy comes spilling out, such sweetness, polyphony of sound that I can't help but cry out too, not words but sounds, sound, the sound of horror, love, crying aloud, loud, the loudest I have ever called, all caught up in the contrapuntal chaos of the room, the song balancing on strange harmonies, rising, rising, until by mutual consent we stop, exhausted.

The meal is served. The *shirayim*, bits from the rabbi's plate, come down the length of the tables. It is as it has been described, a scene out of Chagall, for the whole crowd takes to the air with abandon, glee, wildly squirming into each other's coats, faces, bellies, licking after bits of herring, potato kugel. It's not the food itself but the fun of snatching a spark of holiness that is dancing madly down the room, actually putting our tongue to it, taking it in; leaping upon it like fish with our mouths open—one feels the dreadful shimmer of the mackerel-crowded sea. Who can believe that the awesome solemnity, sobriety of these Orthodox grandfathers could dissolve in such uninhibited merriment as my friend and I gladly give ourselves up to the squeezing, jostling, singing, sniffing, tasting, fighting for the *shirayim*, all our uneasiness melted away, at one with the body of the Bobover.

The rabbi rises to bless the members of the congregation,

one by one calling out their names over the *kiddush* cup to which the Chassidim respond by downing the glass of beer at their elbows.* On the Saturday when I first visited the Bobover synagogue, they asked my name in Hebrew and sent it up for a blessing. Now, weeks later, without any prompting, the Bobover calls out, "Moishe ben Zaav." I am so amazed that I tip my glass to him without thinking, as if we were clinking mugs across the room. A hush falls over the hundreds of white heads, black beards, children: their mouths open in amazement. Am I making fun of the rebbe? Pulling his beard? The Bobover too looks me in the eye, not aghast yet in wonder, but as the blush spreads across my cheeks, his face breaks into a wide grin, and he tips his *kiddush* cup back at me, twinkling. Everyone dissolves in smiles, a low murmur of laughter. Why not, *l'chaiyim!* So the rhythm goes on, lecturing, eating, drinking, three or four times we roll on in the prayer wheel till at last the evening ends, all of us shoulder to shoulder, dancing in the space where the tables have been cleared away, and my friend, who is nimble on his legs, kicks and gyrates with abandon.

"*Ayyyy, ayyyyyy*," we're still singing and dancing on the subway home to Manhattan at one in the morning. For the editor it is the circle of babies and grandfathers, crushed belly to belly, leaping and swaying before the rabbi; for me it is the song rising and falling in their throats, that has rocked us into a far voyage across the mystical waves. Yes, we can feel the glow; the editor, an expert, says it's better than marijuana. I feel the white heat of the angel on my face. Yes, this is it. We have to do something about it.

My friend joins a friendly, "intellectual" West Side temple. I go to one service with him, a pathetic affair with the Hebrew

* My memory may be faulty here and it is possible that we used wine, not beer, for the *kiddush*. It's possible that we drank before eating and that this incident, indeed, happened at a *kiddush* that first Saturday. The events, like the Chassidim, are still whirling through my head, making chronology impossible.

original paid a fleeting lip service and all the obnoxious euphemisms of Reform Judaism bled so pale, a pure tasteless Unitarianism on the tongue. I stare at him after the service. "You have to be kidding."

Am I better? I don't go back to Bobov. It's wonderful, but I can't live in the eighteenth century. I'm afraid to spoil the memory of that evening's holiness.

Is there a synagogue I can go to? I want the intellectual challenge of peers, but I also want the holiness of Bobov. I want to lose myself in a crush of children, old men, as I did at six or seven years old outside the doors of the Chai Odom on Nightingale Street, holding a holiday flag, the Star of David on a blue-and-white banner, an apple stuck to the top of my stick in whose core there swayed a fat wax Sabbath candle, aflame. Simchas Torah! The Torah scrolls swinging with silver plates; blue, gold, cherry velvet covers come down the front steps into Nightingale Street, cradled by men in silk hats, swathed in yards of banded shawls: everyone pressing forward to kiss, kiss the hem fringe, touch it to one's lips, Torah, Torah, Torah, to worship the law as a living thing.

It is not life but death that is my deepest experience of the contemporary synagogue. After my mother dies, eaten alive by cancer in her hospital bed, my father, who is so angry he can hardly stand to walk into a synagogue anymore, takes me to a Dorchester *schul* and shows me what to do for my mother, completes my bar mitzvah lesson at the age of twenty-nine, how to put on the *tefillin*, say the mourner's Kaddish.

Before, the synagogue has been a vicarious experience. Now in order to recite prayers for her, by law I have to attend daily, twice, morning and dusk.* No matter how tedious, rushed, the service, I find myself strangely comforted. Here are men like myself, some seventy, others barely fourteen, who have lost a parent. Our grief is naked, common; for almost

* One recites Kaddish to aid one's parents' souls in the stringencies of the year of purification they undergo after death. One is helping them ascend from the pit.

a year* we will stroke together, rowing the souls of parents over the waves. My mother's ghost, which comes to me at night so that I rise in terror as she wraps her arms around me, grows quiet, assuaged, as I wrap the leather bands around my arms and call out to her: rest, rest, praising the name of God, Yisgadal, V'Yiskadash, Magnified be Thy Great Name. . . .

In the damp thickets of Brazil, Lévi-Strauss ponders the uses of the hall of prayer, how the civilizations he encounters mediate between the living and the dead, their terrible claims. The dead do not bury the dead, as the quote would have it, the living bury them, and ignore this duty at their peril. For the penalty of living without consciousness of death is to have one's body invaded by ghosts, to lose fear, lust, hunger, and be but a shadow, a ghost, bored and gagged by tedium.

Now I understand the synagogue's heartbeat, and I am grateful for it. I need that strange, mixed, unfamiliar company of mourners: salesmen, a bank manager, a pimply schoolboy, an ancient graybeard. I even rejoice in two loudmouths at the lower East Side temple with their intolerant outrage at blacks, welfare recipients, etc., for in the intimacy of death they talk to me with my long hair and strange clothes as if it is understood that despite disagreements we are one, the living, the survivors, the afflicted. One day a young black Jew comes to pray with the morning *minyan* and a hush pervades the room. He has taken his place at the oars with us. In death he has become one of the company, and after the prayers, even the bigots shake his hand with tenderness. Grief has made us lovers.

As the tide ebbs at the end of the eleven prescribed months of mourning, I try to hold on to the synagogue, but irritation

---

* Why don't we mourn a full twelve months? The Jewish Encyclopedia gives one a taste of talmudic leaven reaching even into hell. "Because the full year is considered to be the duration of judgment for the wicked and we presume that our parents do not fall into that category, the practice is to recite the Kaddish for only eleven months."

reasserts itself. At one synagogue I am embarrassed by the clumsy praying, the middle-class homilies; another repels me with its senseless haste, a meaningless rattle of Hebrew, and there is too far a distance between the Yiddish-speaking ancients and myself.

Is there a synagogue I can go to not only in the grip of death, but weekly, to study? When I first came to New York City, exhilarated by the world of old Jewishness I found alive, the pushcarts of Avenue C, the world of Orchard Street, its little synagogues where I spent my first New Year's in Manhattan, I asked friends at *Commentary* and others to join me to create a house of study. It never came to pass, a synagogue of writers, painters, artists, New York intellectuals. One can pray on Orchard Street, but it's too alien to study there. Instead I have sought out teachers, individuals, and the lessons have not hallowed a place. But the impulse to build a synagogue, not a gaudy hall or elaborate temple but a "tent of meeting," a structure that will embody the geography of contemporary Jewish questions, wanderings, where one can meet, think, pray together, that must remain an important dream for me. I have felt the holiness of the ark in strange places: the US Air Force, where in a makeshift *schul*, a classroom loaned to the Jewish servicemen at Gunter Air Force Base we celebrated the Sabbath, each one trying to remember some fragment of the service; the tiny box off a street called Rue des Synagogues, Tangier, where a congregation looking like Don Quixote's retinue, a rowboat full of Castillian Jews who remembered their ancestors' flight from Spain five hundred years ago, snatched me up from the street to make their *minyan*: at the houses of friends where three or four of us at the table suddenly began to discuss the tradition, the law, and were gripped not only by the argument but the holiness that seemed to gather in the air, silent wings beating above us.

2
The Three Gurus

The Three Gurus

VVVVV

At a certain moment, if you do not regard your religion as merely spontaneous heresy, prophecy, or intuition, you must take a teacher. The notion of *guru* has been popularized by the Eastern religions, the master who will make knowledge immanent in you, and of course, Chassidism has its *tsaddiks*, those righteous ones whose influence transcends human knowledge and sets the disciple on the true way. I, too, came at a dark moment in my life to ask from Judaism more than I had gleaned from family, Hebrew school, popular wisdom. Deep in my Litvak bones, however, was a detestation of the idea of guru or *tsaddik*. It was anathema to surrender oneself uncritically to another man. The great teachers, Moses, David, Hosea, were always reported with their warts as a hedge against inflation.

"Don't forget his warts!" a rabbinical friend of mine cries, hearing I am to write some pages on Rabbi Soloveitchik, the only man to be called "The Rav" in this generation, *the* rabbi, the lawgiver. When the *Village Voice* published my eulogy of Harry Wolfson, hailed as "the world's greatest scholar," they printed the sentence "he had his warts," then neatly excised the paragraphs that described them. *Goyisheh kopp*: "Love without reproof is no love," said R. Jose b. Hanina. The impulse to worship is strong in me. Yet the tradition teaches us to take up an iron bar and shatter all our images. That, I think, is the function of the bitter gossip in the Talmud, to render all the sages human. Worship belongs only to God.

Harry Wolfson, Joseph Soloveitchik, and Gershom Scholem; to call myself their student is to defame them. I have hardly begun to absorb their lessons. My Judaism is still a chaos. In my head these three all speak to one another.

Those who are at home among their teachings I hope will read these jottings with the amused curiosity of the native for the stranger's impressions.

Despite one's awe at the depths of their scholarship, each of these men possessed a spark of the guru; that fire that lit the eyes or prose makes the whole intuitively apparent to the student almost in the first moments of study. It was the gift of Hillel, who, confronted with an obstreperous nonbeliever wanting to learn the whole of Judaism while he stood on one leg, smiled and rendered the Bible in one epigram that Jesus was to purloin and turn upside down, a hundred years later, reversing the negative precept: "Don't do unto others what you don't want them to do unto you."

It is the hope for that fire that draws one into the presence of great scholars, the belief that they possess academic magic, more, the breath of the Nabi, the prophet, to make the most complicated of structures, God, the Law of the Universe, suddenly clear, demonstrable, so you "know" before you understand. It is the power of poetry, striking metaphor, and if in Hebrew the word "know" means sexual intercourse as well as understanding, perhaps that is a clue to the excitement with which a Jew approaches his books, his teachers. I have felt it, reading Scholem, Wolfson, at Soloveitchik's lectures, that heady swoon, that bursting of light within the breast. No Chassid dancing, singing, can raise me to the ethereal music that these men, dry, reedy, in the measured intellectual tones, recite.

Turning the Tables
on Spinoza

VVVVV

HARRY WOLFSON sent for me.

To understand why I hung up on my father—who had
called to tell me that the sage wanted to see me in Cambridge
—and rushed back and forth like a baffled bird in my tiny
New York study, knocking into walls, imagining this and that,
you have to know that Harry Wolfson was a household deity.
In the Boston Jewish community, Wolfson, a tiny man, not
much higher than his desk, was a tall tale. In Eastern Europe,
scholarship and holiness were indissoluble, and Wolfson, the
foremost Jewish scholar in America, became, despite his disclaimer "I am an unobservant Orthodox Jew," a prince. In
1925 he was awarded the first chair of Hebrew learning in
an American university, the Nathan Littauer Professorship of
Hebrew Literature and Philosophy at Harvard. Those to
whom Jewish learning was important had to make, at least
once in their lifetime, a trek to his study in Cambridge.

To Boston Jewry, Wolfson's presence savored of more than just intellectual spice. That first Jewish seat* at a university notorious for its clannish, clubby, silent anti-Semitism, for the rankling insult of President Lowell's public antipathy to the wave of Polish Jews at Harvard, was occupied not by an assimilated German Jew, but a representative of the best in the Eastern European talmudic academies, a graduate of the famous Slabodka Yeshiva, a real Litvak. That's what counted to the Orthodox, not Wolfson's B.A. and Ph.D. from Harvard, no—his record as a nine-year-old prodigy at Slabodka.

In my family, he was a very particular hero. My father, who came from Eastern Europe as a child, used to joke with us about the day he deserted his strict adherence to the rules of kashreth, kosherdom. He saw Harry Wolfson, "the world's greatest Jewish scholar," eating ham and eggs in the Waldorf Cafeteria. "If it's all right for Wolfson, it's all right for me!" (My father shook his head over the ham-and-egg story as I repeated it to him. "No, no," he insisted. "It was toasted English on Passover.") Harry Wolfson had been my father's freshman advisor at Harvard, and he loved to embroider tales of his guide's foibles, the absent-minded man who criss-crossed Harvard Yard with the young tutee; first at the steps down to the subway, remembering a letter left behind in the office, then, back at the subway again, almost through the turnstile, a book he was supposed to bring, on and on until the evening he had set aside for entertaining his charge in Boston was over and it was too late to reach their destination—the Old Howard Burlesque & Striptease in Scollay Square.

Now I was climbing the back stairs of Widener Library with my father. We found Harry Wolfson's doorway, knocked on the opaque milky glass, shuffled awkwardly into his study. Wolfson looked at me. Previously I had hidden behind my

---

* That seat didn't come out of the beneficence of President Lowell. A group of non-Jewish professors in Semitics prevailed on a Hebrew captain of the glove industry, Littauer, to endow a professorship for their underpaid colleague.

father's back when we encountered his famous freshman advisor on Massachusetts Avenue.

"You wrote that article about Blue Hill Avenue, the synagogues."

"Yes."

Framed by shelves of books, piles, pillars, a Babylonian brickwork of editions, Wolfson was not the tiny man whom I had seen walking, self-absorbed, in Harvard Square when my father interrupted his reverie to salute the scholar. The head rose from a small chin to a brow that seemed almost as wide as his shoulders, all the strength of his short limbs gathered up into that massive skull, and I felt the eerie force, a giant's, concentrated in those eyes, reflecting the weight of thousands of volumes.

"They were very good, but. . . ."

I bent in to hear his dry peppery voice.

"Be careful."

I looked at him, puzzled.

"Say whatever you like about the Jews. Tell the truth, only. . . ."

A wrinkle in his cheek. "Say it in *Hebrew*."

We both smiled. "I have written poetry too," he added. "Look at this."

Turning to his desk, he picked up a book, flipped the pages, had me read. I saw what he meant; the language of his summation was more than philosophical history. The words, balancing conundrums and contradictions, shadowed Kafka and Borges. Seeing my delight, he pushed out of his chair toward a bookcase. Reaching up, he tipped a heavy volume off the shelf. It almost knocked him down. I got up to help, but he waved me back. Spreading the text out, he pointed to one passage, then another, his riddles.

"Weren't you ever tempted to become a philosopher yourself?" I asked. "You are the most important scholar of Jewish philosophy. Sifting all those sources, evaluating them, didn't you think of formulating your own?"

Harry Wolfson looked at me and his eyes were alight, laughing. He took a volume of his work on Philo, a book that not only rescued the Alexandrine Jew from obscurity, but in the words of Isadore Twersky, established him as the "dominant influence, latent or apparent, in European philosophic thought for seventeen centuries," opened it, put the stub of his finger to a page and, as I read, whispered, "You think Philo said that? Philo didn't say that. I said that."

Reading Harry Wolfson one is struck by his poetry and his originality. The language is not only succinct and ironic but, as he grows older and more assured, it begins to break out openly into a familiar wit. The two volumes on Spinoza are beautifully written, but the voice is formal, echoing Whitehead's dictum "Style is the most austere of qualities." The books on Philo are much more relaxed, as if simplicity had replaced austerity, and in chapter after chapter, pausing in his assembling of the Alexandrian's complex structure of thought, Wolfson, like Hillel, summarizes it all in a few dazzling paragraphs. But in his *Religious Philosophy*—as if anticipating the sands of time running out on him, in his sixties, seventies, 120 years would be too short for the mass of manuscript lying in his files to be properly edited, annotated, weighed and reweighed in his endless revisions in galleys, the whole of philosophy from Plato to Spinoza, and before, after, pre-Socratics, neo-Kantians—Wolfson begins to handspring. In these short essays, lectures—amazing acrobatics, philosopher to philosopher—grasping the rope of an idea, he sails through fifteen centuries to show off the leaps his mind has been making over the handwritten manila pages he accumulated.

In his Widener office, at the end of my last discussion he beckoned me to get up and accompany him to a set of wide green file cabinets. He put my hand on the handle of one and motioned for me to pull. The drawer rolled forward and it was packed, bulging with cream-colored folders filled with manila paper. Prying one out at random, he showed me the large, handwritten scrawl of his thoughts, then bending back to the cabinets, pulled out drawer after drawer with me.

A sea of folders! He looked at me, amused. "The whole history of philosophy is here." I was dizzy. Only an infinitesimal amount would ever see print in his lifetime. It took Harry Wolfson ten, twelve years to publish a single volume. He treated his galleys from the Harvard University Press like the first draft of a typist. There was a staggering amount of knowledge awash in these drawers and one has to go to the epigrams of the Talmud to do it justice. "If all the seas were ink, and all the reeds pens, and all men scribes, they could not write down all the Scripture and Mishnah I studied, nor what I learned from the sages in the academy. Yet I carried away from my teachers no more than does a man who dips his finger in the sea."

The quintessential Wolfson is feisty, funny, a master of epigram, a talmudist. He can cleave the Gordian knots of terminology; his weapon, laughter. One sharp sentence disposes of the endless wrangles of historians of philosophy and religion who see the Arian heresy as a battle betwen Aristotelians and Platonists.* "On the whole, it is not historically correct to arrange the Fathers into groups, to dress them up in the uniform of the Academy or Lyceum or the Porch, to march them under the school banner of Plato or of Aristotle or of the Stoics, and to make them sing their school song. The Fathers did not regard themselves as followers of the various schools of Greek thought." In the midst of drawing the subtle distinctions and parallels between Arianism and its fellow heresy, Apollinarianism, their common shift on the

---

* Arianism, in brief, denies that Jesus was of divine nature, while Apollinarianism denies that Jesus had a human nature. Wolfson characterizes these heresies respectively as "leftist" and "rightist." Both deviations are named after their original proponents, Arius and Apollinaris, fourth-century Christian philosophers. The controversy these points of view spawned engulfed much of Europe and the Middle East in widespread massacre and arson as cities went up in flames over the issues.

question of whether Jesus Christ had an irrational soul, a voice that is almost wicked intrudes.

Had they any reason for first denying to Jesus an irrational soul and then granting him one? Or are we to assume that they had no reason for their change of mind, but acted only as if they were shopping for a Christmas present for the holy child Jesus, and, after debating with themselves whether or not he could use an irrational soul, for no reason at first decided he could get along without one, then bethought themselves further and decided to get him one anyhow?

To appreciate what this image does, you have to understand that the reader is groping through very difficult, almost algebraic, formulation of Christian mysteries and Greek philosophy when a paragraph like this suddenly lights up the page like a holiday tree. Gripped by the excitement of hearing the terminology of the Muslim philosophers turning up in the speech of orthodox Christians like Albert Magnus and Thomas Aquinas, Wolfson swings a baseball bat. "The fourth event is a double header." Dismissing John Stuart Mill's argument against the infinite power of God, showing how it was anticipated by Thomas Aquinas and long before, by Philo, the philosopher drops into the voice of a caterer, his concealed simile, garbage. "What Mill really did here, our hypothetical scriptural philosopher would conclude, was to rake up an old difficulty, to overlook the answer given to it, and garnish it up as a new argument."

A metaphor that he repeats in several essays is the tailor's version of the soul's creation.

In technical language, the views of these three camps (on the soul's origin) are known as those of creation, preexistence, and traducianism. In plain English, they may be described, respectively, as the theory of custom-made souls, the theory of ready-made souls, and the theory of second-hand souls.

According to the custom-made theory, at the birth of each

child God creates a soul especially for that child. According to the ready-made theory, at the time of the creation of the world, God in his foresight created individual souls which in number and variety were sufficient to supply the need of all the future generations of men. These souls are kept in a place the exact name of which is variously given by various authorities who are expert in the knowledge of these matters. At each child's birth, a soul suitable to his body is placed within him—though, judging by the great number of misfit souls in the world, one may infer that mistakes frequently occur. According to the second-hand theory of the soul, God at the time of creation of the world, created only one soul, and that soul is the soul of Adam. All our souls are only slices of the worn-out soul of our first ancestor, which, without being thoroughly cleansed and destained, are cut down and made to fit our own peculiar bodies.

To the canny ear there is biblical echo in this fun. For when God first came down to earth, says the Talmud, He did so as a tailor. "And the Lord God made for Adam and for his wife garments of skins, and clothed them." Why did He do so? The rabbis answer that since now Adam and she had to work by the sweat of their brows, the Holy One, Blessed Be He, wanted to set an example. Harry Wolfson's demiurge is a down-to-earth *shnayder.**

Was Harry Austryn Wolfson an original thinker? As I turn the pages of *Religious Philosophy* I am struck not only by his method but its purpose. He was a talmudist. He wants

---

* I would like to advance a heresy. I hear—if not Yiddish—the spirit, logos, of it in his speech rhythms, though impeccable English. It could be argued that it is the pungency of the Babylonian Talmud we are hearing, not Eastern Europe. Wolfson's attitude toward Yiddish was problematical. He opposed its being taught at Harvard. Despite his delight in his native Austryn (a cousin, Richard Stone, reports that he kept up with hundreds of names from this Russian *shtetl*, births, marriages, careers, and that any Austryner who wound up at Harvard was bound to learn of Wolfson's desire for a book commemorating the town) he refused to admit its language and literature to the status of scholastic legitimacy. And he was equally hostile to other ethnic courses. "Black studies," he exclaimed to my father on the street. "Tell me, what is there to study?"

not simply to state the truth of a particular philosophical argument but to give the point of view that has gone into creating it. Who is it being said to? Who said it before? Who after? He wants to give us the human *structure* of the argument. (The title for the vast work in his drawers of which all his individual books were to be parts was *Structure and Growth of Philosophic Systems from Plato to Spinoza*.) It is not Philo or Spinoza alone who emerges from these pages, but Philo arguing with Aristotle, Plato, Heraclitus: and centuries later Maimonides, Spinoza, Aquinas, Descartes arguing with Philo, so that a whole world, a universe of argument, is bodied forth in the volumes on Spinoza, Philo, a school in which Wolfson is the smiling master of debate, pitting one against the other, much as Rab Ashi and the redactors of the Babylonian Talmud did in the spirit of Rabbi Judah the prince, who had assembled the Mishnah before them: a dozen views of the same problem with a shrewd eye threading them together. The voices are alive and in the books, the "house of study" of Wolfson, St. Augustine takes Philo's side while St. Thomas sides with Maimonides against them. Spinoza reaches over the benches to embrace the point of view of Aristotle, which has lain in the dust for so many centuries, the Holy Writ of one decade of thinkers rescued from the wastebasket of another.

When half the argument is missing, Wolfson jumps in and makes it up.* And when there is no argument, Wolfson creates one, a first mover of philosophical debate, because after all, that's what philosophy is about, *nu*? "Though he slay me,

---

* But the Fathers [the Church Fathers], learned in philosophy as many of them were, knew that besides those philosophers who believed in immortality, there were others, chief among them the Epicureans, who were outspoken opponents of immortality and argued against it. While no formal and direct refutation of the Epicurean arguments is to be found as far as I could ascertain, in the Fathers of the Church, answers in anticipation of these arguments are provided by them in their discussions of the nature, origin, and functions of the soul as well as in their positive arguments for immortality. Let us then see how the Fathers would answer the Epicurean arguments against immortality.

I will argue with him," is what the Hebrew is said to read in the book of Job, not *trust* but *argue*. Even when God Himself comes down to earth to tell man what it's all about, He has to argue. And later, in the Talmud, the Holy One, Blessed Be He, gets a real scolding. Philosophy is argument, not dogma, trust.

If you understand how Jewish Wolfson's point of view is, then you can sense why his books touch me and why his sly whisper is an earnest of his own claims to be Philo. Isadore Twersky, his successor at Harvard, summarizing the importance of these volumes, says:

Wolfson depicts Philo as the founder of a new philosophic trend in whose footsteps followed not only his immediate successors, the Church Fathers, but also his indirect disciples, the Moslem, Jewish and Christian medieval philosophers. . . . Philo emerges from Wolfson's reasoning as a sovereign critic of all schools of Greek philosophy and, consequently, as an autonomous thinker.

Now, however, it is Harry Wolfson who is the "sovereign critic" of medieval philosophy, of Spinoza, and in *Religious Philosophy* he reaches past his scholarship to speak in parables to the modern world. He spanks Hume, John Stuart Mill, their misunderstandings: fools who don't know their genealogies. One set of terms inevitably spawns another. He perches on one foot, an acrobat, a Zen master, and begins to flip the whole history of philosophy in one marvelous parody, mocking in the language of the famous biblical genealogy of man, Genesis, 10 and 11.

And Plato lived forty years and begat the ideas.

And the ideas of Plato lived three hundred years and begat the Logos of Philo.

And the Logos of Philo lived seventy years and begat the Logos of John.

And the Logos of John lived six hundred years and begat the attributes of Islam.

And the attributes of Islam lived five hundred and fifty years and begat the attributes of the Schoolmen.

And the attributes of the Schoolmen lived four hundred years and begat the attributes of Descartes and Spinoza.

And the attributes of Spinoza lived two hundred years and begat among their interpreters sons and daughters who knew not their father.

In Harry Wolfson's lexicon, there are few original ideas under the sun but many mistakes. Monumental shifts in religious philosophy can be traced back to a misunderstood term or a mistranslation. Wolfson's method is based on reviewing the sources that are obvious in a given philosopher's work (borrowings from Plato, Maimonides, Descartes), then focusing on the ways in which his subject alters these inherited ideas. Through the text, we are introduced to the psychology of the man who composed it. Why does a philosopher like Spinoza suddenly become irrational, refuse to carry his thoughts into the logical progressions of Aristotle, whose ideas he has been restating? In catching Spinoza, Augustine, at the moment when they slip or deliberately step aside from their own machinery, Harry Wolfson renders them, their abstractions, human.

Yea, what is more filled with pathos than the moment in Wolfson's corpus when turning back to his beloved Spinoza in *Philo and Religious Philosophy* (Spinoza, who must at times have seemed like his double, the young Jewish intellectual suddenly finding himself feted as a great thinker outside the narrow walls of the Jewish community), Harry shows how the optician of Amsterdam, at the last moment, cannot surrender his individuality to eternity but forsakes his master Aristotle's idea—that only the human race is eternal, not human beings—and comes back into the fold.* Yet he holds on to his unique-

---

* Like Avicenna and Averroes and their followers in the past, he [Spinoza] tries to show that the human mind, though in its origin it is only a part of the absolutely infinite intellect, becomes individualized during the lifetime of man by its acquisition of knowledge . . . on its reunion with the absolutely infinite intellect whence it originally came, somehow, in some inexplicable manner, retains

ness, the hope of it after death. Wolfson smiles because, as he deftly shows, immortality implies resurrection, and once you are into that game, you might as well accept revelation, since you are in the realm of faith, not logic. That stubborn last-minute grip on personal immortality before death brings back the whole host of angels and demons Spinoza had spent his life forsaking.

Turning the tables on Spinoza and his successors, showing how their ideas are no more logical than the ancients', only less clear, all their thoughts anticipated, Wolfson is functioning as more than a scholar. He is a commentator. His wit is the breath of Rabbi Hisda's vineyard, a bit of vinegar, but he is arguing for faith. You cannot doubt it when you finish the last lines of his essay on "Immortality and Resurrection," where he stages the Church Fathers' hypothetical reply to a young modern skeptic who will accept immortality of the soul, "seeing that respectable modern philosophers and even respectable modern scientists with a philosophic turn of mind do occasionally give a nod of approval to immortality," but not resurrection of the body, "seeing that modern science is all against its possibility."

"Dear young man," answers Wolfson. "If you can find consolation in this verbal kind of immortality and if this verbal kind of immortality can serve you as an incentive to do good and shun evil, go and console yourself and sin no more and mayhap the Lord in His mercy will reward you with true immortality, aye, and with resurrection, too.

"And to this, and with this, we say, Amen."

But of course, it is not the Church Fathers speaking, it is the rabbis, because we have heard only a few pages before that the Church Fathers excluded nonbelievers from salvation,

---

its acquired individuality. The human soul is thus immortal, or eternal, as he usually calls it, and its immortality is in a certain sense personal and individual.

immortality, and resurrection. It is the Jews who allow that "a pious Gentile is equal unto the High Priest."

It is religion in its broadest sense, a messianism of the here and now, where pagan philosophers, Christians, and Jews mingle, borrowing freely of each other's insights. That is Wolfson's ideal. Judaism has nothing to fear in such a world, for its special testimony has a hypnotic power, and the burden of Wolfson's song is that again and again, since its message became known outside the boundaries of the Jewish community, philosophy, pagan, Christian, Muslim, keeps coming back to it. So Philo is his hero, the Alexandrine who was able to synthesize Judaism and Greek philosophy, thereby laying the logical basis for Christian, Muslim, Jewish thinking in ages to come. Have we improved on Philo? Not very much, says Harry. Perhaps we accept less of the Scripture literally than Philo did, but he, in conformity with the talmudists, already saw large sections of it as allegory. If you want, as a Jew, Christian, or Muslim, to maintain the logic of Greek philosophy while holding on to the belief in the uniqueness of Scripture as a holy book of revelation, the Alexandrine's propositions in the main are still the best of both worlds.

To believe, despite the obligatory sour grapes, that God is running the universe, this is the quiet direction of Harry Wolfson's thought. Moreover, his sympathies for certain forms of Christian or Muslim heresy: Arius striving to get back to the unity of God;* Pelagius attempting to defend

* The Arian heresy "may be described as leftist. . . . It denied the divinity of the pre-existent Christ, the Logos: and it also denied a divine nature in the born Christ, Jesus" (*Religious Philosophy*, p. 126). Wolfson shows how Arius, in denying the idea of "three inseparable individual substances, called hypostases of persons" within God, was re-embracing the Philonic position. "Philo extended and deepened the scriptural meaning of the unity of God: it was to exclude any kind of logical or metaphysical divisibility, such as divisibility into two substances, even when inseparable from each other, or divisibility into matter and form, or divisibility into genus and species. The unity of God meant absolute unity" (ibid., p. 145).

Philo's definition of free will against an Augustine intent on
making into dogma a much more limited demarkation of
man's freedom—a position that would have been anathema
to most of the Church Fathers preceding;* the careful summation of the battles between Church Fathers, Arab philosophers, their Muslim and Christian successors, over Philonic
terminology (until we suspect that it is Philo who is the
standard in Harry's head for heresy, how far have they deviated?); his shrewd eye for the moments when Jew and
Catholic, Arab, agree, Miamonides and St. Thomas, or even
better, Stoic, Arab, Catholic, and Jew: all are in the spirit of
the rabbis at their most enlightened moments, tied to no specific dogma but to the tradition of inquiry, the thousand
flowers of opinion blooming in the Talmud.

   Wolfson's talmudic background clarifies Philo for him.
(Why for instance does Philo's God create the Universe
through intermediate powers, "without touching it Himself,

---

* "Pelagius maintained that there was no loss of free will in the descendants of Adam as a result of the fall. . . . In contradistinction to all this,
Augustine maintains that as a result of the corruption produced by the
fall of Adam and inherited by his descendants that freedom consisting
of the ability to sin or not sin which was possessed by Adam before
his fall is no longer possessed by his descendants" (ibid., p. 162–64).
   When Augustine, to whom it had been reported that "The Pelagians
believe that the study of law leads to God," shouted at Pelagius, "You
are a Jew in all but name!" one can be sure that Wolfson does not
regard it as an insult.
   Augustine gets a thorough spanking from Harry a number of times
and is scolded roundly for creating dogma out of dog Latin. The
Church philosopher commits the ultimate anathema in the scholar's
eyes, a mistake in grammar. The latter shows how Augustine misunder-
stands the Latin *continens*, a translation of a Greek verse in the Book
of Wisdom of Solomon, "And I knew I could not otherwise be *wise*,
except God gave it." Augustine takes *continens* to stand for "continence"
rather than its explicit meaning both in Latin and in the Greek; it has
been translated from "wisdom." This mistake results in "his belief in
the powerlessness of man to abstain from sin" and the doctrine of
"irresistible concupiscence." The scholar shakes his head: "In our judgment, Pelagius, on the problem of freedom, represents the original
Christian belief. It was Augustine who introduced something new from
without" (ibid., p. 176).

since it was not lawful for His nature, happy and blessed as it was, to touch indefinite and mixed-up matter?" Wolfson's answer is: "These statements . . . through Philo, reflect the many passages in the Old Testament that make it unlawful for the clean and the holy to touch the unclean and for the unclean to touch the clean and the holy.") More important, perhaps, Wolfson's identity as a Jew, a Jew at Harvard, leads him to the Alexandrine's quandary, trying in an assimilated Hellenistic world to hold on to his own tradition, to create through Greek philosophy and its commentators a justification for Judaism. If Wolfson's Philo is Jewish, so is his Spinoza. He draws an ironic portrait of the former Dutch "yeshiva bocher" Manassah Ben Israel's star pupil, among his new-found gentile friends.* In the chronicle of Spinoza's philosophy, passage after passage, Wolfson shows his subject in lonely isolation, arguing with the Jewish sources of his childhood education, Maimonides, Crescas, Ibn Ezra: and perhaps it bodies a portrait of Wolfson too, carrying on an argument with the past, in preference to his Jewish contemporaries.

Why was Harry Wolfson important to me? Difficult texts, touched by his laughter, assumed life. Ancient Greeks, neo-Platonists, they stood up like the exotic crabs of a Lewis Carroll tale, croaking ominous lines, "The stars are animals!" on the seashore, in the ear where we hear time crash. At his

---

* Despite the fact that he allowed himself to enter into the discussion of problems which troubled the minds of his correspondents, he never communicated to them the fulness of his own thought or discussed with them the philosophic problems which troubled his own mind. The congenial group of merchants, booksellers, medical students, and holders of public office which formed the immediate circle of Spinoza's friends had a layman's interest in the general problems of philosophy, but they could hardly serve as stages of his thinking. They seem to have had a more vigorous grasp of the problems of theology, in which they were the liberals of their day, but with all the adventuresomeness of their spirit they were just beginning to approach the liberalism of the medieval writings of Jewish rationalists read by Spinoza in his early youth, which he had long outgrown. (H. A. Wolfson, *The Philosophy of Spinoza*, pp. 22–23. New York: Schocken Books, 1969.)

office, he handed me a reprint of his article "The Problem of the Souls of the Spheres" and I found myself retracing his steps through the ether as I searched in a chapter of my novella *Dorchester, Home and Garden* for answers to my mother's death, her disappearance, the whereabouts, if possible, of her soul. Philosophy was poetry, a language of abstraction that tried to grope after the beyond, the unknown. The far reaches of logic, Wolfson showed, brought one to the same absurdities, unknowns, as the furthest limits of the astrophysicist. As Virgil took Dante by the hand, Wolfson's voice guided me through a foretaste of death, the descending and ascending circles of man's knowledge, theory, alerting my eye, no matter how complicated the terminology, to the simplicity of the riddles. Clarity like Harry Wolfson's is dazzling. If man is about awareness, putting down his meticulous analysis, I felt as if I was indeed stepping from sphere to sphere, ethereal music singing in my head.

Did Harry Wolfson believe in God? Behind the veil of laughter, the answer is clear, "existential," although the scholar might have laughed at the word, for he had watched philosophers through the centuries taking the much vaunted modern "leap of faith." It was either believe, as Spinoza, Philo, Plato, had done, or accept the Epicurean explanation of the "emergence of the world out of the accidental collison of aimlessly drifting eternal atoms." And if one was going to believe, perhaps it was best to follow in the footsteps of that bluff Arab Ibn Khaldun, who, "in the age of old struggle between orthodoxy and rationalism in religion . . . saw nothing but the perversion of reason and, like a goodly number of non-quibblers of every religion, he chose to suspend reason rather than pervert it."

And, like my father two score years before, I caught the scholar's coattails. If Harry Wolfson can suspend reason for a taste of immortality, so can I.

Levitation in the Law

WWWW

"Soloveitchik is recognized as the master of many if not all of the younger traditional writers engaged in theological speculation. Why then . . . the omission of Soloveitchik? The answer is not hard to find. Soloveitchik's literary production is so scanty that those outside his circles have to rely on hearsay for even a glimpse of his position" (Lou H. Silberman, *American Jewish Year Book*, 1969).

"As a talmudic scholar he is perhaps the most eminent of contemporary rabbinic authorities with a masterful grip of Halakah proper" (*Great Jewish Thinkers of the Twentieth Century*).

"Looked up to in North America as the unchallenged leader of enlightened Orthodoxy . . . popularly known simply as "the Rav" (*Jewish Encyclopedia*).

"WHAT DO YOU THINK of Soloveitchik?" I asked Harry Wolfson in the scholar's office during our first interview. He beamed. "A great preacher." At the time I was puzzled. (Wolfson may have added, "The world's greatest.") His enthusiasm was evident, but I thought it a strange compliment, for after all, Soloveitchik was no mean scholar. He had a doctoral degree from Berlin in philosophy, his thesis on the neo-Kantian Hermann Cohen's metaphysics and epistemology. He was professor of Talmud at Yeshiva University. Moreover, the system of talmudic exposition under which he taught as developed by his grandfather, "the Brisker Rav," was renowned for its "incisive analysis, exact definition, precise classification and critical independence."

Now I see what Wolfson meant. Talmud is divided traditionally into two parts; Halakhah (derived from the Hebrew word "to go" or "follow") its legal aspect, laws, regulations, prohibitions; Agada, the stories, anecdotes, epigrams which cluster about the delineation of the laws, sometimes elucidating them, sometimes running on merrily, commenting in an oblique and paradoxical fashion as if a tape recorder hidden in the Babylonian chambers were continuing to transcribe while the justices relaxed and indulged their imaginations. Joseph Soloveitchik's reputation is as an outstanding "halakhist." In his capacity of professor of Talmud at Yeshiva University, his ruling on questions of Orthodoxy, *kashruth*, is law to many Jews. The Litvak tradition is a legal one, and it's not surprising that this spiritual and literal grandchild of the great *Mitnaggedim*, the Gaon of Vilna, the "Brisker Rav" should publish as his first major work an article entitled "The Halakhic Personality," in which he insists on the Jew commiting his whole life to study and practice of the law, that in performing and understanding the commandments of rabbinical Judaism, he not only gives his life meaning, he begins to know God. "By forbidding one type of behavior, permitting a second, and requiring a third, Halakhah engages man's conscious mind and will at every point. . . . Halakhah makes the service of God part of a total life which is suffused with religious significance . . . and gives man a sense of purpose and a sense of the divine purpose."*

What Soloveitchik's contributions as a jurist to the realm of halakhah have been, I cannot judge. It is his genius for the other half of Talmud, Agada, that attracts me. He is not only a "great preacher"; he is, bar none, the greatest storyteller I have ever heard. To appreciate Soloveitchik you must come on a Saturday night about two hours after sunset has closed the Sabbath to the weekly *shiurim* (lessons) he gives at the Maimonides School in Brookline. There in the large hall sit between a hundred and two hundred men and women;

* A. Lichtenstein, "R. Joseph Soloveitchik," in S. Noveck (ed.), *Great Jewish Thinkers of the Twentieth Century*, p. 292. Washington, D.C.: B'nai B'rith, 1963.

bearded rabbis, well-tailored doctors, lawyers, merchants of the Boston Orthodox community, on the right side their wives, daughters: men and women mingling at the back tables where one will sometimes find a friend teaching at Harvard or Boston University, Hebrew Bibles spread out before them, a sprinkling of younger rabbinical students. And often, in this august company, one greets a former butcher from the Dorchester ghetto, others who despite their less imposing occupations have come to hear "the Rabbi." Some are there in business suits, others in flannel shirts and dungarees. Yet all are students in the sense of the old talmudic academies. The doors are open. There is no admission charge, membership, and it is in this mysterious circle that Joseph Soloveitchik speaks.

The frail man with a gray beard enters the room and everyone rises. He walks to a small table on slim legs where he sets down the four or five large volumes he has carried in with him, markers in them, sometimes a scrap of paper, a few notes for two-, three-hour lessons he delivers extemporaneously. A microphone is suspended around his neck by an assistant, and he sits down and stares blankly for a few seconds.

What one is about to hear at the Maimonides is ancient, older than the academies at Nehardea and Pumbedita of the second and third centuries of the Christian era. It goes back hundreds of years before Jesus of Nazareth. It is the oral tradition. Generations passed before the remarks of Rabbi Akiba and Rabbi Meir, which bulk the Talmud, were written down, even codified. They were held in memory first, and only the memorable was passed on.

At Maimonides the advantages of the oral tradition are manifest. Because Soloveitchik's written words—if they are not instantly law—at least have to be considered as a strong legal opinion, his freedom of expression in print is drastically limited. He can't seesaw back and forth, entertaining heresy dallying with it before dismissing the possibility. The contrast of Soloveitchik's spoken English and his written is startling. The two published works in English, *Confrontation* and *The*

Lonely Man of Faith, are set down in a careful, elegant style, balancing the abstractions of philosophical terminology with short bursts of poetry, biblical *midrash*, and personal outcry. Although in the second, *The Lonely Man of Faith*, as if more confident of his English, the Rav gives one a few chords of that dramatic music which fills his mouth on Saturday nights, he does not indulge in that levity which is the salt of talmudic discourse. The Soloveitchik of *The Lonely Man of Faith* is passionate, but the rabbi's humanity, his wit, his breadth can only be appreciated by hearing him within that circle of friends and students where he can think aloud and contradict himself.

There is another advantage to the oral tradition. The realm of the written word is fine for logic. But when you are speaking of a world beyond logic, it is not enough to define, to explain; you must make your auditors *feel* what you are talking about, *believe* in your thoughts. When Joseph Soloveitchik one Saturday night spoke of Adam and Eve in the Garden, he did so with such immediacy, familiarity, even while sifting thousands of years of commentary, retelling, that one felt God bend low and call out, "Adam? Adam?"

That is what makes Soloveitchik so awesome, that spark of the Nabi, the prophet who can make the Holy One, Blessed Be He, palpable; as the story happens in the room, it does become, again, revelation. Nor is the Rav unaware of his gift.* In one of his lectures on the Garden of Eden, he was speaking about the presence of God.

---

* This gift for storytelling is usually accounted a Chassidic accomplishment. A. Lichtenstein in his essay on Soloveitchik in *Great Jewish Thinkers* relates an anecdote which in this context is interesting.

Most of R. Joseph Soloveitchik's early years were spent in the White Russian town of Khoslavitch, where his father served as rabbi. Although the town traditionally elected a Mitnagged as rabbi, its Jewish populace consisted largely of Lubavitcher Hasidim. When the seven-year-old Joseph was sent to study Talmud at the local *heder*, he came under the tutelage of an elderly devotee of Habad. . . . For the better part of a year, young Soloveitchik's Talmudic

"God wrapped himself in mystery and removed himself geographically from man.

"Man heard his steps in the Garden. Outside the Gan Eden man lost contact with Him.

"Outside man has to search for Him, in the garden He searched for man.

"What makes it so difficult for man to find God?

"The orderliness of the cosmos.

"God's will is embedded in the cosmos.

"Man sees only the behavior and not the will.

"He descended to Moses in a pillar of cloud.

"What is a pillar of cloud? The world.

"He lives in the shadows.

"The Russian Jews who left—'We were choking for air.' A Jew can not find God unless he joins the Jewish community.

"Why has God gone into hiding? Because man denied His authority.

---

progress was impeded while the study of Tanya (the central classic of the Lubavitcher Habad Hasidim) accompanied by enthralling stories of Hasidic lore proceeded." Lichtenstein also details "a life long taste for literature from his mother, who led him from fairy tales to Ibsen, Pushkin, Lermontov, and Bialik.

Regardless of its source, it is a unique gift, and its appearance and power in the essays is noted with surprise by the uninitiated.

Soloveitchik reestablishes for himself in contemporary terms, the kind of biblical exegesis that is the foundation and framework of Maimonides's *Guide to the Perplexed*. This should not suggest a similarity between his typology and the philosophical exegesis of Maimonides but it points to the patent fact that both view the Bible as offering man in his existential plight the means of understanding his situation. What makes Soloveitchik's development and use of this way of doing theology so fascinating is the peculiar circumstance that, since the 18th century, the very halakhic school of which he is considered the greatest contemporary master by those capable of judging the matter has all but ignored Scripture as a foundation for a constructive statement of Judaism, if, indeed, it concerned itself with the problem at all (Lou H. Silberman, *American Jewish Year Book*, vol. 70).

"Wherever man is with God, there is Paradise.

"You want a divorce? [He claps his hands.] All right! You can have a divorce. I act out the roles. How few men can act out God with authority."

I believe these are Soloveitchik's words, not mine (although one must be careful. I have reconstructed his speech from lecture notes, and the hypnotic effect of the telling is such that I did not always distinguish between what I heard and what I thought). In an earlier lecture, trying to explain the terrible loneliness of Eve after the Fall, the absence of God, the Rav spoke so that the whole hall trembled with his whisper, leaning forward, grasping into the pillar of smoke. "If a man is holy

> You feel His warm hand,
> You feel His breath on your face.
> All man has to do is humble himself.
> They heard His footsteps but instead of
> Crying out, they hid themselves.

Or in a lighter vein, he eyes that eternal comedian, the snake, the *nochosh*, who represents for Soloveitchik the master of propaganda for a soulless world, a pure materialist, to whom environment is everything, no rules. So the snake puts in Eve's mouth the answer, "He made me do it. The serpent beguiled me." And Soloveitchik snaps, "The *nochosh*—I wish he were around. I would like to argue with him."

Later, commenting on the recent discoveries in astrophysics, the black hole where all known rules of science seem to be contravened and matter is extinguished, he quips, "The *nochosh* must be out there, talking." I cannot forget the evening as the *shiuri* came to its conclusion after midnight, the Rav exhausted from the hours of the lecture, standing leaning against the table, trying to give us the persona of Cain in the Land of Nod, natural man's loneliness as he gropes toward a spiritual hunger he has no understanding of, the fratricide exiled, driven from his farmstead to the Land of Nod, a trespasser, only residing, never at home.

"Cain was an existential provincial.

"He not only cultivated the land, he was a slave to the land.

"Exile for Cain was a very severe punishment. He was very attached to his home. He wanted to strike roots. He didn't want a temporary shelter, a city.

"The land was east of Eden.

"Every time he stepped out of his tent, Paradise was visible from afar.

"Whenever he turned westward, he saw it.

"Whether Cain was born in the Garden or outside (there is a controversy) it didn't matter. It pulled like a magnet."*

I walked into the middle of the *shiuri* when he was lecturing about the moment when Adam and Eve discover that they are naked. The amount of rabbinical commentary on that instant is amazing.

Soloveitchik was complaining, rather conventionally, about the craziness of the modern world, who can understand it? All this sexual business, running around, homosexuality, everything, it's not Jewish, etc. Then his mind begins to jump and leap over the hobby horses, male and female. Women know the boundaries. "Women are by nature more conservative," he said. "Hitler was elected by the women." He went into a long digression about German politics in the Weimar Republic, how the liberals gave women the vote and the women elected Hindenburg, because they were basically conservative, and Hindenburg brought in Hitler. Of course, he said, "This is pure typology."

"The woman is a preserver. She knows the boundaries. Man

---

* It is with considerable trepidation that I publish lecture notes. In the moments of rapt attention much slipped by. It is the Rav's ability to fill his remarks with the dramatic force of his voice and gesture that makes them extraordinary. However, I can't pass on to discuss his uniqueness without attempting to give my sense of those nights.

operates in his mind." He tried to define a woman's intelligence. "A unique intelligence was imparted in [the woman's mind]—*fingerspritzgefühl* [to be able to tell by the touch]." Soloveitchik's face burst into a grin as he pronounced the German word and wiggled his fingers, the texture of life squeezed between his quick thumb and forefinger as if testing the strength of a piece of yardgoods.

Is Judaism against going into space? Is it wrong to go to the moon? No, said Soloveitchik, it's man's nature to be always reaching out. "Man's task is to go beyond boundaries." The moon. "Homosexuality." (I can't believe my ears, but a friend confirms it.) "How far man can get in his desire to occupy new territory, new space."

Suddenly we were in the Garden of Eden. The Rav is talking about the moment when Adam and Eve discover they are naked and drape themselves in fig leaves. "The minute he fell from grace, God told him to put on shorts."

What happened at that moment? To Adam? To Eve? "The presence of shame is characteristic of evil. The lack of shame is characteristic of innocence."

"They discovered a new experience—shame."

And so, into a discussion of sex. Soloveitchik spoke of it as it occurs in the animal, a force, an itch. "He wants to discharge the sexual pressure."

Only man is not an animal but a spiritual being. "Sex life is legitimate if it leads to the establishment of a community. To create a community, to experience in love that bond, in responsibility to the community, to the future.

"If it is between two strangers then it is the most selfish."

A discussion followed of the difference between the Jews and Greeks on the matter of sex. "Aristotle considers sex life something coarse and evil." This is anathema to the Jews, says Soloveitchik, to whom sex is something holy and transforming. Maimonides went along with the Greeks on this, and was stigmatized by Soloveitchik. He cited another famous Spanish rabbi of the medieval world, Nahmanides, "Ramban criticized Maimonides, in that he learns from the wicked Aristotle."

When does Judaism take joy in sex?

"If sex is both forming a community, an existential community, a metaphysical call, the sex is sanctified.

"By severing it, one takes advantage of the other; usually the victim is the woman. The sense of generation to generation, this is sanctification.

"Marriage is not linked with natural man but spiritual man. Natural love by itself is nothing but vulgarity and exploitation. Perhaps man is man because he is ashamed. Natural man is not ashamed. Spiritual man is ashamed.

"Shame is part of the personality. You can't get rid of it."

"Why were Adam and Eve embarrassed?

"They had no reason to be . . . no reason to be ashamed.

"There is shame present in sex life because it is possible to vulgarize it.

"The Fall severed man from the natural life.

"With the appearance of *chayt* [sin] love life was severed from spiritual life."

The Rav paused to cite the large number of pages in Jewish law on sex. The second largest is on diet. "If you take an extra cookie, so what? It's not so terrible. But," he added, his face growing stern again, "Yehoodiss [Judaism] becomes almost ruthless when it comes to sex. Why?"

Here the Rav stood up, his arms outspread, his face glowing through the gray beard; the force of his words seemed to lift him a few inches off the ground. "The power of love life is almost irresistible. When it comes to the male, love life is orgiastic, hypnotic, irresistible!" Judaism's great talmudist, sixty-nine years old, eyes alight, gray beard bristling with electricity. "Orgiastic, hypnotic, irresistible."

He stood there a second as if stunned by dreams, then, settling back to the floor of Maimonides, added, "Discipline in love life is the highest degree of sanctity."

Telling friends about it later, I say, I once saw a man levitate. It was Rabbi Soloveitchik.

Let us come down to more solid ground, however, to understand the intellectual tensions in these lectures. I would like to refer to Soloveitchik's printed words, two essays in the Orthodox journal *Tradition*, for he goes over the same territory, Adam in the Garden of Eden. How formal his voice is! None of the banter of the lectures. Even the strains of romanticism are filtered through an elegant but old-fashioned prose, deliberately abstract, so it sounds dry, dry. Yet the wine is strong, even heady, and a cultivated palate can savor its bouquet.

Imagine that Adam was created twice, first as a dumb beast, then as a philosopher. In his initial state as "natural man,"* in Soloveitchik's tale, Adam doesn't distinguish between himself and his environment. "He is united with nature, moving straight forwards, with the beast and fowl of the field, along an unbroken line of mechanical life activities, never turning around, never glancing backwards, leading an existence which is neither fraught with contradictions nor perplexed by paradoxes, nor marred by fright."†

This is natural man "created out of the dust of the ground." Even the beginning student of Rabbinics will smile with recognition at the stereotypes the rabbi is setting up. Ah, it is an old altercation in Judaism, particularly dear to the Litvak heart, that race of scholars, between the am-ha-eretz (the man of the earth, soil, dirt, who doesn't care for learning) and his opposite, the sage. The "natural" Adam really smells of the dust. "Man, who was created out of the dust of the ground, en-

---

* The following quotes are from "Confrontation," *Tradition* 6 (1964): 2.
† Soloveitchik quotes the passage of Scripture that this image of a man of the dust is based on: "And every plant of the field was not yet in the earth and every herb of the field had not yet grown . . . and there was no man to till the ground. But there went up a mist from the earth and watered the whole face of the ground. And the Lord God formed the man of the dust of the ground and breathed into his nostrils the breath of life and the man became a living soul" (Gen. 2:5–7).

veloped in a mist rising from the jungle, determined by bio-logical immediacy and mechanical necessity, knows of no responsibility, no opposition, no fear, and no dichotomy, and hence he is free from carrying the load of humanity." Yet for a moment, the rabbi stops, peering in wonder through the eye of his unsophisticated Adam, almost nostalgic, at the animal world, the vision of a hedonist. "Before him stretches a vast garden with an almost endless variety of trees desirable and good, tempting, fascinating, and exciting the boundless fantasy with their glamorous colors."

Now, alas, Adam is shaken out of his "glamorous" dreams.* God puts a bit of awareness in his head. Enter the scholarly Adam. The dummy begins to think. Adam in his second state "confronts himself," to use the language of the essay. And there's no question who Rabbi Soloveitchik's hero is.†

The verb to take signifies that God removed man from one dimen-sion and thrust him into another—that of a confronted existence. At this phase, man, estranged from nature, fully aware of his

---

* The advent of the philosophical Adam into the Garden is ingeniously managed by the rabbi. There are two biblical references to man's arrival in Eden: "And the Lord God planted a garden eastward in Eden: and there He put the man whom He had formed" (Gen. 2:8), "And the Lord God took the man and put him into the garden of Eden to dress it and to keep it" (Gen. 2:15). Such a repetition in the biblical text is a natural opening for rabbinical commentary. There is a slight difference in the passages and Soloveitchik seizes on this to weave his account. He argues that in Genesis 2:8, man is just dumped in Eden. In Genesis 2:15, there is preliminary action, he is "taken" and given commands, "to dress . . . and to keep" Eden. Adam as "natural man" was simply placed in nature. Adam as "confronted man" is placed in "confron-tation" with nature and, by extension, God.

† Soloveitchik gives an explanation of this "confrontation" in somewhat technical language. "The second story is of a confronted man who began to appraise critically his position vis-à-vis his environment and found his existential experience too complex to be equated with the simplicity and non-directedness of the natural-life stream. This man as a subject-knower facing an almost impenetrable objective order, was dislocated by God from his position of naturalness and harmonious being and placed in a new existential realm, that of confronted existence."

grand and tragic destiny, became the recipient of the first norm. "And the Lord God commanded the man." The divine imperative burst forth out of infinity and overpowered finite man.

This flash of poetry, sexual "burst forth, overpowered," is the halakhah, the advent of the law so dear to Soloveitchik, the beginning of the body of commandments which bow the philosopher down to the earth again. And the word "confronted" gives the rabbi a key to Eve, her place in Eden.

There is however a third level which man, if he is longing for self-fulfillment, must ascend. At this level, man finds himself confronted again. Only this time it is not the confrontation of a subject who gazes with a sense of superiority at the object beneath him, but of two equal subjects, both lonely in their otherness and uniqueness, both opposed and rejected by an objective order, both craving for companionship. . . . Two individuals, lonely and helpless in their solitude, meet, and the first community is formed.

Someday, I think, reading this, someone will write the story of Tanya Soloveitchik, the rabbi's wife, who had a doctorate in education from Jena and was considered his peer by intimates of the Soloveitchik family. On another level, rattling the bones of this dry language is the power of the word as an instrument of sex.

The community can only be born, however, through an act of communication. After gazing at each other in silence and defiance, the two individuals involved in a unique encounter begin to communicate with each other. Out of the mist of muteness the miraculous word rises and shines forth. Adam suddenly begins to talk—"And the man said." He addresses himself to Eve, and with his opening remark, two fenced-in and isolated human existences open up, and they both ecstatically break through to each other.

This description of Adam going from harmony with nature to encounter, domination, and finally with his mate to a new harmony based on mutual recognition is a parable of the uniqueness of men and women in the human community.* For the purpose of the essay in *Confrontation* is to describe the uniqueness of Judaism as a faith community and to insist on its not surrendering this in an ecumenical world. The Jew, man or woman, is unique. Judaism is unique. Confront! Argue! Be different! This is Soloveitchik's battle cry, and it is an old and thrilling Hebrew shout.

"I am lonely," the rabbi says in the opening lines of *The Lonely Man of Faith*. A somber pessimism runs through this second essay and the voice trembles on the edge of being personal. He comes back to the Garden of Eden. Now he has a new version of what happened, or an old one he has decided to entertain. (Any line of the Bible generally has dozens of stories attached to it. In the public lectures, three or four hours does not suffice Soloveitchik to go forward more than a few words in the biblical text, and he keeps shrugging as lines of commentary and other connections come into his head for

---

* Despite Soloveitchik's typology, his characterization of women as "conservative," it is interesting to weigh his words about Adam and Eve, sentences written long before the rhetoric of liberation became fashionable.

Modern man . . . has forgotten how to master the difficult dialectical art of being one with and, at the same time, different from, his human confronter, of living in community and simultaneously in solitude. He has developed the habit of confronting his fellow man in a fashion similar to that which prevails at the level of subject-object relationship, seeking to dominate and subordinate him instead of communicating and communing with him. The wondrous personal confrontation of Adam and Eve is thus turned into an ugly attempt to appear as master-hero and to subject Eve to his rule and dominion, be it ideological, religious, economic, or political. As a matter of fact, the divine curse, addressed to Eve after she sinned, "and he shall rule over thee," has found its fulfillment in our modern society. The warm personal relationship between two individuals has been supplanted by a formal subject-object relationship which manifests itself in a quest for power and supremacy.

which he simply doesn't have time.) Forget the Adam who went through two stages. Think instead of another two Adams: Adam the first and Adam the second.* Now Soloveitchik does something surprising. The "natural man" who was the unsophisticated Adam of the initial stage in creation for the previous essay, becomes Adam the first, but he has nothing to do with "the dust of the ground." Instead he is the opposite, "a creative esthete. He fashions ideas with his mind and beauty with his heart. . . . He legislates for himself norms and laws because a dignified existence is an orderly one. . . ."†

It is Adam the second who is tied to the line: "And God

---

* In Genesis I we read: "So God created man in His own image, in the image of God created He him, male and female created He them. And God blessed them and God said unto them, be fruitful and multiply, and fill the earth and subdue it, and have dominion over the fish of the sea, over the fowl of the heaven and over the beasts, and all over the earth."

In Genesis II, the account differs substantially from the one we just read: "And the eternal God formed the man of the dust of the ground and breathed into his nostrils the breath of life and man became a living soul. And the eternal God planted a garden eastward in Eden. . . . And the eternal God took the man and placed him in the Garden of Eden to serve it and to keep it."

The Jewish mystics were also intrigued by this discrepancy and talk about the Adam Ha-Rishon, an Adam who existed before the historical Adam, before the dawn of history. Soloveitchik's two Adams, however, are in the nature of "schizophrenic" halves of the same man.

† The most characteristic representative of Adam the first is the mathematical scientist who whisks us away from the array of tangible things. . . . Adam the first is always an esthete, whether engaged in an intellectual or ethical performance. His conscience is energized not by the idea of the good, but by that of the beautiful. His mind is questing not for the true, but for the pleasant and functional, which are rooted in the esthetical, not the poetic-ethical sphere.

In doing all this, Adam the first is trying to carry out the mandate entrusted to him by his Maker who, at dawn of the sixth mysterious day of creation, addressed Himself to man and summoned him to "fill the earth and subdue it." It is God who decreed that the story of Adam the first be the great saga of freedom of man-slave who gradually transforms himself into man-master.

formed the man of the dust of the ground." Dust that signi-
fied the unreflected, humble origin of Soloveitchik's first
reading now stands for humility. The rabbi has turned the
dummy, the am-ha-eretz image, on its head. Why?

A more compelling danger than ignorance has suggested
itself to the rabbi—arrogance, the all-too-intellectual Superman of Nietzsche. Adam the first is bound up not with dust
but power, the cosmos. "His motto is success, triumph over
the cosmic forces. He engages in creative work, trying to
imitate his Maker (*imitatio Dei*)."* Yet, a degree from Berlin
in his pocket, Soloveitchik's awe for all kinds of learning
echoes in his description.

Adam the first transcends the limits of the reasonable and
probable and ventures into the open spaces of a boundless universe.
Even this longing for vastness, no matter how adventurous and
fantastic, is legitimate. Man reaching for the distant stars is acting
in harmony with his nature which was created, willed, and directed
by his Maker. It is a manifestation of obedience to rather than
rebellion against God.

Adam the second, is like Adam the first, also intrigued by the
cosmos. Intellectual curiosity drives them both to confront cou-
rageously the mysterium magnum of Being. However, while the
cosmos provokes Adam the first to quest for power and control,
thus making him ask the functional "how"-question, Adam the
second responds to the call of the cosmos by engaging in a different
kind of cognitive gesture. He does not ask a single functional question. Instead his inquiry is of a metaphysical nature and a threefold
one. He wants to know: "Why is it?" "What is it?" "Who is it?"
(1) He wonders: "Why did the world in its totality come into
existence? Why is man confronted by this stupendous and indifferent order of things and events?" (2) He asks: "What is the purpose of all this? What is the message that is embedded in organic
and inorganic matter, and what does the great challenge reaching
me from beyond the fringes of the universe as well as from the

* Soloveitchik derives this trait from the phrase in Genesis I, "image of
God." Adam the first attempts to become like God the creator, His
image.

depths of my tormented soul mean?" (3) Adam the second keeps on wondering: "Who is He who trails me steadily, uninvited and unwanted, like an everlasting shadow, and vanishes into the recesses of transcendence the very instant I turn around to confront this numinous, awesome and mysterious "He?" Who is He who fills Adam with awe and bliss, humility and a sense of greatness, concurrently? Who is He to whom Adam clings in mortal fear and dread? Who is He who fascinated Adam irresistibly and at the same time rejects him irrevocably? Who is He whom Adam experiences both as the *mysterium tremendum* and as the most elementary, most obvious, and most understandable truth? Who is He who is *deus revelatus* and *deus absconditus* simultaneously? Who is He whose life-giving and life-warming breath Adam feels constantly and who at the same time remains distant and remote from all?

Rabbi Soloveitchik steps into the biblical text, takes the image of dust and tastes it, breathes the life of his commentary into it. He becomes the Adam of the dust, Adam who quivers in the arms of God, who is "redeemed," "overcome," whose humility leads him into almost erotic knowledge of God.

Dignity is acquired by man whenever he triumphs over nature. Man finds redemption whenever he is overpowered by the Creator of nature. Dignity is discovered at the summit of success: redemption in the depth of crisis and failure. "Out of the depths have I called thee, O God." The Bible has stated explicitly that Adam the second was formed from the dust of the ground because the knowledge of the humble origin of man is an integral part of Adam's "I" experience. Adam the second has never forgotten that he is just a handful of dust.*

Adam the second, "the lonely man of faith," is the Rav's

---

* The biblical metaphor referring to God breathing life into Adam alludes to the actual preoccupation of the latter with God, to his genuine living experience of God, rather than to some divine potential or endowment in Adam symbolized by *imago Dei*. Adam the second lives in close union with God. His existential "I" experience is interwoven in the awareness of communing with the Great Self whose footprints he discovers along the many tortuous paths of creation.

image. But here we come to the paradoxical nature of Solo-veitchik's teaching and indeed of Halakhah itself, with its sus-picion of monkish tendencies, its encouragement of the Jew to play a role in the cosmos as Adam number one.* Torn between natural and spiritual impulses, an existential glory in man's predicament is what distinguishes Soloveitchik as halakhist and agadaist, as lawgiver and storyteller in *The Lonely Man of Faith*.

Had God placed Adam in the majestic community only, then Adam would, as it was stated before, never be aware of existential loneliness. The sole problem would then be that of aloneness—one that majestic Adam could resolve. Had God, vice versa, thrust Adam into the covenantal community exclusively, then he would be beset by the passional experience of existential lone-liness also provided with the means of finding redemption from this experience through his covenantal relation to God and to his fellow man. However, God in His inscrutable wisdom, has decreed differently. Man discovers his loneliness in the covenantal community and before he is given a chance to climb up to the high level of a complete covenantal, revealed existence, dedicated in faith to God and in sympathy to man, the man of faith is pushed into a new community where he is told to lead an expanded

* Witness Soloveitchik's excoriation of Soren Kierkegaard, from whom he has visibly borrowed ideas and terminology:

> For Kierkegaard, faith supersedes the majestic posture of man. The world of faith rises upon the ruins and debris of the world of majesty.
>
> This thesis is unacceptable . . . to the Halakhah which insists upon the dialectical movement between these two worlds. They do, indeed, exist concurrently according to the Halakhah. More-over, Kierkegaard lacked the understanding of the centrality of the act of objectification of the inner movement of faith in a normative and doctrinal postulate system which formed the very foundation of the Halakhah. The Halakhic world of faith is "terribly" articu-late, "unpardonably" dynamic, and "foolishly" consistent, insisting that feeling become thought, and experience be acted out and trans-formed into an objective event. Kierkegaard's existentialist world, like Schleiermacher's pietistic world, is a place of silence and passivity, far removed from the complex array of historical events, not hungering for action or movement.

surface existence rather than a covenantal, concentrated, in-depth existence. Because of this onward movement from center to center, man does not feel at home in any community. He is commanded to move on before he manages to strike roots in either of these communities and so the ontological loneliness of man of faith persists. Verily, "A straying Aramean was my father."

What does the community of "majesty" mean to Joseph Soloveitchik? It quite clearly resounds in his decision not to accept the post of chief rabbi in Israel. His refusal to wield very real political power in world Judaism has puzzled many. And many too are the voices raised against him. To the ultra-Orthodox the Rav is suspect as being too lax, too secular. To the Conservative Jewish rabbinate he is a disappointment because he has not made any of the radical halakhic decisions which would adjust Orthodoxy to the new social conditions of the twentieth century. The most biting criticism I have heard comes from within the very walls of Yeshiva University, in a study that appeared in 1968 in the *American Jewish Year Book*:

Students were asked to select from a list, or write in, the name of the rabbi who best reflected their own religious-theological-philosophical thinking. Most significant was the finding that no more than 28 percent of the students chose Rabbi Joseph Solo-veitchik as the only such person. Yet Rabbi Soloveitchik is YU's leading religious personality: is considered by most Orthodox as the world's leading talmudist: and is the foremost leader of vir-tually all modern Orthodox organizations, most particularly the Rabbinical Council of America. It is to Rabbi Soloveitchik that one would expect the students to look for intellectual and religious leadership, as well as for personal guidance, and it is indeed to him that students say they would like to look.

After drawing a picture of rabbinical students disturbed by the widespread disregard for Jewish law, wanting "guidelines" both philosophically and practically in terms of their relation-ship to the non-Orthodox community, finally, hungry for a personal friendship with the Rav, the article continues, "The image of Rabbi Soloveitchik as an exemplary figure persists because such a figure is so desperately sought, and no one else appears to be as qualified to fill that need."

These are messianic expectations. What would the Rav answer? For it is not only the rabbinical students who are asking, but much of the serious Jewish community.

Two evenings in particular seem to have been agitated by his quandary, one on the rabbi's namesake, the biblical Joseph who almost became the Messiah and the other on Moses negotiating the covenant at Mount Sinai, the beginning of the "covenantal community" that is so precious to Rabbi Soloveitchik, the life lived under the halakhah.

"Joseph.

". . . a dreamer!

"What was Joseph's desire? [The prophet] Daniel anticipated Freud. Your daytime desires break through at night. He was searching for something—what was it? Power.

"In stating [the image in the dream of] the sheaves bowing down, power. We are oversimplifying: he was motivated by love of his brothers.

"Joseph feared two things. The falling apart of the covenantal community. That it would not survive after Jacob's death."

Now the rabbi speaks in his own voice. "I thought that Judaism would fall apart after twenty years in America but I never said it. Joseph was afraid that it would fall apart, haunted by that fear. The twelve brothers, they may spread out over a large area, disintegrate.

"Judaism survived in America in the big cities, not in the small towns. It troubled him like a vicious ghost.

"Another dream, the I.O.U., 400 years of slave labor, Abraham's [God had foretold the troubles in Egypt to Abraham]. Joseph was sure that God would collect, a mighty technological country, life under a cruel dictatorial pharaoh who tolerated no diversity. Joseph had a feeling of doom. He saw in power the only solution.

"We were all gathering sheaves in the middle of the field, why the center? We were all in the center." The rabbi's voice breaks on *ahnuchnoo* (we), half crying, the Lithuanian Jewish voice of the Mirskys. "I was dreaming a unity, the *ahnuchnoo*. I did not raise the sheaf, somehow the sheaf stood up. I didn't drag my sheaf into the center, against my will, against my plan, in its place, it remained steady, it wouldn't move, not only my sheaf acted automatically, your sheaves automatically, only I'm afraid, willy-nilly it happened, I'm frightened by it but it looks like the Kodosh Boruch Hu (The Holy One, Blessed Be He) acted without consulting us.

"It's funny, Joseph says, usually a person dreams of realities that are close to him. I should have dreamt of sheep not of sheaves. The profession of Abraham, Isaac, Jacob was herds. Agriculture was from Egypt. Joseph has never seen a sheaf. What kind of a hint? If it had been a simple dream, it would have been sheep. The Kodosh Boruch Hu is about to make us leave a pastoral country for an agricultural one, it may have a disastrous impact on the house of Jacob unless we are united.

"No separation in the covenantal community between the economy and morality. Between the meal and the synagogue —a teaching community. The manager must set an example. Joseph dreamed of teaching and managing. Who is the central figure in the spiritual community? Maishe Rabenu [Moses, our teacher]. Three lands suffered from a famine, Arabia, Phoenicia, Palestine. Joseph managed to feed the whole Middle East.

"The first dream is of economic unity. The Torah has never preached poverty or begging, wanted that a man should earn a living. Beggars cannot form a covenantal community.

"Why did Pharaoh accept Joseph's interpretation? He was the only one who gave him some plans, how to organize: all the Pharaoh's priests had no plans to avert the fallacious interpretations, six daughters, sons. One cannot impose oneself as king upon the people, he must be elected, accepted. Our messianic hope is that God will be accepted by us all voluntarily. He [Joseph] wanted the moon and stars, that the spirits of people bow down. The body bows down because a person is afraid; when I have God, the spirit bows down.

"The first dream was told to his brothers. The second dream was told to his brothers.

"He didn't need Jacob's consent for him to be economic czar. Jacob had the power to veto the choice of spiritual successor. The final choice is not up to the Heavens. Malchis [kingship] in Judaism means to be the teacher of the community. What was Jacob's answer? Nothing. He did not sanction it. He rebuked him [Joseph].

"Joseph's main desire was fixed—to make Jacob accept the dream. In fact, Malchis went to Judah, not Joseph, the martyrdom of the Messiah was assigned to Joseph, an experiment, short-lived—the opportunity was offered to Joseph when the brothers came to buy food.

"The first dream came true—how modest the dream, how fantastic the reality, they'll all buy land, cultivate, pay him homage: now he's the economic czar of the Middle East. He remembered two dreams. He wanted to be the King Messiah, that through his descendants the eschatological dream [will] come true. If Jacob will bow to him, the kingship will come to him. The minute the brothers bowed to him, Joseph was preoccupied with getting Jacob to come to Egypt. Protocol would demand that Jacob prostrate himself before the viceroy —the strategy revolved about getting Jacob to come to Egypt without knowing his identity. The old man will come to petition before the governor for Benjamin."

In the terse epigrams of the rabbi's commentary, one can see the contradictory tensions of the messianic role. Joseph's very strengths as a man of "majesty," as a figure in the economic cosmos, have coarsened him, made him unfit for the spiritual kingship. For kingship in Israel, as Soloveitchik points out, implies the responsibility to teach. Not to teach only from experience of the world of "majesty" but from experience of the spiritual one as well. The Jew cannot render unto Caesar, what is Caesar's, because the covenantal community does not accept such a split in authority. What is the rabbi's definition of his own responsibilities? For a fleeting moment in the lecture on Joseph, he refers to the ideal teacher, Maishe Rabenu—Moses our teacher. In the lecture on Mount Sinai, Soloveitchik draws a vivid picture of the genesis of the covenantal community against the background of a pagan world. First Abraham, who initials the covenant for a family, then Moses, who signs it for a people, come into focus.

"Maimonides' view—to understand Abraham you must understand idolatry. Abraham was born into an idolatrous world.

"Maimonides—one may still have faith in God and worship idols, stars.

"At the outset worship was spontaneous. People were overwhelmed by nature, the astral world.

"To watch the skies, the heavens, is overwhelming; the loveliness and beauty of nature is almost maddening, but these are only mirrors in which God is reflected.

"There were no statutory laws. Each individual adored God in his own way—commendable to admire beauty. Admiration was transformed into adoration.

"Adoration of nature became a cult. Institutionalized. Anything can become an idol—man can become an idol.

"A child can become an idol. The first generation in America of Jews worshiped their children too much.

"In Jewish annals there was never such a rich and enlightened community as there is in the United States.

"I was raised in abject poverty. I was dressed in rags. My mother promised me a new suit for Passover. She called me in. Beryl, I can hardly pay for the *matzohs*. Children can be cruel. They laughed at me. I studied with my father by the candle through the long nights. My father bought a new Sefer, then we had no [money for] candles. We studied by moonlight.

"Don't idolatrize. Even the state of Israel should not become a deity—our relationship to God is above the state of Israel—

the state is not a substitute—you may admire it but not adore it. Giving unlimited trust to a finite being—Maimonides' definition of idolatry.

"We paid a high price of idolatry, a commander like Dayan. What is the punishment? Disappointment and disillusionment.

"Man likes to standardize, organize.

"Sensitivity to beauty was the impulse of adoration. Ugliness was the characteristic of the idols.

"The uglier the idol, the more inspiring the idol was.

"At the outset, the motivation was beauty, but once [man] began to misinterpret it, it deteriorated into ugliness."

Behind the beard, he dances in his childhood.

"As a child I never had an opportunity to see the sea. At twenty-four, in Danzig, my reaction to it was complete intoxication, all I wanted to do was recite the psalm upon it.

"An intoxicating, redeeming effect on me.

"The Russian woods, dark blue. I thought I was seeing the woods of my childhood again. (Shade—the green tree—a hot sun—a tree is a place of assembly—the top of a mountain.)

"I became accustomed to it.

"Man becomes brutalized by routine.

"They stooped so low as to worship a monster as a substitute for beauty, contrary to the original motivation.

"Man is not capable of worshiping idols unless he is brainwashed. Paganism placed emphasis on multitudes. Paganism is based on myth, not knowledge. It severs man from the cognitive—the mob is gullible, and cruel—you can sell things to the multitude that you cannot to individuals—emotions are more powerful in the mob, greater cruelty—the individual cannot indulge in orgiastic rituals as the mob.

"The first covenant was reached with Abraham, an individual, not a multitude.

"Judaism is trying to teach, not indoctrinate—you cannot teach a multitude.

"We are not anxious to conquer the world—we had opportunities, we rejected them.

"We were afraid that they would vulgarize it."

(Speaking in God's voice.) " 'I wanted individuals.'

"Abraham tried a few times to convert the many. He went to Egypt not just because of famine.

" 'Just teach your son, Yitzchok [Isaac].'

"I never felt responsible for Boston. I felt responsible for my family, the children at the Maimonides school. I haven't tried to convert the world or the entire Jewish community.

"The second time on Sinai, only Moses [was called up]. 'Your job is to teach.' "

Many years ago, I am told, there was talk of Rabbi Soloveitchik coming to the Jewish Theological Seminary, that bastion of Conservative Judaism. Perhaps there, the bold, almost heretical voice in him would have found freer expression. On the other hand, he might have been swallowed up in the compromises and clichés of suburban Judaism; which is not to defame the rigorous atmosphere of scholarship at the seminary but only to point out that the "covenantal community" which exists around Joseph Soloveitchik at Maimonides in the midst of the Boston Orthodox is not the same as the pulpits to which the graduates of Conservative Judaism's institution go. It is only in Orthodoxy that Soloveitchik can find a community that will wholeheartedly follow the halakhah. Whether he could have created a new halakhah for the mass of American Jews, that is a difficult question. Because he is the only one in this generation brilliant enough to reformulate the law and prestigious enough to make his rulings stick, the disappointment is enormous, and this disenchantment outside the Orthodox community can be heard in the lines of the article of the *American Jewish Year Book:*

In its very broad outlines, his philosophy or way of life finds great resonance among the modern Orthodox, who see in it a vindication of their own involvement in the secular world. But when Rabbi Soloveitchik attempts to apply this philosophy of life to reality, his position is often indecisive, vacillating, and quite contrary to expectations. It is the Orthodox who made of Rabbi Soloveitchik a charismatic leader: he disclaims this role for himself.

I feel the force of this criticism. But Rabbi Soloveitchik's charisma is manifest. Commuting weekly from Boston to New York City to fulfill obligations as a teacher and leader, his dilemma is to deliver a messianic message to the modern world, while not losing the source of that charisma.

Man of faith must bring to the attention of man of culture the *kerygma* of original faith in all its singularity and pristine purity in spite of the incompatability of this message with the fundamental credo of a utilitarian society. How staggering this incompatibility is! This unique message speaks of defeat instead of success, of accepting a higher will instead of commanding, of giving instead of conquering, of retreating instead of advancing, of acting "irrationally" instead of being always reasonable. Here the tragic event occurs. Contemporary majestic man rejects his dialectical assignment and, with it, the man of faith. . . .

Modern Adam the second, as soon as he finishes translating religion into the cultural vernacular, and begins to talk the "foreign" language of faith, finds himself lonely, forsaken, misunderstood, at times even ridiculed by Adam the first, by himself. When the hour of estrangement strikes, the ordeal of man of faith begins and he starts his withdrawal from society, from Adam the first— be he an outsider, be he himself. He returns like Moses of old, to his solitary hiding and to the abode of loneliness. Yes, the loneliness of contemporary man of faith is of a special kind. He experiences not only ontological loneliness but also social isolation, whenever he dares to deliver the genuine faith-*kerygma*.

What is the consolation? Like the prophet Elisha:

Many a time he felt disenchanted and frustrated because his words were scornfully rejected. . . . Elisha was indeed lonely, but in his loneliness he met the Lonely One and discovered the singular covenantal confrontation of solitary man and God who abides in the recesses of transcendental solitude.

Is modern man of faith entitled to a more privileged position and a less exacting and sacrificial role?

Over the Abyss

‹›‹›‹›‹›

Was there ever a Jew who was not a mystic? Whether it is through halakhah, philosophy, esoterica, there is that hunger to get at God, imagine Him, identify with Him. Rabbi Akiba, second-century stalwart of the law, bureaucrat of Talmud par excellance, deft originator of a thousand legalisms and one, standing on the head of every letter in the Scripture, walked into the mystical garden and out through it drove his companions to lunacy, apostasy, and death. It was the same Akiba who proclaimed the Jewish warrior Bar Kochba as the Messiah. (He was the Messiah, said Soloveitchik, quoting Maimonides. The problem was that the Jews did not recognize him. The generation has to be ready if the Messiah is to act.) Mysticism in Judaism is bound up with messianism, with the here and now, not just transcendental solitude. The lonely thirteenth-century man of mysticism and Hebrew acrostics, Abraham Abulafia, finds himself knocking at the pope's door demanding action now. Without mysticism it is doubtful that Judaism could have survived. *"Denn der Zohar hot mich*

derhalten bein Yiddishkeit (The Zohar has helped me to remain
a Jew)," cried the Chassidic saint Rabbi Phineas of Koretz.

I can say aye to that. Jewish mysticism has brought me
home. And the teacher of Jewish mysticism in this century has
been Gershom Scholem, he who rescued its corpus from the
dump heaps of ridicule to which the nineteenth-century historians of Judaism had consigned it.*

While I was still an undergraduate at Harvard, Ben Zion
Gold gave me Scholem's *Major Trends in Jewish Mysticism*.
It lay on my shelf gathering dust for ten years. I leafed through
some of the chapters, interested, but the prose was too dense
for my experience. The sages caution us not to read the book
of Ezekiel, with its difficult dreams and images, before the age
of thirty. The warning is not superstitious. Mystical thought
depends on a certain sophistication about one's dream and
erotic life. It can either unhinge or bore the young man or
woman who has not gone through enough revolutions of love
and despair to grope with its symbols as metaphor for the
riddle of one's own behavior.

At twenty-eight, twenty-nine, with the death of my mother,
the realm of the unknown began to reach out toward me again
and speak in voices that I had separated myself from since
childhood. It was impossible to ignore the presence of my
mother's ghost. I took Scholem's book off the shelf and began

* "By his strict historical and philological methods [he] inaugurated a
new era in the study of Kabbalah and Jewish mysticism, placing it on
a firm scientific basis." *Jewish Encyclopedia.*

Scholem is the third in a triad of twentieth-century German Jewish
thinkers who have had a profound influence on the intellectual life of
the community outside Orthodoxy. I admire the other two: Franz
Rosenzsweig, whose final years are a modern martyrology, like the
medieval rabbi dismembered by fanatics, lying in a basket composing
hymns to God—Rosenzsweig, crushed by paralysis, dictated books,
articles to his wife by flicking an eyebrow; and Martin Buber—not so
much for his philosophical books or even his popularization of Chassidism, but rather textual work like *The Prophetic Faith*, a work of
biblical exegesis which makes clear the world of prophecy in ancient
Israel.

to dabble in its first chapters in an offhand way. The language and terminology are fascinating, but they are not simplified or made easy. Clear as the scholar's prose is, even poetic, the text requires, like Ezekiel's vision of the heavens, that you bring a full heart to appreciate its import. It was not death but love which suddenly unlocked the book.

At the age of thirty, a woman I had lived with for six years left me after a cruel and unhappy string of estrangements and reconciliations. When we broke finally and I went off from New York to Cambridge, Massachusetts, while she departed for London, my dreams turned into nightmares, vivid, actual, and the woman appeared in them with the force of a destroying angel, innocent, uncanny, a medieval succubus, threatening to overwhelm me. She wound herself around me until I woke up screaming, on the edge of panic.

I was afraid to sleep. Haggard, close to nervous prostration, fearing the sudden onslaught of a ghost who bore less and less relation to the actual woman but would leave me shaking in tears, unable to eat, thinking of the window ledge, I needed a guide to dreams that would drive the fantasy back into the hours of sleep.

It was not Freud but Scholem who gave me insight into myself. Such craziness was a gift. I had the key into *Major Trends in Jewish Mysticism.* The pages caught fire, accounts of men whose dream life was more powerful than the sights and sounds of the real world around them. I understood the impulse behind the sages who rose from heaven to heaven.

With the fascination of one who reads his own biography in the tale of another, dead centuries, milleniums before, I followed the accounts of the German Chassidim of the twelfth and thirteenth centuries, constructing the angel who sits on the throne of the heavens, the original of the Golem or clay man, the Red Adam, to make dreams palpable out of prayer, clay, and water: the image of the Spanish Kabbalist Moses de Leon, who elaborated on the hints in the Talmud that there was a female Presence of God, the Shekinah, who could be drawn down into ecstatic union with oneself. I grasped what Abulafia in the thirteenth century was doing when he scrambled Hebrew letters in his head after hours of prayer and meditation, waiting for secret words to illuminate his imagination.

And in the efforts that Scholem detailed of Isaac Luria in Safed (sixteenth century) to explain the presence of evil, the skimming of the Holy One, Blessed Be He, and his dross, in a series of bowls whose blinding light like a nuclear explosion shattered whole universes, I touched corners of the galaxy which had lain in darkness before my eyes. But this was not only an education in metaphysics but insight into the irrepressible eroticism of my Jewish ancestors. The false messiahs, Sabbatai Zevi, Jacob Frank, were like dangerous Jesse Jameses of the Jewish consciousness, revolting against the excesses of a long capitalization of morality and ethics, taking Jewish heresy into wife swapping, deliberate fraud, ritual murder, dwarfing my own perversity.

What a powerful cure against the claim of one's own solipsism was the history Scholem unfolded. And what a different light it cast on all the major Jewish rationalists. I recognized echoes in Maimonides, Wolfson, Soloveitchik; this drug, this dream, was at the center of the tradition, dangerous, real, in the threat of its claims, but also intoxicating. Images swarmed out of Scholem into my own fiction. It is a chronicle not merely of historical but of poetic event, and its metaphors moved like charms in my troubled imagination.

The irrational was the subject of rational discourse by thinkers and practitioners of mental health long before Freud sanctified it with "scientific" terminology and brought its study into modern medicine. Jewish mysticism as it unravels in the pages of Scholem from the earliest recorded work of the Merkabah, scholars who ascended to the halls of the Seven Heavens in the first, second, third century, so sure of their vision they stationed stenographers beside them to record as they uttered them: the ecstatic sights—to the split between Jacob Frank and the followers of the Baal Shem Tov, modern

Chassidism, black and white magic—is one continuous parchment. Its insights are startling for the modern reader. All the insanity he can imagine has already been attempted within the tradition, if not in every particular, in general outline. Contemporary Satans like Charles Manson and his tawdry band appear as no more than benighted, ill-informed descendants of madder Frankist ideals. *Major Trends in Jewish Mysticism* is a source book, withal a dangerous one, with precedents for any number of spiritual adventures. Why should it be important to know that one's great-grandfather may have been involved in this? Because somehow, modern Judaism as it represents itself in too many Reform and Conservative temples, organizations, public organs like *Commentary*, *Midstream*, has excluded the irrational from Judaism (though they honor Scholem, whose scholarship is too impeccable to be ignored), forcing those of us who are moved by the spirit of madness abroad in the land ("your land, by land"), to make a false choice: rational Judaism or leave the modern fold. Many who put on Buddhist robes or end up mindlessly chanting songs that will always sound forced and awkward to me in a Jewish mouth might have acted out a life-style equally strange, but I suspect more satisfying, in the costumes and formulas of Spanish and Polish forebears. Now if you don't believe that an inherited gesture is more natural and mysterious, spiritual, than an acquired one, despite the contemporary revelations of DNA, RNA, bodily acids inheriting the acquisitions of centuries, cellular wisdom, and all the testimony of years spent breeding horses, dogs, cattle for characteristics—there is no possibility of agreement between us.

I need madness, mysticism, God. Suprisingly, as I began to read Wolfson, listen to Soloveitchik, I discovered that they were in tacit agreement. Despite the efforts of Heinrich Graetz, that towering Jewish historian of the nineteenth century, and his followers ("A book of lies," he called the Zohar) to exclude mysticism from Judaism, to advance a faith without prophecy, a polite if somewhat sad superrationalism, sitting in the pews with Aristotle's unmoved Mover, Unitarianism with a five-thousand-year-old historical tradition—*no*, there is simply no great rabbinical figure who is not a mystic. That pillar of strict legal scholarship, the Gaon of Vilna, the bitter antagonist of the Chassidim (who are always romanticized as the inheritors of Jewish mysticism), admitted to Soloveitchik's grandfather Rabbi Hayim that as a boy he had indulged in Golem making, "But when I was in the middle of my preparations, a form passed over my head, and I stopped making it, for I said to myself: Probably heaven wants to prevent me because of my youth." To be involved with God is to try to shape an image, even though human and animal faces are forbidden. With sympathetic understanding Scholem shows generation after generation of thinkers attempting this difficult double task, to maintain the essential unity and unknowable as a real conception of God while attempting to approach and grip some aspect of the *Ayn Sof*, the One Without Limit.

Two great anxieties plague man and create the world of the irrational: life and death. Mysticism as detailed in Scholem (and Wolfson too) answers the terror of death with the vision of an afterlife.* In the pages of Philo it is an austere, intellectual life; in the columns of the Zohar it is an afterlife filled with tensions and emotions. To the terror of life, Philo, the rabbis, the Zohar answer with laws, halakhah. The Kabbalists, especially the Zohar's reputed author, the thirteenth-century Spanish mystic Moses de Leon,† are absolute Freudians on the

---

* I'm not sure what Rabbi Soloveitchik's thoughts are on the afterlife and death. I suspect his answer would be to concentrate on perfection in the present. I heard him say that the promise of immortality that was implicit in the Garden of Eden would be made good when man was ready.

† In *Major Trends in Jewish Mysticism*, Scholem makes a convincing case that the bulk of the pages published under the title the Zohar, The Brightness, or The Book of Splendor, in "artificial Aramaic" that is an Aramaic that was never spoken by the sage Simeon ben Yoha in the first half of the second century, A.D. (the Zohar claims Simeon as its author) were penned by Moses de Leon between 1275 and 1286.

issue which, as we have seen in Soloveitchik's remarks, is central to halakhah, sex. Seed, sex, underlies everything. The fear of its abuse in the Zohar is extreme. Masturbation becomes a form of murder.

Him who wilfully spills his seed. . . . Such a one is thrust down lower than all the others in the world. All others have a chance to ascend, but not he. Is he even worse, it may be asked, than a murderer? Even so, because a murderer kills another man's children, but he kills his own, and he spills very much blood. . . . Every sin admits of repentance barring this, and every sinner may hope to see the face of the Shekinah barring this one.*

Is it the attempt to overcome these two mighty terrors, death and sex, that have given birth to the idea in Judaism of the Messiah, the figure who will mediate between the realms, subdue death and sanctify seed? The dream that he will come, can come, may even be coming now if only man will make ready, has created some of the most tormented moments of hope in Judaism. One cannot help but thrill at Sabbatai Zevi in 1665 in Turkey, trying to take the burden on, declaring the end of the strict sexual prohibitions because the era of blessings was here and the forbidden was henceforth permitted: Women's Liberation bursting forth in the unlikely precincts of the Oriental Jewish community. For all his sadness and sickness, Scholem's Sabbatai Zevi has the lineaments of the human, and inhuman, hero. When Don Quixote rides out of the Jewish stables he imagines he is the Messiah, the Messiah ben David, or Jesus.

The surprise that comes in the pages of Gershom Scholem's *Sabbatai Sevi, The Mystical Messiah,* is that Sabbatai Sevi, this "false Messiah," was a true prophet, his attitude toward women in the context of a rigid Oriental Jewish community simply amazing. He calls them up to read the Torah, gives them equal rights with men, has both sexes dance in front of his table at

* The Zohar, Vol. II, p. 312

banquets, and, according to rumor, offers his wife to a few favorite disciples.

Sabbataianism and its promise of "political and spiritual freedom" was not to end with the apostasy (Sabbatai, under threat of beheading, embraced Islam) and death of its founder. Out of the pages of Scholem come darker knights of faith who carry out Sabbatai's blessing, "Blessed art Thou O Lord our God, King of the universe, who permittest the forbidden," which they interpreted as the deliberate commission of evil. The scholar gives us the intellectual context of the attempt to "cram the maw of impurity with the power of holiness until it bursts from within." His voice cannot conceal its lyrical sympathies for these "warriors"; "What daring labyrinths of the spirit are revealed in this new creed! What yearnings for a regeneration of faith and what disdainful negation of the exile." Now the true Quixote of mystical Judaism gallops into the world, Jacob Frank, "a man who did not live at all in the world of rational argument and discussion but inhabited a realm entirely made up of mythological entities."*

Unlike the captain of La Mancha who, dazzled by knightly romances, was content to tilt at windmills, Frank struck at Judaism, the whole of the halakhah, God himself. Jacob Frank carried on the ritual exchange of wives among his followers that Sabbatai Zevi initiated (and which was practiced by a sect of Sabbataians in Smyrna well into the twentieth century), and advocated conversion to Catholicism as a conscious attempt on the Jew's part to commit an act of heresy, to do evil, and in doing evil to exhaust or purify it. But his ultimate act of horror was to take the ancient blood libel, the charge that the Jews used the blood of murdered Christian children for their

---

* The treatment of Jacob Frank in *Major Trends in Jewish Mysticism* is rather brief. This quotation and most of the others in these pages on Frank come from the article "Redemption Through Sin" in Gershom Scholem's "The Messianic Idea in Judaism" (New York: Schocken Books, 1972).

Passover supper ceremony, and to declare publicly, in Lvov, that it was true. Such wickedness, which could easily have brought mass murder down upon the whole of Eastern European Jewry, was beyond even the imagination of Sabbatai Zevi. With fascination Scholem follows this wild horseman, raising the banner of nightmare. " 'Wherever Adam trod a city was built, but wherever I set foot, all will be destroyed, for I came into this world only to destroy and to annihilate. But what I build will last forever.' " At this apocalypse, the devil himself is speaking. " 'It is one thing to worship God—and quite another to follow the path I have taken.' " The scales glitter in the scholar's prose:

There was a man who was not afraid to push on to the very end, to take the final step into the abyss, to drain the cup of desolation and destruction to the lees until the last bit of holiness had been made into a mockery. His admirers, who themselves fell far short of him in respect of this ability, were won over by his intrepidness, which neither the fear of God nor the terrors of the bottomless pit were able to daunt, and saw in him the type of the true saint, a new Sabbatai Zevi and an incarnate God.

Scholem's researches do not end with the details of Frank's madness, conversion with his followers to Catholicism as a way of sinking to the bottom of the "abyss" (whence the Messiah must go before the new world can arise); erasing the prohibitions against incest, sexual taboos, the institution of ritual exchange of wives; testifying in public that Jews use the blood of Christians for religious ceremony; trifles in that depth to which Frank sped crying, " 'all laws and religions are annihilated.' " They rather attempt to understand and plumb the psychology of the followers who clung to the archheretics' skirts.

"A new type of Jew had appeared for whom the world of exile and Diaspora Judaism was partly or wholly abolished and who uncompromisingly believed that a "restored world," whose laws and practices he was commanded to obey, was in the process of coming into being. . . ." Scholem shows how Jacob Frank anticipates in his absolute nihilism a new age. The critique of a corrupt world dominated by evil "Rulers," the angels of life, wealth, and death, who were to be overthrown by Frank, is prophetic of the French Revolution. His successor at the head of the movement he created was to die on the guillotine with Danton. The Frankists became the enthusiastic supporters of the *Haskalah*, the "enlightenment," which indeed swept Judaism up in a mighty revolution.

At the very beginning, Gershom Scholem has cocked his eyebrow at us, excoriating the historians to whom Frank was "nonsense" or "grotesque, comical and incomprehensible," asking if we have not inherited a holy part of that shadowy knight's mantle. "We owe much to the experience of Zionism for enabling us to detect in Sabbatianism's throes those gropings toward a healthier national existence which must have seemed like an indiluted nightmare to the peaceable Jewish bourgeois of the nineteenth century."

By uncovering the radical tradition within Judaism, those teachers who were bold enough to carry their ideas into revolutionary action, by identifying their texts and giving a clear and unbiased account of their lives and theories, Scholem has stretched forth the tent of the Jewish covenant to include many who were homeless under the narrow canopy that occupies the middle and the right of the road. One of the most profound insights of *Major Trends in Jewish Mysticism* is the traumatic effect of the expulsion from Spain on the imagination of Jewish theosophists. The early Kabbalists had concentrated on the beginning of the world. Now "redemption," the promised end, looms all important, rather than "creation." When the redemption that should have been the reward for enduring the catastrophe of the expulsion does not come, "the flames which had flared up from the apocalyptical abyss sweep over wide areas of the Jewish world until they finally . . . recast the mystical theology of Kabbalism." We are in exile? Okay, cry the pious Kabbalists of Safed, God has to be in exile

too. It's the only explanation, *nu*? From Himself. Only wait.
Wait till He comes back! The Jews begin to bang the drums
of mystical prayer, behavior. Everybody help! Liberate the
sparks of the Messiah in yourself, separate good from the dross
of evil. He's coming! He's coming!

Who came?

Sabbatai Zevi and Jacob Frank.

Who are they to us?

Messiahs?

I am not suggesting that we create in modern Judaism a sect
of wife-swappers (although a few Israeli kibbutzniks tried it)
or deliberately go about committing evil. What we inherit
from these forebears and the Zohar is not a specific theosophy,
interesting as it may be, but poetry, a poetics of religious action, the drama of man through deliberate sublimation and
release of sexual impulse attempting to come into the arms of
God. To enact this drama with one's Eve, *both* in the covenantal community of halakhah and one's own lonely imagination, this seems an important task for the twentieth-century
mystic. The danger of a self-centered mysticism is grave.
Turning outward from this encounter to the world, we must
call again for the Messiah. Not out of frustration and unhappiness with our union, that source of inner anger and spleen
which in the name of messianism, Stalin, Hitler, the Inquisition
spreads terror, but out of bliss to fulfill the talmudic dictum,
that the Messiah will come one day after he is no longer
needed.

Yes, Scholem says, Sabbatai and Frank went off the track,
but look at the energy in their madness. What is that madness
but the old craving for God, God manifest to an entire
community?

Is Gershom Scholem a mystic?

In his book, *9½ Mystics*, Rabbi Herbert Weiner teases
Scholem in this regard, calling him an "accountant" and re-
cording the remarks of a disappointing lecture where the latter
holds out such secular phenomena as the modern state of Israel

as the realm of mysticism today. But Weiner's real question is does he believe in this stuff and can he make magic? It reminds me of a hitchhiker I once picked up who was a student at Yeshiva University. We started talking about Rabbi Soloveitchik. "No one really knows whether the Rav really believes in God," the young man asserted. Now, anyone who has seriously listened to Soloveitchik knows that he believes, albeit he had doubts, and a Judaism with no doubts is no Judaism. So Scholem believes, not in any specific doctrine, I imagine, but in the subject. His hunger is real. Does he make magic? Yes, in his books. Like the Kabbalists who preceded Sabbatai, his work has planted seeds. "The story is not ended," he declares at the conclusion of *Major Trends in Jewish Mysticism*. "It has not yet become history, and the secret life it holds can break out tomorrow in you, or in me." Like Dracula, the Messiah will return. Frank Rosenzsweig (whom Scholem gleefully identifies as a resurrector of Kabbalistic theology) has the pungent last word on this subject.

The expectation of the coming of the Messiah, by which and because of which Judaism lives, would be a meaningless theologumenon, a mere "idea" in the philosophical sense, empty babble, if the appearance again and again of a "false Messiah" did not render it reality and unreality, illusion and disillusion. The false Messiah is as old as the hope for the true Messiah. He is the changing form of this changeless hope. He separates every Jewish generation into those whose faith is strong enough to give themselves up to an illusion, and those whose hope is so strong that they do not allow themselves to be deluded. The former are the better, the latter the stronger. The former bleed as victims on the altar of the eternity of the people, the latter are the priests who perform the service at this altar. And this goes on until the day when all will be reversed, when the belief of the believers will become truth, and the hope of the hoping, a lie. Then—and no one knows whether this "then" will not be this very day—the task of the hoping will come to an end and, when the morning of that day breaks, everyone who still belongs among those who hope and not among those who believe will run the risk of being rejected.

In this century of the holocaust, hearing the selfish hammers of the nations beating on the body of Israel, halakhah and philosophy are not enough. Only together with mysticism can the holders of the covenant remain sane. Between "hope" and "belief" we must push for the "End of Days." In rendering authentic Jewish images like the clay man, the Golem, which misused and neglected fell to sentimental popular folklore, back through the careful mirrors of his scholarship into bold and daring intellectual creation, limbs fashioned by classical philosophy and theology, Gershom Scholem has returned to Jews the heroes and territory of a secret world—that terrain and those champions who have sustained us through centuries when no inch of the real world was ours in safety.

When I first began to read in Jewish sources as an undergraduate at Harvard, it was difficult for me to respond to the mystical heartbeat of Judaism. Like the conservative Sadducees I could sympathize with the older Judaism in which there was little or no mention of the afterlife, only Sheol, the place of darkness, dust, the hopeless Babylonian netherworld: "For in death there is no remembrance of thee: in the grave who shall give thee thanks?" (Psalm 6:6). Only after the death of my mother, my own growing anxiety before the prospect of Sheol, did the ribs begin to form, did I begin to understand the art of theological construction.

That ark built to float out over the seas of death, the engines of man's conduct, the nuclear power of seed, generating the driving force.

Natural man constructs science fiction. Spiritual man constructs theological fictions. While the world of space, dreams as pragmatism, as a vision of the future without God, have always depressed me, the idea of space filled with my craving for the Holy One, Blessed Be He, populated by angels rising and falling, demons, witches, cherubs, seraphs, is endlessly delightful. More and more I want to know of the travels before me. What is the God of philosophy but such a creature, beyond time and space. The riddle of existence puzzled out in

Wolfson's histories, Scholem's, Soloveitchik's—to analyze, to psychologize, to bring the Unknowable, the First Mover, the Ayn Sof, Without Limit, into the arms of man—why, this is reaching beyond storytelling, philosophy, into theological mechanics.

Mysticism, philosophy, halakhah, in Judaism these are all ways of apprehending that fourth dimension in which we step through the limitations of mechanical knowledge, death, chance.

3
Israeli
Journal

Between My Teeth

WWWW

For MANY YEARS I LAUGHED at the notion of Israel. I was interested in myself as a Jew, in the history and literature of Judaism, particularly the Eastern European experience, and Israel seemed to me a side issue, a distraction. I began to write about being Jewish at Harvard, and teachers inevitably asked me, Have you gone to Israel? I would shrug the question off. It's not important. Certainly the dinky little Israeli destroyer I remembered touring with my classmates from the Beth El Hebrew School, somewhere in the early fifties; the assorted junk that uncles and aunts brought back from their trips, cheap brassware and candlesticks; the harsh wines my father and Ben Zion Gold served, as a patriotic duty; did not feed my appetite. Israel, it seemed to me, served as an excuse for American Jews to ignore their responsibilities for a living intellectual culture in the United States and instead lose themselves in sentimental dreams far away from home.

Prior to the 1967 war, it seemed to me that Israel would only be a bad joke, a mistake, a family closet where one would be stifled in old coats, castoffs. Whenever one criticized American Judaism, the answer was, everything is being saved for Israel. Who could help resenting the place? And Ben Gurion's temper fits, come over and settle or else forget it, you're not Jews, didn't help. *Gay kucken af'n Yom.* Apart from there being a lot of Jews there, what's so Jewish about Israel?

After 1967, as has been told a dozen times, the Israelis discovered that they were Jewish. That, frankly, the only ones who really cared about them were the other Jews in the world. All their contacts in Africa, Europe, could vanish overnight if circumstances shifted, and only their brethren would risk life, limb, and pocketbook to bail them out. But what is not so generally understood is that the American Jewish intellectuals were also shifting. I don't particularly count myself as a thinker, but friends in the philosophy, English, political science departments at Stanford, Harvard, City College, began to feel responsible for Israel. The traumas of Jews in America before World War Two when they were discriminated against, assigned to quotas, excluded, were suddenly in their nostrils, and the victory of the Israelis against overwhelming odds was a personal victory for many of these older friends of mine. It wasn't the Arabs they had won against. It was all those snobby descendants of the Pilgrims and the DAR who had made them feel mean, weak, threadbare, the custom pedlar's children. With the war in Vietnam going so badly, the tables were turned. America looked shoddy.

Mixed with this warlike redemption, however, was a sense of Israel's fragility. The ark that the Jews were sailing in the Middle East could come apart at any moment, no matter how cocksure the Israelis appeared. "Why are you so arrogant?" I scolded my Israeli cousins.

"How long do you think we would last, if we weren't?" they replied, smirking and wincing at once. It was true. What can you answer? If the Arabs call the bluff, we're in trouble. So one bit one's lip but began to love them, a peculiar, wary love.

Moreover, with the capture of The Wailing Wall, the Old

City, something very ancient that transcended Israel, modern Israel, came back into our possession. Israel became once more the Holy Land. It seems as if all Israelis were touched by this. A mystical center began to radiate in our consciousness. No one can adequately explain why the Wall and the old Arab city should work so on the imagination of a secular generation, but it did and it continues to do so. And it is for the very reason that the Jews laughed at the notion of going to Uganda (rightly so, you can imagine now under General Amin what a disaster that would have been) and said, no, no, we will return to that barren desert and swamp, Palestine. Because they, we, are in search of a fable. Judaism for me is a balancing act between the rational and irrational. You cannot justify to any American Jew on a rational basis his return, his allegiance, to the land of Israel. I began to understand after 1967 the pull of that land on my bones.

In the wake of the Yom Kippur War, my visit to Israel just before it, I have come to realize that the state of Israel is bound up in the very center of Jewish existence. Yes, it is a borrowed land, country of Perizzites, Jebuzites, Rephaim, and we are the wanderers, the river crossers, but our covenant was struck here. You cannot have a mystical Judaism without an earth to depart from. Chase us out again. As long as the idea of Judaism remains, Jews must return to the dream of an earthly paradise, a place to enact the drama of the Jewish idea, righteousness, messianism, both Koran and New Testament realize that it cannot be until the Jews are in their place. Not to love that place is only to be a half-Jew. And to love it is already to be half a Jew. *Nu?*

Disaster is always lurking behind me waiting for a moment of distraction to slip its hand into my pocket. The Talmud defines madness as loss: "You begin to lose things and one day, you lose your mind." This trip I have lost my beloved Spanish army knife, two favorite pens, and (I count what is coming in Eilat as robbery, not loss) at the last moment, in the act of writing out postcards to friends in the post office in Athens, O treachery, while smiling over an Irish girl from Attleboro, Mass. I met in the labyrinth at Knosses, weaving a web before her between the Brown Bull of Cuailnge, the fabulous Celtic monster, and this present haunt of the Minotaur, not the bull but the trickster pulled the wool of forgetfulness over my eyes and I left my journal behind on the desk, not to be remembered until I landed in N.Y.C.—a notebook containing two months of jottings on Israel, Bedouin folktales, the beginning of a story (this I mourn most, the magical thread with which I begin a story, this once slipped away can never be recovered: I stare at a dozen corridors into an unfinished tale, horror) plus addresses, companions, the paths to whose houses are now gone forever.

So these pages which I intended to write out of my jottings on the Holy Land, the Promised Land, must now be composed entirely out of my head.

"You think it's a beautiful green land," said Soloveitchik one night at his lecture in Brookline, "No, it's brown, dusty, hot, not such a paradise, Eretz Yisroel." And he spoke of the attachment he felt to his verdant backyard in Brookline. There is the real Eretz Yisroel, and the promised Eretz Yisroel, the actual Israel, and the dream of Israel, so perhaps it is appropriate that I should lose my notes on the actual Israel, made while I was in the presence of the land, and here in America have to reconstruct that world entirely in my head. For it was not the real but the unreal Israel I was after, and no one can understand the real Israel's existence without understanding the unreal Israel, which is in many ways much more palpable and powerful so that even in Israel most people are living not in the real but the unreal country.

How shall I explain? In some lands, for a while, the dream life of the people overwhelms them and they live in a fantastic world. This is what happened to the Germans. They conceived or believed in a bad opera of Wagner for fifteen years, and no wonder the priests of the dream could not abide Jews.

All their invocations, super race, supermen, blood purity, were old Jewish clichés, they had stolen everything except the one valuable antidote to those dangerous hallucinatory poisons, self-laughter—oh, blockish Aryans, that Semite tribal remedy, insistent mockery of one's night visions, that those melancholy dyspeptic Allemands could not swallow. Nevertheless, all through modern Israel I remembered the angry reaction of one of my gentile American girl friends: "They're Germans. Just like Germans."

No, it is not true. At their own valuation they might like to be mistaken for Panzers, but at the best, after a few weeks, one discovers that the Israeli is only a super Semite, a different matter—for, in the case of the Arab and Jew, Super Semite does not lead you up, up, but around, around, implying not Superman mounting above the clouds with a bulletproof impervious chest, higher and higher, up to Krypton, but rather around and around until you get a whirling dervish, personification of a dust storm.

"It's good that the war lasted only six days," my cousin says to me. "I was at Suez and by the seventh day, it was enough already. For six days you went on fighting without thinking but on the seventh day, I realized I couldn't have gone on with it another hour without collapsing. No water to bathe in, shave in, ridiculous. The Rabbinical Council sent a truck down full of Coca-Cola in appreciation, because we were 'good boys and had captured Jerusalem.' But the cokes were hot, no refrigeration. Israel!"

Another cousin, in Tel Aviv, tells me about a neighbor whose son was a colonel in the air force. The officer gets up out of a sickbed to fly thirty-eight missions during the war.

"What's going to happen?" the colonel's father asks him in Yiddish.

"Papa, I promise you, not a single bomb will fall on Tel Aviv." On the third day of the war, my cousin calls the house to find out how the son is.

"It's finished," says his mother, in a terrible voice. "My

Shlomo has finished the war." The irony of the aviator's death, even in English, is strange and personal. This is a country of tribes, families, everyone rushing off to see an aging father or mother who for twenty years has been at death's door, a country where at best you can live only an hour or two away from parents.

A country which for thousands of years existed only in the Jews' heads; in Africa, Europe, Far Asia, America, the rabbis quarreled over its laws, how much land each Jew was entitled to, the dates of its holidays, the facts of its commerce, agriculture. A trickle of them, Maimonides, Judah Ha Levi, Isaac Luria, my great-great-great-grandfather Reuben, managed the trek to the wasteland to weep among the ruins of the dreamland in which they had lived through infancy and adulthood. Talmud, Zohar, Zionism, Israel, a synonym for Paradise. "The Land." Modern rabbis in America, unconscious of the irony, using the language of Indians, Hopi, Zuni, Pawnee, "Have you been to Eretz? Have you visited the land?"

Chanoch Bartov, an Israeli writer, listening to, anticipating my carping, bends over the table at lunch, his lips twitching sarcastically. "You have to realize it was founded in desperation. Jews no longer believed in religion, God, in Europe. Yet they wanted to remain together as Jews. Israel was the last hope. They came to Palestine because it was the only chance for them to survive as Jews, a last desperate chance. It was an experiment." He shakes his head, points his finger at me. "And we're not sure it's succeeded. It's still desperate, believe me."

That desperation you feel everywhere in Israel. "You can't get along here unless you shove. You have to be aggressive." Again and again I heard that in Israel. Then indeed I was shoved, right off a bus in Tel Aviv by a crowd of eighty- and seventy-year-olds, after a particularly frustrating three hours at a bank finding that Israeli pounds were a desperate currency and could not be changed back into American dollars without incredible red tape, my *bobbas* and *zaides* elbowing in front of me as the vehicle pulls in, shoving Maishe to the rear of the queue and as he finally squeezes into the door, putting forth aged hands and buttocks to bump him out onto the sidewalk. Enough! I lost my temper and started screaming, "Miserable! Miserable!" in a rafter-shaking voice, feeling the flush of Isaiah at this ugly stubborn mob. The whole street suddenly came to focus on me, not as they would in New York City (Jesus, who's that nut?) but rather shamefaced, half inquiring, curious, even the bus driver, sticking his mug out, abashed, acknowledging anger. What's up? Something wrong? They knew what I was talking about, like parents who have pushed a child too far. Anger was not only holy here, it was an everyday necessity.

Here I began to understand the scolding tone of my cousins —how come you don't come to Israel to live, you American Jews? Soon your time is up. Try to come over in ten years. Sorry, too late. The door is shut, *Die in Galut!* Always talking, desperate, desperate, a country living on the margin, on charity, constant gypping by merchants in the street; in Eilat the Rent-A-Car salesman starts to warn me about trying to fool with the odometer, then smiles and says, "You're American. It's only with the Israelis we have trouble. . . ." And the rudeness, the chaos of queues for the bus, the open sourness of salesmen, ticket-takers, waiters, the arrogance—again and again people thinking they know English refusing to let you repeat or explain, completely misunderstanding your questions—and Israeli directions, a kind of hand wave over a forty-five-degree arc, one end of which will take you to Australia, the other to Siberia, given with such firmness and assurance that there is no possibility of appeal for more specific details.

I ask my cousins who have scolded me for not coming about the Israeli economy. "Terrible. The technology is good but the labor force is lazy, impossible, no one wants to work. Frankly, believe it or not, the American worker is more efficient."

They are summoning me to the dream land, but inevitably the real land contradicts it. They themselves keep fleeing Israel for other places, and in New York, Paris, London, they re-create it in their heads and weep over their withered right arms.

Why did I come to Israel?

Because.

Because of the Christmas stocking I hung up on my bureau when I was three years old for Santa Claus, hoping for all the bright baubles I had seen in the windows of Jordan's and Filene's, railroad trains, huge teddy bears; that I found stuffed like an Indian quiver full of arrows, warnings, with picture postcards of Palestine, a book full of colored engravings of Jerusalem bound in olive wood that I had already torn apart in my father's desk drawer—my parents' message to their baby coming into consciousness, this is your North Pole, toy factory, this land of too bright sun and late afternoon shadow.

Because of Hebrew school and all those boring Saturday afternoons at the Chai Odom Nursery where Mrs. Chansky's daughters dragged me for Israeli folk dances, songs, everything Israeli stamped, sanitized, sexless, so that the land seemed as if it was full of the heavy thick stockings of the Chansky sisters, Orthodox and unappetizing, approved by your parents, grand-parents, great-grandparents, 100 percent *glatt* kosher, a land of heavy, sleepy goodness as burdensome as an endless afternoon nap.

Because of rows of aunts, uncles, cousins, rabbis, fellow Jews, Jewish professors, etc., who cried, "Have you gone? What, you haven't gone? How come? Not yet? When? When?"

Because my mother, dying, left me a thousand dollars to go there.

Because Yakov Lind told me that on every street in Tel Aviv there were fifteen Isaiahs, twenty Jeremiahs, and a hundred Messiahs, all crying out at once; that half the population was obsessed with visions of solipsistic holiness; that by King David's tomb there was an authentic holy man who lived entirely on the leaves of trees which he detested but about which he was the absolute gourmet; that the students of a crazy yeshiva for former whacked-out drug addicts and hippies were running around the streets of the country proclaiming milleniums and quoting Zohar. . . .

I finally decided to go and kiss the Jewish blarney stone.

I began by preparing. I read or in a sense consulted my traveling guide, touchstone. In the library on Sixth Avenue I removed Agnon's books from the shelf and read them to the holy number three.

In *In the Heart of the Seas* I read of a trip to the Holy Land by Eastern European saints by boat. Let them come from Yemen and Morocco on the wings of an eagle, after this reading, nothing would do but Mirsky of the Mirskys of Pinsk, Slonim, following in the track of his great-great-great-grandfather Reuben should journey in a holy vessel over the waves to the Land.

Now we will skip a tedious journey out of which Agnon almost wrings a masterpiece (alas, his book grows tedious too) and come at once to the landing at Haifa, or about four hours before the landing at Haifa, when Mirsky, through a veil of morning mist, sights the holy mountain of Carmel and begins a furious debate in his head. Will he kiss the ground when he first gets off, publicly or privately? Is it showing off to do it right in front of all the other passengers and therefore an abomination, or is it false pride even to be thinking of the other passengers when he has an opportunity to put his lips to Holy Soil? Will they let him do it right away? Will it cause a scene? How should he do it? Memories of Gideon, prostrate on his face, or bending on his knees. If the dock is wood does it count as Holy Soil, or if it's metal, etc., this and a thousand talmudic curlicues go through his head, sustaining and bedeviling him through the long, long security check and wait on the boat, until finally at the very end of the passenger list, he goes down the gangplank and finds himself on his knees kissing asphalt.

Why asphalt? he wonders as he gets up. (Nobody has paid

the slightest attention to him, he sees in a quick look around.)
Ah, he has the answer, shouldering his bag toward customs,
isn't his name, Maishe, Moses, and didn't Moses get his lips
scorched with a coal, wasn't that his real kiss with the divine,
and Isaiah, wasn't his mouth cleansed with a live coal, and
what is better for him Mark (Moses, Maishe) Mirsky than a
bit of bitumen, it's an omen for a writer. But later, on the way
from the custom house, just to be sure, he plants his lip in a
windowbox full of geraniums and gets the real authentic taste
of dust in his mouth, tongue, throat, grit between his teeth.

And the dust sticks to his palate right through his first meal,
which is out of "Israel on Five Dollars a Day," Farm Foods in
Haifa, a restaurant, which serves him a gefilte fish which is
pure myth so that his mouth waters with joy of horseradish,
his eyes too, and he eats manna.

First moments. He sees that the girls are beautiful. They do
not look like his cousins, the mannequins of Long Island, and
he rejoices and sends forth a song of praise. Where there are
lovely, lovely women, there must be culture. And he thinks,
maybe Momma's thousand dollars is prophetic and will lead
him finally to middle-class happiness; he will take that first
agonizing step Franz Kafka was longing for, "that one, first,
high step, that step which it is impossible for him to climb
even by exerting all his strength, that step which he cannot
get up on and which he naturally cannot get past either,"
toward a decent, sane life, marriage. He treads a land of his
own making.

Yes, I can address myself as Mirsky, a third person, a second
person (here we are treading on dangerous trinities) in Haifa
because I am living in hallucinations of Israel, talking to myself. "Why did you go to Israel?" they asked me last night,
here in New York City. "To enter a hallucination." They
shake their heads, unbelievers, yet it's true, the first days I am
talking to myself as if I were a character in a dream, watching
myself, half floating above my body, abstracted, my soul flut-
tering detached, drawing me up on the mountain where Elijah

faced the priests of Baal, kindled fire on the brow that beetles over a vast, fertile plain. Standing in the prophet's place on the stony forehead of his mountain, I too feel like calling the Almighty to witness, striking my sense of him into flame against the flint of this towering hilltop. "You are crazy, Mirsky," the voice whispers in my ear (but not so loud as it might in Massachusetts).

"And some fell on the stony ground," that sentence of Jesus rebuking the deaf auditors of the divine message which fell like seed, it echoes in my ear on the way up to Elijah's mountain from the village of Muchraka, for here in the country of the Druse it marks him as a city boy, a carpenter's son. My sandals crunch over the rocks as all around me out of the hillside flanks, fields of stones, red, brown, orange pebbles, the mustachioed wizards, Druse, have coaxed fat, leafy vegetables out of gardens of gravel. The stones burst into flower, the seed in Israel is triumphant, cleaving the rock. This stony ground that refused Jesus, these northern hills, I love them, their bony, white ribs cropping out of green grass. Stubborn bare ground, my tongue dry with heat, I jump off the road, seek a path of my own; in the midst of deserted valleys climbing up, I hear the tinkle of goat bells and am in the ancient land of Yom Kippur where the tug of hunger in your head late in the afternoon lifts the Jew out of time and geography into the fast vision. I praise the black snake gliding away from me into the bushes, not Faulkner's "Grandfather," but Patriarch.

Later, in Galilee, these hills will rise over even Elijah's head. I will understand not only Jesus, the Galilean, but Isaac Luria, Ari, the Lion, a country of Messiahs, not only the top of Israel but somehow, the top of the world, as if you could, if only enough conviction doubled in your breast, on one foot leap singly into heaven. The upper world closer to you than the lower. Staring down from the shattered doorjambs, the broken window shutters of Sfad, the old streets creaking in the wind, I saw Isaac Luria's Kabbala in the landscape, the bowls that skimmed good and evil out of the might of God, cupped between the mountaintops, in the valleys of his mountain fast, the Lion had congealed God, beginning, end, and felt the icy shudder of His presence breaking the ribs of crockery.

"Galilee, Galilee, thou hatest the Law."

My nation of idol-breakers who dreamed of God shattering the very earth and universe as insufficient to His might, the complexity of His good and evil.

"Give me my vision!" I cried on Carmel, in Galilee, Sfad, Sinai. Instead I got a good kick in the pants.

In the immigration hall coming into Israel, under the picture of Theodore Herzl, his words, "If you'll believe, it won't be a fable."

Late at night in Haifa, sitting on the iron railing of the pedestrian guard at a street corner, watching pretty girls go in and out of an ice-cream parlor, I start to talk to a young Israeli. "I'm from New York."

"You Jewish?"

I nod. He relaxes. Begins to complain about Israel after 1967. Everything has changed since the Six Day War. His father is a contractor. Now everyone is trying to make a big killing. The government has sold out to business. For the first time, he says, sadly shaking his head, you can make a lot of money in Israel.

Before 1938, my cousins tell me, it was a different country. No one in Tel Aviv locked their doors. You didn't need a key for your home. The Jews who had come to Israel came because they believed in a dream, Zionism. In 1938–39, however, Polish Jews began to arrive, horse thieves, crooks, not like the earlier German immigrants from Hitler, and for the first time they had crime in Israel. Now with the Moroccan, Yemenite, Iraqi immigration, prostitutes, etc., Israel has changed beyond recognition.

On the beach in Tel Aviv, some very tough-looking Iraqi girls motion me over to their towel on the rocks, try to start a conversation in Hebrew. I mumble my limited vocabulary. One takes my hand and leads me down to the water. We splash each other laughing, the water too shallow here to really swim. She directs me in our wading and as we stand up from our dog-paddling, I note her full bosom, the taut line of her dark body. We return to the rocks and I stretch out in the sun, only to hear in her throaty English, "I want to go to New York."

Tel Aviv

VVVVV

TEL AVIV, that dumpy little mock-up of Miami, Tel Aviv fills me with good feeling, laughter, enthusiasm: its bustle is the beat of Blue Hill Avenue, my father's, the politician's, lost kingdom in Boston. Bubbling over the first few days in Tel Aviv, I tremble as the Iraqi, Moroccan, Yemenite horses go by, and I long to fall on those dark mares' flanks and make whole tribes of Israelis. Still, I remain celibate in an Eretz that seethes with sex. Worse than Blue Hill Avenue, here is the fountain of fulfillment—the avenues of brown Middle Eastern beauties, Roumanian and Hungarian pastries, such a racial plentitude, I want to jump into the middle of it and integrate the world. We Jews are the International, I shout to myself, thinking of Isaac Babel's Gedali, buttoning the three bone buttons of his green frock coat in bloody Zhitomir, "the founder of an Impossible International . . . an international of good people," sitting in the cafés, with the survivors from the four corners of the earth, sipping "a little of that pensioned-off God in a glass of tea." In this Palestinian sun, I have been baked overnight into orange, and except for the few old and young tenaciously clinging to the pale hues of yeshiva existence, I am at one with the crowd that overflows Dizengoff Street—like an old New Year's celebration in Times Square. All ages, even the babies, out at midnight, and the whole of them, to the most succulent Scheherazade of Jewish Arabia, *shlepping.* I swear, twenty thousand people dancing that unique Jewish step, not parading but *shlepping*, that slow kibitz of a walk, half shuffle, half skip, *shlepping* back and forth before the café tables, ancients poking among the adolescents. A book on my table attracts an old man. I tell him I'm reviewing it for an American paper. "Do you know so-and-so?" he asks. "Of the *New Yorker*, in 1941? The *New York Times*, 1945?" His connections are decades too early for me to make any sense of them.

"I'll see you again," is his farewell and why not, I think, aren't we all in the same family? *Vey iz mir*, all these girls in my family, take me home, I want to beg them, take me home (but not to New York, where too many of them, as I found out on the beach, would like to head).

If Jerusalem is the austere capital of the old Kingdom of David, Tel Aviv crowns the modern Israeli state. There's nothing to ruin, bleak Judean hills, or as in Haifa, the shape of the Carmel mountain range. There was nothing but flat dunes when the Jews arrived here at the turn of the century, an old port to the side, Jaffa, and a small river. One can revel, untroubled, in the glut of stucco, the noise of the bazaar, food stalls, traffic tearing down and pushing up. This it it, *nu?* Judaism today. Such a human place. "Watch your pocket," even strangers warn you. "Tricky fingers." The tears go back ten, fifteen years. "When poets, artists, actors, really sat at the cafés." But they still do, and pacing the street, Dizengoff, with Israeli writers, Yoram Kaniuk, Chanoch Bartov, we keep bumping into directors, journalists, stopping for another cup of coffee.

At the legendary Dahn Ben Amotz's, another Israel unveils for me. "This is the Israeli Allen Ginsberg," my friends tell

me, taking me there. In a house in old Jaffa, the sea lapping
outside his windows, writer, radio personality, the aging dean
of the native beatniks, holds his court, attended as the tales
have promised me by the adolescent nymphs of an enthroned
king of the vineyards. We engage in a brief literary sparring
match, at which I become painfully aware that Dahn, like my
other acquaintances among the writers of the Jewish State,
hasn't read anyone after 1950. His "hipness" is almost quaint,
though he tells powerful anecdotes about the Sinai wars, when
after the battle he quietly immured himself in St. Catharine's
Monastery. And after snapping at each other all evening, he
bawls out the friend who has brought me for not trying to get
a Hebrew publisher for my novels. Across from us as we sip
wine and squabble, a lovely seventeen-year-old girl dressed in
a wrap that fits as loosely around her as a silk towel unrolls
like a scroll of Esther, showing breasts, thighs nonchalantly
before the company. Occasionally, one of the men rises, takes
her out to another room for a backrub that is evidently from
the land of fable. Oriental, opulent, something more than
"liberation" is the musk of these Scheherazades. Yoram tells
me tales of hundreds of young kibbutzniks, girls and boys,
dancing naked under the waterfalls.

"Take me to them," I beg. But he shrugs his shoulders. It's
not for a four-week tour, a trip into such exotic subterranean
caverns takes a while to arrange. But it's not eroticism that
Yoram talks about when he describes his journeys among this
new generation of the kibbutzim, rather the idealism, the hope
they have, the dreams. "They are the future of this state," he
says, eyes glowing.

The old, however, as much as the young, seem to me to have
the poetry of idealism in that Israel within Israel, the communal
settlements, kibbutzim. Chanoch Bartov, an Israeli novelist,
journalist, takes me to a poetry reading at Abba Kovner's, a
poet who lives in a kibbutz outside of Tel Aviv. The room is
crowded (his living room—for here as in other friends' houses
in Europe, the poet is not ashamed to read in his own quarters)

with farmers, mechanics from the kibbutz, cooks from the kitchen, many of them comrades from their days of fighting against the Nazis as partisans in the forests outside Vilna. As you look at Abba and the other men and their wives, now old women but with young eyes, women who fought as girls alongside their husbands-to-be, a glow spreads over the proceedings. In New York City, Abba's leonine silver prow would probably be towing a young girl or two in its wake. They tell stories, Abba, Chanoch: of Bialik and Shlonsky, the Hebrew poets, laureates of the generation before—how manufacturers and businessmen came first to Bialik, and after his death to Shlonsky—to get names, words for things: buses, trains, that had no equivalent in Ancient Hebrew. They banged on the wordsmiths' doors, holding presents under their arms, begging creation, and the poets gave them a name. (In the case of the bus it was *Egged*, connections, a baptism in exchange for a bottle of brandy.) On the ride to Abba's, Chanoch began to lament his own separation from the kibbutz, agonize over it. Did he do the right thing? he asked his wife. Could they go back? I felt often among these middle-aged friends of mine the questions of their childhood, still active, unresolved, a fountain of youth in their features.

In my greed to see old Tel Aviv, Jaffa (which has been turned for the most part into a sanitized tourist tearoom), I walked so hard in a new pair of sandals (they wear like iron, a friend assured me, yes, yes, into my flesh) I tore my feet up and now can hardly limp to the corner. This is no place for running. Slow down, my feet warn me. Only I want to see everyone. Among the brown mini-skirted girls of Dizengoff, the boys in shorts, the older couples in short-sleeve shirts, an old Chassid in heavy silk coat and with a fur hat unbelievable in the June heat picks up cigarette butts from the sidewalks, wastebaskets, and surreptitiously bears them away. I sit dazzled by contrasts at the cafés, lumpy rabbinical couples, hippies, Long Island debutantes, Arab beauties in tight pants, Hebrew dwarfs, a train of old men, girls in their military uniforms, fat, skinny, misshapen, shaped beyond one's hopes. I rise screaming in their midst, my family, my family.

Yet Eilat is coming and all this sentimentality is to be smacked right out of me.

Up Against the Wailing Wall

VVVVV

Three-fourths of a mile from Jerusalem, from the place where you begin to go downhill by a path descending in terraces, we saw the holy city, the citadel of our delight. There we rent our garments in accordance with the law. And after a little time we saw the broken house of our sanctuary and glory, and we rent our garments a second time for the sake of the sanctuary. Thus we reached the gates of Jerusalem (Obadiah of Bertinoro, 1488).

"How MANY DAYS did you spend in Jerusalem?"

"Five."

"Only five?"

"I wanted to maintain myself in a state of euphoria. I could not maintain it for more than five."

Not entirely true, this answer I gave a friend. I had to hurry back for an appointment in Tel Aviv. True to form, the Israeli novelist Yoram Kaniuk had forgotten about it when I arrived. Yet Jerusalem was a city that demanded of me a holy effort, that I live not in the present but the past, imagining at every moment that I was in David's city, Solomon's city, Herod's city, the city of the War of Independence (in the jitney taxi coming up from Tel Aviv, an elderly passenger pointed to the hulks of burnt-out tanks by the side of the road, stark monuments of the bitter battle fifteen years ago to supply the beleaguered town, so that I was required to mourn as a visitor, to count the cost in lives, every inch of the ascent), city of the Zionists at the turn of the century, every city but the present one glaring down from soaring new hotels, and that was the other effort, blotting out the city of Teddy Kollek, trying to cast it like a concrete mote from the eye as it marched over the coronet of bare Judean hills, cement teeth of the dragon.

Stony hillsides, sheep ranging through miles of abandoned terrace, and I felt the holocaust that had engulfed these mountains and left them bare of inhabitants, the hand of Roman desolation, an ancient shattered countryside, history as eerie as science fiction; but there is also something of Lhasa about Jerusalem, especially if you wind up to it from the east, where the golden and silver domes of the Old City appear in the distance from the narrow, tortuous path of the road, a forbidden citadel. A high, arrogant place, the touch of ice in the air that gives its citizens a mocking edge. This was no town for Jesus to come to with his dreams of resurrection; that is for a soft, balmy coast where the hope of spring is alive even in biting December. "He that sitteth in heaven laugheth/ The Lord hath them in derision/ Truly it is I that have established My king/ Upon Zion, My holy mountain." A rock town, half sky, both above you and below you. "In Haifa they work, in Jerusalem study, in Tel Aviv play," the proverb sings, and the scholarship of Zion takes its cynical, detached looking-down on man's folly from this height. "For in death there is no remembrance of thee," a tag of ironic supplication that must have slipped across the harp strings of the psalmist, circling the promenade of his crow's nest, an earthly kingdom at his feet. It was not merely trade routes that brought David to this spot, but the desire to sit on high. Ha!

Dumping my valise in a hotel, I rushed downhill into East Jerusalem, Old Jerusalem, the walled Jerusalem, blissfully ignorant of the buses that would skirt the tangle of gates, streets, blind avenues, a labyrinth of routes, signs that sent you doubling back upon your footsteps again and again, until you cried out in despair; a bus that would merely, by the back gate, dump you there. The Dung Gate!

Pulling a black velvet yarmulka out of my pocket, I jumped in through one of the massive towered entries of the Crusader battlements bounding across the moat into a village bustle as thick and hoary as Esau's beard, a crowd of robed Arabs, Long Island suburbanites in Bermudas, Hungarian Orthodox in mink caps, black frock coats, a motley rabble of hawkers and babblers swarming over the cobbles of old Palestine as I stopped, a Jerusalem as absolutely faithful to one's Hebrew school imagination as a stage set, its tumult held between thick walls of glazed soil, an architecture that has not changed much since the days of Ur of the Chaldees. The noise was as sweet to me as Mogen David Extra Heavy Malaga, but cloyed at last. I plunged on in the direction of a sign toward the Holy of Holies, seeking a way and straying from the way, not knowing how to find . . . but toiling desperately through back alleys, the Armenian quarter, the long, covered market street jammed with Americans, Germans, Swedes, Arabs, goats, donkeys (in the shade of the grassy moat under one of the bridges into the gate, sheep were grazing); still a Jerusalem of the Bible in which Jesus, stripped to a loincloth, could be goaded, hooted, mocked, shoved up and down one tortuous, winding avenue of tiny stalls, busy merchants and their customers, turning for a moment to this municipal sweetmeat, a condemned man, naked, trying to drag a heavy cross along the steep inclines of the narrow thoroughfare. The procession to Golgotha might have gotten lost, for the arrows to the Temple, Via Dolorosa, sent you in circles, pointed you into a knot of streets where fleeing too eager hawking, bumped and jammed on, at last one was content to be absolutely without bearings and stepped away into the side streets. So I found myself in back lanes, the orange earth sifting into my shoes. Gray, weathered shutters, silver with age, wood like fig bark, falling out of the clay walls. Down the end of one avenue where the shops have petered out, an Arab boy is beating a goat's back with a switch, laughing, calling to two or three friends to witness his tyranny, until it kicks him hard and he bursts into humiliated tears to the smiles of swaddled grandfathers in the doorways: a village, not a town. And the map in my hand is useless. These byways have no names and no one knows where when I ask; or rather they all know and motion me in so many ways that I might as well put my nose to the crumbling citron rubble and smell the footsteps to the Temple. Which I do.

I start to climb, guiding myself into higher streets to take a look over rooftops, trying to direct myself east by distant mountains. I intrude into an abandoned, hushed old city. Clambering over fences, poking down side alleys, the quiet of dusty gardens, weeds, falling house fronts, I push through an open gate, mount a rooftop. Hills rise across from me and stare down.

The wall.

I know it's the wall because that is all there is, a big empty space in front of it, with two little boxes and a few black frock coats pressed against it. A blue-and-white Jewish flag in the foreground. I would know it was the wall even if it had still been plunged in the garbage of the Dung Gate a few feet away. You could smell all the sadness that had been pressed against it and those pockmarked stones had been rocking Mirskys to sleep through the Exile from Alexandria to Dorchester. Under the Israelis it is twice, three times the height that Jews have known it for the past few thousand years, as if our grief had grown in stature, digging down to the foundation stones. It used to be a little backyard wall. Now its shadow is impressive. Still, only a wall, only a wall.

A writer in America, Leo Litwak, sober, a rationalist, told me how he had come for three nights to it at a distance, only to look staring for hours, not wanting to approach.

I've pushed open someone's gate, walked into his backyard, and am standing on his roof staring down in silence. When I begin to think again, to hear through the hum of insects in my ears the faraway sound of human voices, feel the blanket of heat drawn away from my chin, I know it's time for me to go and touch the stones. For I stood in the hot sun for half an hour, not able to think, dream, make any fantasies, up against a wall.

Slowly I walk down through the alleys, approach the Chassidim, young bearded rabbis who after trying out Yiddish and Hebrew on me lapse comfortably into pure Brooklynese. Abandoning my leather handbag in their damp hovel by the guardbox (their garments distill a melancholy dew even under the fierce Palestinian light) I adjust my velvet skullcap returning from its exile, missing the pert button on top, a crumpled crown out of Lifshitz's Religious just off Orchard Street. What fabulous price would the tailor have asked if he had contemplated its present hallowing? The Chassidim wrap me in the leather straps of the Tfillin (my fingers shake, forgetting how to twist the black binding around my arms and head although I have been doing it four, five times a week since my mother's death) and prayer book in hand, I tread air, toward the wall.

Put my hands against it, slowly, tentatively, feeling the stone, then unable to stop, I come closer, put my lips to the slabs, slide my cheek against the grain. It is the face of my father, my grandfather. I open the book to begin the Eighteen Benedictions. But I am crying; I can't stop, the tears are thick in my eyes, throat; I cough, my mouth full of mucus. Only a wall, a wall, no fancy cupolas, arches, churches, mosques, a blank wall. I hug it, crying hysterically, my dead mother, grandfather, all the Jews, generations of us, thousands of years of us, our family, up against a wall. I can't stop, and I blunder on through the Eighteen Benedictions wailing, out of control, amazed at myself. Mirsky! Mirsky! A voice in me is shaking its head.

At last the Benedictions are finished. My fingers let go of the cracks stuffed with paper prayers. I brush my cheek against it one last time and, exhausted, trying to stop crying, turn away.

A little man, hatless, runs up to me. "Mister, I got a picture of you."

"Please," I croak.

"No, it's good . . . I took a picture. Very cheap. . . ."

"Go away, please, no, no. . . ."

"I got a good one."

"No, it's bad . . . bad . . . please." I fall back into the arms of the astonished Chassidim who (*o vanitv*, ever present) I can see through dimmed eyes are impressed by the American's flood of grief. They take me into their cell, unwrap me away from the buzzing of the photographer jumping like Rumpelstiltskin, shaking his camera. "Good, good!"

It is forbidden to make images, and here at the Holy of Holies is an idolatrous pest, creature of Sodom and Coney Island. Later, when I told the story to my Israeli cousins, saying that I had been grateful for the presence of the Orthodox, that at least they had retained some sense of the need for holiness in approaching the wall, and perhaps even the separation of men and women might be justified in the sense that male and female would find their emotions less inhibited, laughter broke into my tale.

"Those holy Chassidim." My cousin smirked. "They're in cahoots with the photographer. They probably get a cut of his take."

Often I thought of going back and beating the cameraman: Jesus and the moneychangers, Mirsky and the photographers. Still, there is something so Jewish about the mingling of vulgarity and holiness, nothing sanctimonious, no incense about the sacred places, only the faint scent of urine where dogs have peed, as in the caves of Elijah and Simon the Just. Like the shouting and tumult in the synagogues of Dorchester, Eastern Europe, only a saint could concentrate on the Divine, no help from nice surroundings or brethren in discipline.

The peoples and their kings will come together, will come together on business to Palestine, and they will say, "Since we have troubled ourselves to come hither, let us look at the business of the Jews, and what its nature is," and so they will get to Jerusalem, and they will observe how Israel worships . . . and they will say, "It is well to join this people," and they will not budge from Jerusalem until they are made proselytes, and they will offer sacrifices and burnt offerings.*

* Sifre *Deut. Berakah*, Rabbinic Anthology, p. 565.

In the Heart of
the Heart of Jerusalem

WWWW

A COOL MORNING, a hot afternoon, one day in Jerusalem rolls
into another and I cannot distinguish them on the scroll as I
circle the Old City. Jerusalem from the slopes on either side
can be held in the hollow of your hand, weighed for its sins,
its preciousness; when you walk round from the Valley of
Hell, Gehinnom, to the Valley of Redemption, Kidron, the
whole of its bulk is before you, a sphere you can take and
lay to your heart. "Jerusalem that art builded a city that is
compact together." It is a child's city, and one is reminded
of the Jewish story that God created a perfect universe, though
now it's cracked. What happened? He couldn't resist, He
played with it.

It is a wall, Jerusalem, first you go over it, around, under. . . .

An Arab city, fortunately, most of its streets, as in Fez, are
closed to automobile traffic. This irony, constant in Israel—
only the Arabs, Druse, preserve for us Jews the real sight, taste

of the ancestors we have come back to honor. It is they, in their peasant, desert robes, that you want to reach out and hug, mysterious as the snake that glides out from the trash in the Valley of Kidron.

The sun in these valleys is hellish. The northern bend around the old city seemed minutes away when I started, and an hour later I turn finally from the western to the eastern side and walk down, then up the flanks of the Mount of Olives through the sea of overturned graves where the Arabs wrought sacrilegious havoc after the war of 1948. Somewhere here that oldest ancestor, Reuben, my great-great-great-grandfather, beyond whose name neither my father or his cousins can trace their line, is buried. A man who came at the end of his years to the Promised Land to join his daughter Channah Malka. For a while I roam through overturned stones hoping for a miracle.

And only a month before, in Brooklyn, my father and I combed through an equally ravaged graveyard by a rusting subway spur, trying to find his mother's, Devorah's, grave. Lost, we had to go back to the marker office, then to a nearby florist, pay the fee for a search and restoral of the monument. A grandmother who died before I was born, in the hour her ship first touched America, in the arms of my grandfather who was waiting for her and his children. "Hello, dear Mother," my father said to the stone.

After an hour of climbing and clambering over defaced stones, searching the inscriptions, envious of the monuments zealously replaced by family who have recovered ancestors, I stop and recite the mourner's Kaddish over the whole hillside, calling out my pedigree in Hebrew first to my *zaide*, Reuben. "I am Maishe, the son of Zaav, the son of Israel, the son of Maishe, the son of Reuben."

Then I start down to the tomb of Absalom, that strange conical tower that looks like the cap of a Babylonian Golem, historically a Herodian tomb, but I prefer the fable and I stop to throw a stone at it. It should be my father, for this is the ancient custom of those who abhor a disobedient son, and who worse than me? "Daddy," I whisper as my stone clangs against the round wall, a proxy. "For the plastic siding I refused to help you tack up last year on your porch."

Down into the Valley of Kidron, my feet aching, hours I've walked, my tongue dry, when turning to look at a cluster of dilapidated houses, an Arab boy runs out, grabs my arm, and pulls me into a yard.

Some older Arabs rush out of a sunken cellar hole, drag me after them with excited cries. What is this all about? Have I violated a taboo? Where am I? Water is splashing below me. One grabs my belt buckle and starts to undo my pants. Another thrusts a candle in my hand. Between confusion and terror I tremble in my underwear. Is this a unit of the P.L.O.? Far off I hear the voices of other tourists. The Arab boy who took my arm in the first place shoves his open palm in my face.

Again, below me, I hear distant voices, muffled, as in twisted English.

Now in the dim cellar I see steps in front of me. The Arab boy's palm quivers under my nose, wanting a reward for bringing me here. I slip out of my pants, fingers are helping with socks, jabbing: five or six men in headcloths shouting at once to my questions in English, broken Hebrew, "What is it? *Mah zeh? Mah zeh?*" I cram my clothes into my leather bag, sandals squeezed under its strap. I can decipher one or two of the words they keep repeating . . . Arabic, Hebrew? It echoes with a familiarity I can't explain.

Shaking a few Israeli pounds out of my wrapped-up pants, I pay off the boy, the man with the candle, who gives me a firm shove down. I slip, trip, skid a few steps into a pool of dark, water splashing up to my knees, waist, grope first down a blind channel, then back away, trying to follow the faint voices farther down, stepping through another hole across the pool, as the waters creep up above my rib bones soaking my shirt, rising to my nipples, only able to see a few feet ahead in the low tunnel, going as slowly as possible in order not to gutter the candle flame, having to bend my head and shoulders to keep from knocking my brains against the top, sloshing ahead but wondering if I have missed the main shaft and am wandering down a side channel, realizing that the floor under me is uneven as the waters rise to my neck and fall to my waist; four, five, six, seven minutes, the voices in front of me fading away, and now it seems like hours I have been toiling forward, creeping more and more cautiously as the candle flickers dangerously, seeing the chisel marks on the walls in the yellow light, the cold of the water seeping into me, and I remember now I am in the heart of the heart of Jerusalem. Hezekiah! They were shouting at me, Hezekiah! I am in Hezekiah's shaft, as deep as one can descend into the ancient Jerusalem, the biblical Jerusalem, it is the stream Gihon, that ancient spring pulsating like a heart, welling between my legs. These are the waters that drew the Jebusites to the site, that shaft the Arabs drew me into was the opening through which David slipped and climbed up into the Jebusite citadel: the blind channel, Solomon's work, and now, step by step, I feel my way, drawing my fingers along the chiselings of Hezekiah's artisans, as they drew the source of Jerusalem, its living waters, the bubbling soul of this place among the barren Judaean hills, deep into the rock away from the Assyrians. A wind blows out my candle.

And in blackness, the water colder now, rising and falling against my body, I inch forward, sightless, praying that there are no more blind channels because I cannot say for sure that I am going forward and not backward, no voices ahead or behind, it's the end of the day, my back cramped and painful. I go on and on, wondering if the Gihon, Hebrew for "gushing forth," will rise suddenly and flood the foot of air in which I breathe; now I remember the description of its miraculous welling, a surging up of waters, then a falling off. In the pit I pray, reciting the "Hear O Israel," step by step, wondering how long this tunnel can go on and whether I have not some-how turned myself around and around in it, the prospect of even a cavity in such blindness enough to confuse me out of any confidence in my direction, and I curse the Arabs and their candles, feeling little wax stumps floating by. It was late in the afternoon when I started down. No one has come after me, and the people before have already left. It is a tunnel of horror, like the ones that floated through papier maché mock-ups in the amusement parks of my childhood. Who could have thought on the hot sunny hillside a while ago that I would be shivering in water up to my chest?

I hear voices again. They do not fade away but seem to get louder; then a pinpoint of light, gray, pearly light. I hurry forward and, picking my way over the final few feet, find myself in the entrance to an open pool among shouting Arab children and an older man who tries to hush their shrieks of laughter out of consideration for the young man emerging rather pale from the tunnel, all of them ducking naked in the waters. It is the pool of Siloam, the place where Mary came to wash her clothes.

Later, Yoram Kaniuk tells me that before the forty-eight war, this shaft was the test of a young Israeli boy's courage. He had nightmares about the passage as a child. It is at the spring of Gihon that Solomon was anointed.

David's city, lying outside the walls of the Crusader Jerusalem, around the pool of Siloam, a ruin of crumbling Arab houses, is still, ironically, intact; an archeologist's, a storyteller's dream, no modern houses yet, no hotels, churches, mosques, synagogues; only shards to construct an unobstructed city of the past.

Damp, gleaming with my passage through the waters, I put on my pants, sandals. Going up the path I must look eerie, for some girls also climbing toward the familiar Crusader walls regard me fearfully, skipping together for protection. They look like gypsies, but from their dark stockings I realize that they are Jewish, not Arab, though olive and wild as the fierce daughters of Kurdistan. I call to them in Hebrew and they look at me amazed. "Are you Jewish?" the boldest asks, then breaks into giggles and hides in the midst of the Orthodox coven.

"Yes," I answer.

"Aren't you afraid?"

"Of what?"

"Arabs," they shriek, break away, running, and reassemble up the road like nervous zebras.

Hebron

————————

VVVVVV

AFRAID OF ARABS? Even alone in desolate East Jerusalem, as I came up from the pool of Siloam on a hillside of straggling huts, I remembered my trip through Morocco, meeting Arabs, Berbers, on the buses, making no secret of being a Jew deep in the deserts where I could have been bundled off in a burlap bag and never heard of again. I sought out Arabs as my blood brothers. I gripped their arms, and I felt the common pulse between us.

So I left Jerusalem to jump off into the old Palestinian West Bank for Hebron, taking an Arab bus (half the price of the Israeli) to Hebron, jogging up and down in the half-sprung carriage with women tattooed and swathed in white linen, dangerous-looking farmers and sheepherders of the villages who squinted at me and the four other tourists sticking out like extraterrestrial visitors; jubilant at traveling through Judea, the homeland of the remnant which had become the Jews. Rocky bone outcropped through a threadbare green coverlet. Stony hillsides and fields of gravel robbed the acreage of farmland, giving a nomadic cast to the inhabitants. I believe, like

Yakov Lind, that these shepherds, gardeners, were probably the descendants of the poor Jews who did not go into exile.

Hebron is a door into the Bible, tribal Israel. Here you can see the lineaments of the town where David set up the first capital of the Judaean kingdom, houses baked in sunlight, clustering door to door, window to window, almost a single structure, castle, drawing whatever vegetables, wheat, goat and sheep flesh, cattle, hides, wool, the district scratched out of its fields and hillsides into its half-hidden, jerry-built fortress. Not the high crowning glory of Jerusalem, no, that is a city, a place in the clouds where, whipped by cool breezes in the burning afternoons, one would dream of heavenly kingdoms. Hebron is a town, low, humble, a nomad's oasis, a market bazaar where Abraham and God could bargain over souls, haggling how many to save Sodom and Gomorrah, make a price, *nu*, make a price, a hundred? Fifty? Twenty? Ten?

The buyer slinks away, ashamed that he can't find the last, absurdly low quote in his pocket.

Blood is on the lintels of Hebron. Its townsmen slaughtered the community of Orthodox Jews in the twenties, and so one walks through the long, twisting market street buried in a maze of alleys and backyards, a mud and wood city too cramped for cars and motor traffic above its main highway like Fez and the old quarters of other Arab cities—a mud, brick, and wood accordion, squeezed into an antique music that dies away at the first auto horn tremor; fear faintly in one's ear. A few days after my visit, an Israeli soldier standing guard at the tomb of Machpelah—where the patriarchs and their wives, Abraham and Sarah, Isaac and Rebecca, Jacob and Leah, lie— was stabbed in the back and robbed of his machine gun. But I'm too happy to be afraid—found, at last, the past.

The tomb of the Patriarchs was not open at the hour I arrived. The restaurant which an enterprising kibbutz nearby had set up in the heart of the Arab town was full of tourists whose tours had paid in advance for all available meals. I escaped the bustle, familiar whining of American teenagers,

and fled up the darkest, most dangerous-looking alley of
Hebron I could find.

In shorts, sandals, hugging my leather shoulder bag—work-
men look up in surprise at me poking my way through backyards where blacksmiths blew on the fire of open forges and
wool flew in bits from stalls; threading into collapsing streets
of buildings that supported each other's demise, staving off a
common fall, until I thrust my head into the snaking market
street, paced its length in the crowd of townsmen, the sprinkling of tourists. An Arab called to me as I walked by. "Sit
down, you look tired."

A young man with a moustache looks so directly into my
face that despite my nervousness it would be impolite to refuse. I nod, and crouch on the box he proffers for my bum.
"Where are you from?"

"America."

"Ah, I have friends in America, postcards."

"You speak good English."

"I learned in Jerusalem."

"What do you do here?"

He points across the street. "A barber." Wedged in between
two other shops was a small green room with a barber's chair
and a few utensils of the trade. "Would you like some tea?"
He waves to a young boy sitting next to us.

"Wait." I reach into my leather satchel and pull out some
spearmint leaves I had bought in the market at Jerusalem.
"Good for the tea." The boy takes them from my hand, starts
off to the local café.

Another youngster approaches, speaks to the barber, and he
rises, beckoning me to follow. We enter his shop across the
street. His customer settles into the chair, I am motioned to a
seat against the wall while the deft fingers of the barber ply
razor and scissors about the child's head. I watch as a white
patch of skin where the hair is cut away spreads under the
razor's edge. This dark boy is actually lighter than I.

"How did you learn to be a barber?"

He points to a photograph of a handsome, white-mustachioed face. "My father was a barber."

"And now you?"

He shakes his head sadly. His father was sick. He had to come home, interrupt his studies. Before the war, he worked in a business in East Jerusalem. Now the business is ruined. He wants to learn English better. He brings out the postcards of friends in England, the United States. One, he says, has promised to get him into a college in England. He wants to study business. Rummaging in his drawers, he brings out the letter, asks me to read it. Painful, his earnestness, hunger to get out of this backwater into another world. The letter is friendly but frankly equivocal, suggesting a place to write to, but hardly setting anything up or offering the barber any real help, finances, a place to stay, job, scholarship.

"Where do you stay tonight?"

"I'm going back to Jerusalem."

"You can stay with me."

We look into each other's black eyes. To let myself fall into Hebron, its alleys, through the door of the barber, lose my way in the byways of this Arab hospitality and learn secrets of the land from its ancient inhabitants, I imagine the faded green walls of the bedroom, sisters, meals, feel days slipping away in the shade of close rooms, the danger of my Jewish blood throbbing, tickling now in my throat. I want to say yes. Yet too hopeless in this barren shop, life, a business career, stopping the foreign strangers that pass by his door to find a lifeline out; the fake jolliness of his correspondents by card. The barber's warmth is naked, his curiosity simple, I want to respond, disappear into this other Hebron. Sisters, his sisters, the handsome wild women I have seen in Morocco, the West Bank, keep me in a crumbling whitewashed room lit by fierce brown sunlight of a Judaean town of clay. Draw me into their arms. I know them. I cannot refuse their invitation, leave, and

I draw myself to the keyhole of the door, but at the last moment, cannot turn in under the lintel. I hold on to his sisters for a last kiss, the fantasy fermenting in my nose, half blinding me, sleepily inclining my head to the side, trying to thank him even as I reluctantly turn away.

"I would love to . . . but I have an appointment tonight."

I hold his tattered postcards in my hands. "Thanks for a great time! Thinking of you!" A splashing waterfall in upper New York State on the obverse side.

The tea arrives. I take a cup from the brass tray wondering whether to sip while his fingers are still employed on the boy's hair. He motions me to begin. "I would like to study English," he repeats.

"You speak good English."

"No." He shakes his head. And it's true, his English is painful and awkward. The card from the friend who promises help is addressed from Oxford. This barber with his slow pathos is not destined for such elegant promotion. Embarrassed, I let my eyes wander about the room as he talks of his brother in Kuwait, hopes of a business school. I am attracted to the dignity of the white moustache.

"Is your father alive?"

"No, he died a few years ago. Now I support the family." Something about the pain in his eyes makes me wince. "And you, are your parents alive?"

"My father, yes. I lost my mother three years ago."

"Was she a Christian?"

"No, Jewish." The answer is out of my mouth without thinking. I feel the barber, his customer, a neighbor in the shop shift slightly in their seats. They don't ask me about my father, perhaps to leave the question politely half open. Knowing perhaps that a Jewish mother is the definition of Orthodoxy. I swallow my tea with a tightness in my throat, feeling the strange tension in the room. The barber bends to his task about the hair of the boy. The conversation goes on but in short, lackluster sentences. Finishing my tea, I wait for the barber to drink his, a slow sipping every few minutes when he puts down his scissors. At last he has done.

I rise, pull out my notebook. Earlier he asked me to send him a postcard and now, determined to maintain our pledge, I thrust it out. Ask for his address. Yes, yes, he answers, and with agonizing lassitude he putters about, finds a postcard with his address, watches me copy it out, takes the slip of paper with my name and street. Listens sleepily as I talk about the possibility that City College might have a program. I remember before he spoke of how someone from a kibbutz had offered to teach him Hebrew in return for Arabic. So it is not simply animosity toward Jews but perhaps the misunderstanding that is making him drowsy with defeat. I wave good-by heartily, thanking him for the tea, a big American clown, I hope.

I go back to Machpalah. The mosque is open to visitors now that the Moslem prayers are over, and a flood of American Jewish groups are being herded through. I listen to the guide's spiel, identifying the resting places of Isaac and Rebecca, Abraham and Sarah, Jacob and Leah. In a passageway of the mosque, the Orthodox have set up a synagogue, since technically it is not a Moslem prayer hall; waves of bubble-gum-chewing kids pack the tombs. One fat girl, her gums working away furiously, stares through the grate of Abraham's bier. "What's this?" she asks her pals, who shrug T-shirted shoulders with indifference. It's just a summer-camp trip. I think of twisting her plump neck around the grate. Shouting, joking, not listening to their guides, these children of Long Island, New Jersey, Connecticut synagogues are making me angry. And the parents who brought them up obnoxious, unholy, shipped them off for a cheap summer with religion thrown in. Miserable! Miserable!

The clamor is even uglier than the rigamarole at Rachel's tomb, a sanitized garage where you parade fast past a dull slab. This is some joke as if the Holy of Holies which the high priest entered once a year was now thrown open to general admission, just enough room in it for a revolving door. "Hurry, hurry, folks, get your five cents worth of the Unknowable."

Thank God and the Arabs that the actual cave underneath the mosque is sealed from Jewish eyes. These biers are only mock-ups. I hear one of the guides from the local kibbutz tell his group that the sherif of the mosque goes down into the cave once a year but is forbidden to tell anyone what he has seen there. A famous Jewish traveler, hundreds of years ago, snuck past the guards and has testified to the existence of real tombs. So with grim satisfaction I feel the secret of Machpalah safe under my feet, under the slabs of that pious Idumean Herod. Would that all the mysteries of the Eretz were buried deep in the earth away from the fingers of this generation.

I try to get a kosher meal in the restaurant which is now deserted, but most of the food is gone. Before my walk, I went in and when no one would show me to a seat or take my order, I started shouting. The waitresses ignored me and I got so angry that I raised my voice and thundered curses on Israel. A manager rushed over and politely apologized. All the seats were taken, could I come back later? Only a tribe of locusts has gone before me.

Who do I belong to? Are the gum children my brethren? As I walk back to get a bus, an Arab taxi stops, and since the fare is only a few cents more I get in, seeing a woman nursing a baby on her breast in the back seat as I step into the front. I remember the taxi I took deep in the deserts of southeastern Morocco, in terrible dry heat, a red-haired, freckle-faced Berber woman swaddling a tiny child in heavy woolen clothes at her nipple. Only an eye poked out of her garments as she drew into her clothes away from my inadvertent stare. The infant whimpered once and no more, for a shudder of displeasure went through the woman so stern and absolute that the baby hushed at once. The Arab child in back makes no noise either, even when it is drawn away from the breast and the nipple of its mother bound up again.

My stomach is empty. In my ears is the clamor of American

tour groups, disobedient modern babies grown up into teen-agers with mouths full of sticky pink. I shudder with the matriarchs at Machpalah. Today's lesson seems to be com-pounded of Arab sadness, Israeli waiters, and my own bore-dom in Hebrew school. Abraham, my head is full of bubbles!

The Female Jerusalem

VVVVVV

WHERE DID THE SHEKINAH, that Female Presence of God, dwell in the land? The tourists had chased Her out of Machpalah. Jumping from the taxi that brought me from the caves of the Patriarchs, I set out from the Arab bus station in East Jerusalem to savor some sacred dust. I would find the Cave of Simon, a spot ambiguously marked on the maps which took me two hours to reconnoiter. Yet the smell of it, the look, was just right. Off a spur road, buried between two highways in the valley to the north of East and West Jerusalem, an orange dirt path leads between two tiny ridges to caves concealed in a no-man's-land. No sign points the way. Only the feel of the landscape sends you one way instead of the other. Which Simon does the cave belong to? Is it Simeon ben Yohai, that talmudic sage who hid from the Romans for years in a rock crib (famous as a paragon of piety, a rabbi who warned Jews about looking at trees, nature a distraction from the task of keeping your eyes on inner piety)? Simeon's real fame, however, came as the author of a book written over a thousand years after his death (according to Gershom Scholem in

Jewish Mysticism)—the Zohar. So one is not only visiting Simeon's cave but an imaginary cave as well, the one in which Moses de Leon,* a mystic of Granada, created the fantastic kabbalistic gardens of Jewish literature.

I suspect that I have confused my Simons and that this is the shrine of some earlier scholar, but the caves do not disappoint me. Damp, neglected, they smell of the crypt. Not as deep as Indian Joe's fabulous hiding place, still they are redolent of secret troglodyte life. In Simon's cave, where I admire his hollowed-out sleeping chamber and imagine him leaning down to his son's chiseled-out crib to check a point in the law, an old woman is praying and weeping. The earth is wet and moist, candles gutter in white wax on the table, and I too can believe that we have poked a hole into God's head and can talk to him more easily down here. I start to mumble the mourner's kaddish under the gray-haired grandmother's wail.

A black-suited Chassid appears out of nowhere in a soiled silk frock coat and knee breeches, creamy socks yellowed by ages of soap. He jingles a circle of rusty keys and admits me to the little sanhedrin next door to Simon's cave where I can see the Palestinian sages perched on the ledges, warming themselves around a fire pit. They are debating clean and unclean, laughing deep in their stone chamber, ruling Israel under the Roman noses.

I took my steps from the grotto of the real and pseudo Simon to the house of the master in these studies, to touch his hem. For as I descended to the old Jerusalem in the depths of its rock and spring, now I ascended to the new Jerusalem, its messianic hopes, on a quiet side street hidden among comfortable houses, the chambers of the greatest scholar of Jewish mysticism, Gershom Scholem. "Have you met Scholem?" I asked the writers in Tel Aviv. No, was the inevitable answer. Of course they had heard of him, read him, but he was ob-

* See footnote, p. 99.

viously living in another world—to me, the real world, but to them, an imaginary one. Scholem's scholarship returned half of the Jewish soul to us who were outside the tradition in the twentieth century. He put flesh on the bones of Jewish myth. The clay man, the Golem, was not a ghetto joke, a fable for children, but the consummate vision of mystical dream exercises. In making us realize the intellectual daring of the medieval German Jewish rabbis, the original Chassids (not to be confused with the movement called Chassidism which started in seventeenth-century Europe), whose speculation was so intense that in rituals of dance and prayer they actually called up the figure of a man, and left handbooks on how to do it: Scholem, as in so many other areas of Jewish mysticism, revolutionized our understanding of the Jewish past and its relevance to the life we were leading, work we were doing. Scholem's Judaism was not a religion of nostalgia but of a direct and dangerous stare into the unknown. So of course I wanted to spy out the scholar himself and see if I could smell the smoke of magic in the wizard's skirts.

Max Frisch, the Swiss writer, had provided an introduction, and I called the Scholem home, talked to the scholar's wife, pushing names—Max, his wife Marianne—ahead of me like calling cards. A few hours later I spoke to Gershom Scholem on the phone. He seemed interested in the claim that I was "an American novelist." But he was leaving Israel in a few days. His house was at sixes and sevens. Could I come on Saturday afternoon? I had made an appointment in Tel Aviv for Saturday with my cousins. Could I come tomorrow? I asked.

Well—he paused—actually, another Mirsky was coming over, a Roy Mirsky who was a librarian at the university. The concurrence was too ironic to let pass. It would be the first time he had two Mirskys under his roof.

So I arrived about five o'clock on a Thursday afternoon, and was shocked at the man who greeted me at the door. The other great scholar of the Jewish world I had met personally,

Harry Wolfson, was tiny, all the knowledge of philosophy contracted into a tiny body, a Litvak nut. Scholem, the mystic, was enormous. Even stooped with age he seemed to scrape the ceiling. He hovered over me as if his arms were wings about to flap him into the air. He fairly jumped and leaped about the room with enthusiasm.

Manuscripts of which I have seen only fragments, he has stuffed in between the books of his library: books surround you on all sides, not only the four walls, but cases of them run it seems along the ceiling, their images reflect off the floor. If one is not in Borges's circular library of endless concentric stacks yet the rooms of Scholem's house are at least the base of a ziggurat, the Babylonian star-gazing tower, its bricks, volumes. We spoke in the one corner where I had some smattering of information, the quality of his English translations. Scholem has the gift of tongues though he denied it, disparaging his English, despite its apparent elegance. One book he has written in German, another in English, a third in Hebrew. He has the whole of that archdemon Jacob Frank's autobiography. His wife is translating it for him. "Written in bad Polish, a Jewish coachman's Polish, a Yiddish Polish written down by Chassids who thought in Yiddish so that all the rhythms belong to their mother tongue." I begin to question him about Frank, and he refers me to his articles in Hebrew. I am flooded with the old humility of my monogamy with English. Just as well that I don't speak any Hebrew though, because he goes on to complain about all the American rabbis who speak "taxi-driver Hebrew."

We talk about the interest in his books, in Jewish mysticism. In some countries there are no readers, in others many, according to the national character, the difference between the French and German imaginations, the American. Scholem remarks that he came from a family which had assimilated completely into German culture. For him, the study of Hebrew, Judaism, was a revolt, a rebellion against his parents.

I leave after three hours, my head spinning with titles of

books, articles he has referred to. Yet like Wolfson, Scholem
has the gift of simplicity. He renders the most complex ideas
and their history into a few sentences of poetry. It is ironic
that Scholem's greatest influence on literature in this century
should have been on a non-Jew, Jorge Luis Borges, the captain
of modern Latin-American fiction. "A mystical novel,"
Scholem calls the Zohar. In the wake of the scholar's work,
the rise of the novel for the Jew must begin in the thirteenth
century with Moses de Leon's pseudonymous text.

These scholars, Wolfson, Soloveitchik, Scholem, fill me with
such joy that I almost cannot bear it and have to go running
from the room shouting, Enough, enough! I sense how my
ancestors imagined the whole world created out of words and
searched in the alphabet, its combinations, for the power to
command creation. If abstraction is man's genius, the ability
to make abstraction holds a palpable emotion—that feat holds
such an attraction for us as human beings as to almost promise
immortality. The circular world that is the nightmare of Borges,
one of the demiurges of the astrophysicist, these scholars trace
the rainbow of its circumference, laws, codes, colors, in their
studies.

I leave Scholem's house dancing. There is no basketball
court in front of it like at the Wailing Wall. No tour buses
rumble past with drivers announcing that inside one of the
mystical brains of Israel is toiling.

I see all Jerusalem through the veil of the Holy of Holies.
I can't stop dreaming. Agonizing over it when it—She, to fall
into the female apostrophe of the prophets—falls away from
my dreams. "Going to Jerusalem?" Chanoch, Yoram, my
cousins, the hotelkeeper in Tel Aviv ask, and sigh. "It's beautiful." Everyone in Israel wants to live there, it seems. Yet its
beauty is that it is hidden high up in bare Judaean hills. One
feels this even more coming toward it from the east, the bus
rumbling up from the Dead Sea, sweeping past Jericho: almost
a Tibetan city, gleaming golden, crowning the mountains.

Should anyone live there? A few Arabs, perhaps, as grounds-keepers? Who would promise to live the life of their great-great-grandfathers? Jerusalem as the pinnacle of the Jews' dream of the Holy Land exists only in our heads. A city awaiting Messiah.

All the mysticism of Zion, that tiny hill on the corner of David's city that has become a synonym for the whole of Judaism, begins for me in the love of women. If Jerusalem is female, let us speak of the real women of the city. Bathsheba, the chambermaid at my hotel . . . I delayed my departure each day only to catch sight of her on the stairs. Nineteen, with eyes of such black witchery as to engage me as hopelessly as Jacob. I spoke with her through another chambermaid, Mary, an Arab girl whose French was about equal to mine. I tried to carry off Bathsheba through the tongue of this emissary but despite the flashing of our eyes, she was still the daughter of a strict Moroccan Jewish home and had to return promptly to her father's gates at five in the afternoon. In Tel Aviv, a Yemenite girl took care of my chamber. Her uncanny sweet-ness evoked lost worlds, gestures from centuries past—I felt like bowing to the floor. The carriage of these young women from the Oriental Jewish world transported me into the thoughts of the Patriarchs, Isaac, Jacob, and I wished for their elaborate courtesies.

In a land of orange cheeks and sensual movement, a land of honey and oil, of dark people, dusky, warm with the purple of grapes, the white, blanched faces of the Chassidim float like upturned fish bellies in the street, an omen of death. In New York City the black costumes and beards appeared quaint. In Jerusalem their complexions are a perversion. Why re-create a Hungarian or Polish ghetto with its pale, unearthly flesh in the Holy Land? What have they done to their women? The women of the Chassidim, girls of seventeen, eighteen, walk about like old ladies, stooped, warts breaking out, anger draw-ing their faces tight. Mea Shearim is a slave quarter, hobbled females clomping about. And the men, vain in their adolescence, silly, strutting about like roosters, their scholarship mere plumage.

One begins to understand why the Israelis are so contemptuous of Orthodoxy. While I was in Israel, a woman who had converted, married an Israeli, then served with her husband as a spy in Egypt, was caught with him, tortured, finally released only to die a few years later of the injuries she had endured in prison—was refused burial by the rabbis on the basis of a faulty conversion. Fortunately, a kibbutz was found that the couple had been associated with which would open its graveyard to her. The incident stuck in my throat. We are here because the land is holy. Is this holiness? Is this the compassion of the best moments in talmudic jurisprudence which bound us in common sweetness through years of trial?

Oh, my confused country, an ignorant Orthodoxy, a labor movement that is compromising its morality for the sake of political power, a country that only exists because of an unshakable dream where materialism is defended with a fury that is reserved for idealism in other lands. "I want a nice house, furniture, children!" my cousin insists. Her parents were Communists who had to be driven from their dream in Poland after having suffered in exile through their youth and early married life for Marxist ideals. Now their daughter is caught between the respect she feels for her parents' nobility and her own determination not to be betrayed by ideas. It's not only "Never again" in terms of gas chambers, Hitler, but too often "Never again" for compassion, charity, dreaminess, art, mystical, messianic hope. Yet the rhythms of these traditional Jewish values remain, the energy of them. So the cheapest materialism is being insisted on with an almost violent irrational insistence. A pretty girl at a travel agency in Tel Aviv, arranging a ticket for me, tells me she once studied piano and singing at Music and Art High School in New York City. And now?

She shakes her head. No more. "Now I want a house, a car. I haven't got time for music." There is something alive, alert in her features. Like my cousin, who confesses to me that she still dreams of going to live on a kibbutz, she hasn't surrendered sleepily to the drift of married life, its comfortable objects. Aggressive in her defense of turning away from music and books, as she watches the sadness creep over my face, she remarks, "I can't afford it."

Mysticism, architecture, women—Jerusalem is not just a city but a metaphor.

We captured the Old City just in time to prevent its despoliation at the hands of the Jordanians who were about to carry out a 1964 plan to cover all the hills and valleys with housing apart from a mean strip around the walls. Then, like a 20th century anti hero, once we had saved the maiden from the dragon we proceeded to rape her ourselves.

A crash program of building, embodying every idiocy of contemporary architecture and mindless copying of the sort of bankrupt town planning which has already been discredited in Europe and America was embarked on—mostly in secrecy—to create political facts, to enrich contractors whose vulgarity was already a byword and to create a prosperous "modern" city at the expense of every human value which does not figure in a balance sheet. . . .

It's come to the point where I even welcomed a patently Anti-Semitic article entitled "The Rape of Jerusalem" in a recent issue of "The Sunday Times."*

* Alex Berlyne, *The Jerusalem Post*, July 10, 1973.

Bedouins

WWW

Two DREAMS I wanted of Israel—to speak to Gershom Scholem and to meet the Bedouins.

I enter the desert, Moses, son of Zaav, son of wandering Aramaeans. Who knows, they might have gotten so far with the greening of the Negev that there would be nothing left but a few strips of sand under the waterpipes. I might have had to imagine Abraham in the midst of the concrete housing projects of Beersheba and Moses in the shopping plazas of Eilat.

The road to the desert begins in Tel Aviv. Because of a few articles in the Boston *Globe*, a little finagling by an Israeli writer, Chanoch Bartov, and the motherly charity of a Mrs. Fishman in the Government Tourist & Press Office, Mirsky, to whom a free trip is manna, found himself classified as a journalist and given a free car and guide to go wherever he wanted, and his heart yearned in only one direction—south into the sands.

In the press office they promised me two days. I wanted to speak to Bedouins? They had no guides who spoke Arabic. However, in the Negev, the Bedouins were fluent in Hebrew.

Unfortunately it was the summer, schools were closed. So, they couldn't show me all the progress being made under Israel. . . . Please, I interjected, I don't want to see schools, clinics, progress, improvements. I want to meet the least improved of the Bedouins, the wilder, the better.

They stared at me. Who is this? What's going on? You don't want to see improvements?

I'd like to meet some unimproved Bedouins.

They shook their heads. Who were they giving a car to? A meshuggeh? A phone call interrupted the ominous silence, and, profusely thanking everyone, I hurried out before they could change their minds.

The driver arrived at my hotel twenty minutes late, making apologies, also asking if I could, please, since his car was being washed around the corner, carry my bag a few streets to his automobile. Okay, I thought, Israeli self-reliance, why not? The agreement at the press office had been that I would spend a night in Beersheba so that the next day we could penetrate into Sinai, as I wanted to see the Bedouins there. The farther south, the less improved, I assumed. Where were the wild Bedouins? That was what I had been asking everyone for the last few days, and as if they were an elusive herd of unicorns, each person had a different answer.

The driver, who was also a guide, seemed about my age, maybe a few years younger, puffing manfully on a pipe, already parading a middle-aged paunch. As we drove off, he started in on American tourists, what a bunch of softies, always wanting to quit at one or two in the afternoon and go to the swimming pool while Israelis on a tour kept pushing the guides past five or six, wanting to go until nine or ten at night, ready to get out of the car and hike, etc.

Well, I thought, we'll see what we'll see, putting aside the pang of suspicion I experienced as I *shlepped* my heavy bag around the corner in Tel Aviv for the convenience of the driver. We stopped after the first hour and he insisted on treating me to coffee. Okay, a regular fellow. Another hour's drive and we pulled into a collection of tin huts. Here, he said, lived the fabulous Sheik Suleiman. This Suleiman was a legend in Israel, hundreds of wives; women came from Europe, the United States, to live with him. He was somewhere in his late eighties, early nineties now, yet just a year ago he picked up some young girl of sixteen, seventeen, hitchhiking and brought her home to be his wife. There were jokes about his having to be careful about bumping into great-grand-daughters in bed. The guide was nervous about the next day in Sinai because he didn't speak Arabic, but he had been to this encampment before.

About six Bedouins were clustered around a fire of burning faggots. Sheik Suleiman was away. Would we like coffee? They put a brass and tin kettle in the flames and, stirring up the coals, poured out a thick, sweet coffee in tiny cups a few minutes later. Several young men lounged against the benches with older men. These boys were the sheik's sons. The elders were dressed in robes, the youths in western clothes, black shirts and pants.

"You don't live in tents?" I asked.

"No, mostly houses," came the reply.

"You like the houses better?"

"Sure." Then they began to complain about the Israelis who had dynamited some of their houses because they were built without a permit. There was a kibbutz across the road from them, and the Israelis wanted to push the Bedouins far away from the road back into a planned settlement. Suleiman, however, was stubbornly clinging to his tin huts by the highway.

"You like the new houses that are being built for you?"

"The new ones are good," they said, in a half-hearted manner. "But"—now their voices rose—"we've been here by the road from the beginning. Ten thousand dollars that house they blew up cost the man who built it." (And, by me, the houses they build themselves are a lot more attractive than the modern garages the Israelis throw up.) What a contrast, however, the bare ground of the Bedouins, like the backyard of a New York City slum lot, trampled into dust by countless dogs, children, goats, sheep, while across the highway, a green paradise, the waving grass and grain of the kibbutz sits on the horizon, a mirage.

"What do you want to see?" one of the boys asks.

"I'd like to see a tent."

Buzzing among the three boys. There was one "Cushi," a black Bedouin, living in a tent. Did I want to visit him? Sure. So we all hopped into the guide's car. (All the legendary love of horses and camels has been transferred to cars. The Bedouin adolescents stroked its fenders like a thoroughbred's flanks.)

We arrived at the tent of the black Bedouin, but this morning he was working at the medical clinic. (Later I found out that there were other tents too. A huge one had been put up for a wedding party that was still going on from the night before when I left the encampment, late in the afternoon.) Two old men were seated in the Cushi's tent, and we squatted down on rugs with them while one of the boys ran to get a pot of coffee for us.

"What do you want to ask them?" the guide queries, puffing with self-importance on his pipe.

"Do they know any stories?"

"What's the history of the tribe?" he asked the eldest of the two ancients.

The reply, which comes back in Arabic, translated into Hebrew by the boys, then relayed in English for me, is that the tribe came out of Egypt with the Jews under Moses but had taken the wrong *wadi* (dry valley) in the Sinai and wound up here.

We all smile. "Anything else?" asks the guide, preparing to get up.

I'm looking for a thread of the flying Arabian carpet. I want a hair of the surreal beard of the Patriarchs. I've given up a normal life to tell tales, and I take a stab in the dark, hoping that they are hiding an old lamp, concealed from the casual tourist, whose demon I can collect. "Do they know any ghost stories?"

"Ghost stories?" The guide shakes his head, looking at me, disparaging.

"Ask them if they know any." He grudgingly repeats my request in Hebrew.

"They are pious Mohammedans," says the guide, as the boys wag in the negative. "They don't believe in ghosts."

The boys shake their heads at me. "Ghosts, *no* ghosts," they chirp.

"Ask that old man," I insist, "if he knows any ghost tales."

"Yes," says the old man, his face withered, arranging the folds of his white robes. "I have heard of a ghost." The other ancient, who had gone to sleep, opens his eyes. "There was a ghost in the Garden of Eden. God threw him out and put Adam in instead. The ghost was very angry and asked God, 'Why do you put him in the Garden and throw me out?'

" 'Because Adam is good and you're bad.'

" 'If I can make Adam do something bad, will you throw him out?'

" 'Yes.'

"That's how Adam came to do bad in the Garden of Eden. The ghost tempted him."

"Ah, that's a good story." I sigh, everyone nodding. "Have you heard of any ghosts around here?"

"Yes," says the old man. Himself, he hasn't seen any, he wants me to understand, but ghosts had been annoying some girls a few months ago by one of the *wadis*.

"That was my sister," one of the boys exclaims. "The ghost threw stones and dirt at her and six other girls who were riding on donkeys by the *wadi*."

The guide and I exchange looks. The other boy smirks but confirms the story. He is the older, in fact, the village school-teacher now, at nineteen. The younger one is insistent despite the ironic grin of his brother, details on how the djinn has disrupted the village pouring out of him. "You want to hear about it?" he asks, jumping up. "Come on. We'll talk to my sister."

So, thanking the elders, we pile back into the car and head for the house of the sister, a young married woman, to hear about the djinn.

At the door of a tin corral fencing the yard of a small compound, a plump girl with a pretty face greets us. No sooner are we seated than she is away for the traditional pot of coffee. I am hopping with caffeine. On the walls are stuck a collection of photographs, family portraits: one of her brothers in the Israeli Army, a tiny official picture of Nasser (juxtapositions that introduce one to the complexities of the Mideast). Cups in hand, we settle back on chairs and she begins to speak in Arabic, more and more excited, her brother rapidly translating into Hebrew for my guide, who renders half of it to English.

"Yes, I was riding with six other girls," the words bubbling up in a breathy, singing Arabic. "From the *wadi* came stones. Huge stones, clumps of dirt, hitting us. We thought it was the wind. Then, drinking our coffee, the men discovered lumps of dirt and camel shit in it. The next morning when we woke up there was dust on everyone's face.

"I went to my father-in-law's house. The djinn threw stones on the tin roof. All night we heard them. Other houses too. Again there was dung in the coffee.

"Now other houses in the village suffered too. Everywhere the djinn was throwing stones at people, filling houses with dust.

"Now up on the roof in broad daylight, we heard the djinn throwing stones, dirt, but there was no wind. Some of the doubters called out to the djinn, 'If you're really a ghost, show us! Throw us some sweets!'

"Down from the roof came all kinds of sweets, sugar, candies, dates.

" 'Give us a salad!' the people cried.

"A whole bunch of tomatoes, carrots, squash, came tumbling down.

"But you know—when we rushed forward to get them—the sweets, the vegetables, were too hot to touch. They burned your fingers.

"Everyone was mad. One night in my house the djinn came during a party and threw dung and stones, put them in the food and coffee. My husband got angry. He shook his fist and cried. 'Come out and fight, djinn, if you're so strong. I'll beat you!'

"After that, the djinn disappeared for a few weeks.

"It came back though and kept bothering everyone."

"How did you get rid of it?" I ask in a lull, the first one in about an hour of nonstop exclamations about this local devil's mischief. An old man, a wizard skilled in getting rid of djinns, was invited to the village. The sister gives a long description of the magical charms and ceremonies of the magician. At last, she relates, the ghost was clapped into a jug and stoppered up.

"You know," adds the younger brother, "that man died just a few months later."

We all, skeptics and believers alike, considered this in silence.

Storytelling over, the young woman insists that we stay for lunch. We abandon our chairs as they bring in cushions, rugs, bolsters and eat with our fingers a selection of stewed vegetables, fishes, and fricassees. The young teacher begins to speak a little English with me. He talks about coming to New York City in the fall. I ask him to visit me. I'll invite rabbis for supper to help the conversation. This Arab is more fluent in Hebrew than some of my friends among the New York rabbinate, or rather not an Arab but a real Hebrew, a wandering Aramaean. After the meal, we ride around the Bedouin encampment. The boys want to show me the wedding tent, but since there is still some activity there, it's considered impolite to show up and gawk. The teacher asks if we are coming back.

There is a wedding later on in the month to which we are invited. Where are we going tomorrow?

"Sinai," the guide replied. "Would you like to come along?"

"Sure."

What unexpected luck, an additional guide, a sheik's son who spoke Arabic. We drove away whistling and went into Beersheba nearby to arrange for a hotel room. I had tried to pay the Bedouin boys as the Israeli guide had instructed me, at the end of the day, but they were adamant, no. No. "We are friends. No." My curiosity about hallucinations had mingled the blood of our dreams together.

I had arranged to leave early and the guide picked me up at seven in the morning. Stopping at the Bedouin village to pick up our friend, we headed down into Sinai through the Gaza Strip. For the first time I was nervous. The streets felt hostile, angry. Most of the older men were away during the day, working in Israeli agricultural or industrial projects. It is among the children that the rock-throwing and vituperation erupts.

The average Israeli town is filthy. Jerusalem, Tel Aviv, Haifa, their streets resemble the backyard of the old Beth El Hebrew School in Dorchester, a wasteland in the literal sense. Paper, fruit peels, boxes; the motorist thinks nothing of tossing these from his windows, and as for the pedestrian, ice-cream cups, paper bags, whatever is disposable he drops as he walks.

Gaza is a dung heap. In Gaza you sense the misery of the refugees, a shack and box town, Tijuana nightmare. We hurried through with closed windows despite the heat. Out along the road you can see the villas of the wealthy landowners of the Strip. It seems like some bad movie of Mexico before the Revolution. How could the Egyptians talk about socialism?

A few miles farther and we see the camels and robes of Bedouins. Our friend thinks he knows the tribe, so we stop the car and get out. The people are shy, but the teacher's Arabic reassures them. They draw near. I'm offered a ride on a camel but demur. "What's their story?"

They are related to the teacher's tribe but were foolish enough to believe the horror tales circulated by the Mufti before the forty-eight war and fled with all their goods into Gaza. Now the Israelis won't let them go back. Their home is in the Negev. There is no pasturage for them in Sinai, and here in Gaza they live by working as agricultural labor.

How sad the camels seem, wandering in circles, useless in the empty lot by the fields of vegetables where their masters have thrown up rough booths of thatch. We all shake our heads. The pathos is undeniable, especially during winter, when they go into the clutter of a refugee camp.

No ghost stories here.

A half-hour later we stop by another cluster of Bedouins. Again, rather than many tents, the intense heat or poverty has dictated hutches of palm fronds. Answers are evasive, curt, at the first one where we inquire. The people don't want to talk. We walk on, seeing a waterhole ahead. There, under a tree, a biblical scene, girls giggling, a few boys ogling them while younger children jump about loading cans and jugs on donkeys. There are one or two older men talking in this shade, the only shade apart from the hutches that is visible for miles around.

The teacher greets them in Arabic. They are wary, but slowly respond. What's their history? They came from Egypt hundreds of years ago. Now the Israelis have pushed them off the land across the road and shoved them here. Across the highway is a large military reservation. They begin to complain bitterly. The land on this side is arid, impossible to cultivate. The Israelis have stolen their traditional grazing and farmlands.

As we leave, the Israeli guide turns to me. "Our friend asked them how they lived. You know what they answered? 'Like dogs.'"

Getting back into the car, I notice that we are headed back to the Negev. It's only ten o'clock in the morning. "Hey," I ask, "aren't we going down into Sinai?"

"The roads are closed."

"How do you know?"

Silence.

"Let's at least try."

"Look," says the guide, puffing on his pipe, "by the time I drop you in Beersheba and get the teacher home, it'll be one o'clock. I have a three-hour ride to Tel Aviv. I want to be home at five."

It's ridiculous. We have a guide who speaks Arabic. The press office promised to send me down into northern Sinai. What was that malarky about American tourists quitting early? The chutzpah of the guide so overwhelms me that I am speechless. We are both aware that the press office will pay him overtime. I treat him to dinner with the Bedouin, who blushes through the meal, ashamed. I feel the rage in my throat that my father who was always getting gypped in business with his in-laws used to roar in the bedroom at my hapless mother. The sun of Beersheba boils black in my eyes.

Eyeless in Sinai

VVVVV

I PLUNGE INTO A COLD blue sea from sands of white heat. The harbor at Eilat is deep. Down on the beach a breeze cools the blistering ground. Above, in the cement streets of the town, water is boiled out of the body so fast, life is a constant trip to the soda fountain. One shares the counter with the drugstore cowboys of Israel, in town for the kill, rich American girls, sick Israeli ones, stewardesses, secretaries, boneheads, community college dropouts. The easygoing hippies of the Eilat legend in the United States have deserted its beach, the shacks of the "Beats" torn down to make way for public bathing and the adventurers gone on into Sinai. Elbowing me at the café tables are faces familiar to me and only a shade darker than the *shlemiels* and *shmendricks* who used to parade in front of Dorchester's Roger's Drug, same hitch to the pants, sporting the bulge of manhood in a swagger of self-love, muscled arms of the sybarite athlete to whom clothes, car, suntan represent the limit of imagination and conversation. There is some poetry in the banter, the aggressive display of male feathers, but it is the empty world of my teenage, and this parody with Iraqi,

Moroccan, Yemenite chords to its tin-pan-alley dancing gives me the lower-middle-class, Dorchester blues.

I rent a car immediately and flee into Sinai. A whole automobile to myself? I stop at a beach a few kilometers out of the city and, finding three girls who were robbed in my youth hostel in Beersheba, try to lure one away. They are sticking together, however, and I offer, at last, to take them all down with me to Sharm El Shiekh. I make two conditions: that I don't have to drive them back; that they don't talk much during the ride.

"It is holy to me," I stutter. "I want to speak to the land in silence."

They nod, willing to please their eccentric free ticket to land's end.

A hush falls over us without my admonition as we sweep into the rocks of Sinai. Only an occasional "Gee" and "Wow" as we pass beyond earth, into a field of the moon, the edge of human existence crossed; only a trickle of water here and there through the stone garden makes it possible for a Bedouin family to cling like insects to the moisture and live. Sinai is a country of death, a platform on which to stand and sense the insignificance of the heartbeat, the damp mucous membrane, the bacteria that finally clot in human life. Here is that suspended chemical universe that mocked Job and his outcries, made him feel small. "Can you bind the chains of the Pleiades?" Small, I felt so small, and it elated me. I was a slave, a servant to something so much larger than me that the anxiety of death passed away and seemed ludicrous. And I understood why my namesake Moses had brought his stubborn band of slave laborers into the ancestral holy places of the Aramaean wanderers so they could touch the old awe, the single God above them and beyond them. Lord of emptiness and death who mocks all images of Himself, Herself, in distorted human mirrors, mocking even pleas, gifts, exhortations, gives them only one supreme gift, to be alone and free and a taste of Its own vast emptiness.

Sinai is a taste of an inhuman landscape, gas and vapor, the music of nowhere, organ chords of it going up through the boulders, red, black, green rocks swelling in mountain range after range, bare of vegetation, a soundless, monstrous music after death that makes one scream and hold one's breath.

"Maishee," I cried in my chest, tearing in my breast, "Maishe, Oyveeenoo, our father."

"Why do you keep looking around?" One of the girls asked nervously as my car swerved off the road for the third time, my head constantly turning over my shoulder to try and keep one of the hills we swept by in view.

"I'm looking for Mount Sinai."

Sinai is not to be found.

Later, we were taught a lesson seeking a literal Mount Sinai on top of Jabal Musa where St. Catharine's Monastery was emplaced a mere fourteen hundred years ago, more or less, by the Emperor Justinian. This is one of the thirteen possible Mount Sinais, according to contemporary guidebooks.

Let Sinai be like the mount where Moses died, somewhere and nowhere. It is perhaps Mount Nebo and perhaps not: for its characteristic is that it cannot be found because it marks the spot where a man disappeared into the Unknown, a prophet who dared the Jews to worship a God who would have no outline, leave no bones, footprints, traces to be worshiped through. Moses was warned to go off into the wilderness and die in an unmarked grave so no more than his laws would be left behind: only through his ideas would the Jews be able to reverence him.

One scholar puts Mount Sinai to the north, another to the south, and there is not one crag or peak of Sinai where you could not imagine Moses coming down with light bursting from his face. Everywhere and nowhere, you are worshiping, seeing a crowd of Jews clustering in the valley beds below the splintered bemas of countless rock clusters. After an hour of driving through Sinai, we had to stop because my neck was stiff.

A donkey wanders down the asphalt road, wobbly, heat crazed? We stop the car and pour out water in a tin for it, but the animal stumbles on without paying attention. Two or three Bedouin girls appear from the rocks and we pour out candy into their hands. I can't see herbiage for goat or donkey here. Only along the sea is there an occasional patch visible to the eye. The ocean on our left is so blue it seems shot through with diamonds, an uncanny aquamarine. The girls looking at it lean forward from the car windows. I want to reach out and smear it on their cheeks, pigment. On the right, somber colors of the rocks. We see valleys disappearing into the interior of Sinai, and out of one of them churns, unexpected, a yellow bus.

"There must be something down there," I say, breaking the silence. And without waiting for assent, turn the car off the road down a creek bed, thinking if it can support a bus, why not this little Volkswagen? All the way down from Eilat, I have been plotting to find the road to Saint Catharine's and take a look at Justinian's guess. This is the road to the monastery, in fact, unmarked, a dry wadi, and we don't go more than a few hundred yards, not even disappearing behind the first range of mountains that flank the passage, when our wheels bog in sand.

We all get out. My companions, giving me disgusted looks, tug and push, shove stones under the tires, throw out all the luggage, spare tire, irons, hoping somehow to make the car move. The sun is sinking. The sky is red. We are going to be alone in the dark, if no one helps. We have been waving at the cars that pass every fifteen minutes or so, but no one will stop. I send one of the girls up to the highway to flag assistance. Not one but two bus loads of Yemenites pull up, charge out, and we are surrounded by friendly, scolding faces.

"What were you doing?"

"Where were you going?"

"Saint Catharine's in this thing?"

"There are mines all over Sinai. You're lucky to be alive."

"Think this is the Negev? Here the Bedouins are no joke."

The two buses carry one Yemenite family, back from an outing, over a hundred and fifty people. An American has married into the clan and he translates. But the bus driver jumps into the Volkswagen and starts to maneuver with the help of thirty or forty young men.

"Listen," I say, bending over to explain.

"Shut up!" he shouts. "You got yourself into this mess. I'm getting you out. Please, no advice."

And he quickly rolls the car out of the sand and zooms off leaving us with all our baggage strung out on the road. "Wait, wait," everyone calls, seeing our dilemma, but the driver is already out of earshot.

We pick up the sleeping bags, valises, bags of food, tires, back seats and carry them on our backs to the highway.

There is a girl from the family who flirts with me, a bikini halter and bottom on her slight body. I can't take my eyes off her and dream among the backslapping of the Yemenites who are trying to make sense of one man and three girls off in a sand pit, winking and elbowing me, of marrying into the family. The American and his wife exchange their addresses with me, and the girl who has been watching me is still waving from the back window of her bus as it disappears along the highway to Eilat.

That night, my companions and I sleep on a beach midway down Sinai. Some campers from an American Zionist group, attracted by my harem, bring us hot food and extra blankets from their tents. Sinai is wonderfully cool at night, unlike Eilat, and we wrap up gratefully.

The next morning we arrive at Sharm El Shiekh, shiny new motels and a military installation whose beach is closed to tourists. We all groan and backtrack to bathing facilities about a mile up the road. I feel bad dropping the girls off here at the end of the peninsula, but I want to be alone. (And I had wound up in the morning doing the housekeeping, filling canteens, cleaning plates, etc.) So after a swim, I turn around and head back up the highway. Late in the afternoon, I realize I have left my sandals behind on the beach. I curse; am I being punished? I pull into a gas station. A plump German girl and her boyfriend with faded dungarees and long hair are sitting at a table by the food stand there. They tell me that the beach just across the way is a good one, lots of people, so I offer them a ride back to it. I like the collection of stray tourists, American Zionist organization campers, Bedouins, soldiers, vacationing kibbutzniks, and last, a colony of "hippies" in open shacks and tents, echoing an Eilat of bygone days.

Walking along the shore past the date palms, I noticed two young men bathing in the sea, naked. Sodomy?

An Israeli runs down the dune toward me. "What are you?" he calls.

"An American."

"Come on." He grabs my arm. "I got something for you. Something good. Come on."

He pulls me up one dune, down another. What is he doing? Well beyond the earshot of any respectable citizens, we burst into a glade of palm trees. A group of twenty young people are lounging in front of tents and shelters of woven fronds. They are all nude. "An American!" the Israeli announces enthusiastically.

No one even looks at me. I try to glance about discreetly. The girls are attractive but rather tough. And their boyfriends seem more seasoned than the average, happy-go-lucky hippie in the buff. "Speak English to him," cries my guide.

A handsome blonde princess with flowing locks shakes her head, hardly curious enough to take a bored, peremptory blink in our direction. My friend, letting go of my arm, bolts into the dunes like the White Rabbit. I stand in the middle of naked women pretending to be interested in the foliage of the date palm. Slowly I start to walk forward, hoping for a friendly invitation for a cup of coffee from one of the campfires. It is

French, however, rather than English that is being spoken and it feels like a chilly day on a cold Parisian boulevard. My entrance is obviously not "cool."

As I trudge, shamefaced, up the dune on the opposite side of the camp, four Israeli soldiers call to me in Hebrew. I squat beside them, answering in my broken Beth El Hebrew School dialect. Disregarding it, they respond in fluent English.

"What do you think of this?"

"What do you mean?"

"Good or bad?"

I attempt to straddle a middle position, indicating that I am neither in favor nor against the proceedings below.

"You want to take your clothes off?"

I shook my head, still not sure of *what* was going on here.

The Israeli soldiers, boys of about nineteen, were frowning at the mirage of the shapely young ladies of Marseilles and Paris strolling nonchalantly back and forth without a stitch. It was too much. They jumped up and began to tear off their fatigue shirts, trousers. "Us too!"

"We want to be naked too." Clutching rolled up trousers and underwear, they thundered down into the camp. An older Israeli girl with breasts hanging below her belly button ran out of a tent shaking a spoon, scolding them in Hebrew, driving them off.

Three Bedouins leading a camel appeared at the top of the path into the camp. They walked down into the center of the tumult, looking neither to the left nor the right, staring straight ahead as they progressed through the pasture of nakedness. Three dunes away they sat down and began to jabber furiously in Arabic.

Intoning to myself that it was all silly, I wandered away, inch by inch. Later, on the way back, I found my footsteps irresistibly skirting the edge of these voluptuous dunes.

In the evening, I was told that the camp was a center for the drug trade in Israel: hashish smuggled in from Saudi Arabia across the narrow sea. Sleeping in my car, next to a few camels in the parking lot, I started up with the first streaks of dawn and rode on. At length, I came to the Crusader castle that lies on Coral Island. The sea of Aqaba is so clear you can easily see to the bottom, forty, fifty feet down, with a mask. I wanted to swim out to the island, floating on the surface with snorkel and flippers, rather than taking a boat. There are acres of coral reef to skim. Usually, I'm bored after a few minutes in the water, but drifting below the waves in a sunny sea of bright banded fish, flocks of white and black zebras, orange striped, blue and red pastels, miniature turkeys feathered in waving brown fins, sudden brilliant spots of emerald like flashes of colored electricity, ducking in and out of caves and valleys of coral: not until this poor mammalian flesh was water-logged could I drag myself from the glut of brilliance.

The island itself, with its miniature lake, ruined towers, cistern, first a Crusader stronghold, then the fortress of Saladin, glows like a fairy tale as one jumps off into the buried treasure of its reef. Anointed to the mastery of these kingdoms, at length I rose, surrendered the tokens of frog princedom, sped on to Eilat to get the car back before the appointed time.

Now the sandals play their fatal role. It was too hot for leather shoes. Since my expensive handmade sandals are behind on the beach near Sharm El Shiekh, I decide to get a rubber pair. It is noon and Eilat is boiling. I try one store, then another, finally climb up to a shopping center high on a hill and find the bargain one-dollar pair I am looking for.

I come down, mail some postcards, pour down a quart of various soft drinks, and go to the bus station. Checking for my ticket, I realize my wallet is gone.

I pour out the contents of my leather bag. Where can it be?

The shoe store? The bus is leaving in half an hour. Grabbing my heavy bags, I run uphill, the sweat pouring off my forehead. Have you seen a wallet?

"No."

Were they lying? I was carrying over a hundred dollars in Israeli money in my wallet, and another seventy in American cash. Would it be too much temptation?

There is no time to argue. Frantic, grabbing my bags, bathed in sweat, cursing the circumstances that had forced me to change so many traveler's checks, a misunderstanding at the rental agency, I run downhill toward the post office. "No." They haven't seen a wallet there. O my God! My bus ticket! My Master Charge, traveler's checks, are in the. . . . "My wallet was stolen the other day," says the girl behind the counter, seeing me wobble visibly.

I gallop toward the soft-drink place. "No." But they sympathize. "Go to the police. In fact, our wallets, two of them, were lifted just a few weeks ago. . . ."

At the bus station, they won't even listen to my question. They are busy. "Are you sure you haven't found a wallet?" The ticket-takers wave me away from the window. I am obstructing traffic.

Back to the rent-a-car. "No." They, too, tell me to go to the police. I remember now. I left my leather bag on a bench for sixty seconds while I filled a bottle with water at the fountain in the bus station. Again I rush back, looking in the bushes around the terminal, hoping someone has just stolen the money.

As I run up and down in front of the bus station in hysterics, a woman and her daughter from the soft-drink place come by in a truck. "Hop in," they call. "We'll take you to the police."

So I jump in the back, noting with despair as I get out at the police station that an iron hook in the back of the truck has torn a hole in my luggage. What was this? Mockery?

It is Friday afternoon. The police are about to close up for Sabbath. They are already getting into bathing suits. The woman police sergeant is impatient, insisting that I have lost my wallet, that it hasn't been stolen. Nothing can be done today or tomorrow. I can come back Sunday morning. Maybe it will be turned in. Abruptly she leaves. I am left with police officers who speak only Hebrew and French.

I stagger off with my torn baggage. I go looking up and down in the streets, behind the shopping center, for wallets. "Have you seen a wallet?" I cry at stand after stand. And wallets are brought to me. I collect three in the space of an hour, one full of identification papers. Faces sigh as I ask them, tell me how, last week, last month, last year, *their* wallet has been stolen. I bring the wallets back to the police station where an atmosphere of country club levity now crowns the desk. Without looking up or asking questions, the clerk receives the wallets and tosses them into a corner. Ignoring me, he noisily sips a coke.

Later that night, at the youth hostel I check into with my depleted funds, I realize that my Eur-Rail Pass is lost too, non-refundable. The total is now five hundred dollars, at a crack.

"Why are you doing this to me?" I scream, the dust and sun thick and clotted in my throat, straggling up the side of a hill with my luggage to the youth hostel. "Why? Why?"

A good swift kick in the rear I got from Our Father, Our King at the gateway to Sinai.

I woke up from all my sentimental dreams of Israel. Holy Land, Promised Land. No mirages in front of me now.

Did You Cry?

WWWW

O Judah, what shall I do unto thee?
For your goodness is as a morning cloud,
And as the dew that early passeth away.
Therefore have I hewed them by the prophets,
I have slain them by the words of My mouth.

MARTIN BUBER POINTS OUT that Israel for the Jews is a living substance, capable of being "slain" by terrible sayings, in a paraphrase of Hosea. Woe unto them that bring back an evil report of the land. Their fate will be like the timid spies who returned from across the Jordan with tales of cruelties and dangers in the Promised Land and were condemned to die in the wilderness.

"Did you cry?" a friend, Hebrew scholar and rabbi's son, asks. "When you arrived?"

"Yes."

"Did you cry when you left?"

"No."

My friend smiles, "Next time you won't cry when you land. And afterwards, you won't be disappointed."

Always, at the end of a torrent of abuse, recalling robbery, arrogance, foolishness, I interject, still, it's my family. I love them.

Finally, looking at the Golan Heights, the wide bleak nothing of Sinai, the hills of Shechem, Jerusalem, my heart beat wildly. No matter how much I felt for the Arabs, it is in my blood, this land, a deep, inexplicable lust. It has been promised to me, my grandfathers, through stories in childhood, a landscape of dreams. It would be too hard not to see it again. I wanted it not to build on but simply to stand on. To know there was an end to the wandering of my family.

My family. Israel is not a land but a family, mine. It is a living substance. Two young boys I met on my trudge up to the youth hostel and asked, "Have you found a wallet?" met me as I walked down the next morning. They insisted, as if they were cousins, that I come with them to the beach, share their blanket. They had hitched to Eilat, yet they shook out their meager coins to buy me soda, popsicles, shared their lunch. On the phone, the telephone operators at the lost and found in Tel Aviv sighed like mothers over my missing wallet. A police inspector I finally contacted to check up on it when I had returned from Eilat asked me for my address and, when I gave my father's cousin, Reuben, as a forwarding address, knew him. Please give him my best, he asked and of course, he would do his best to find the wallet. One set of cousins gave me money, another found me a free apartment. I was taken out to lunch, dinner, the Israeli writers insisted on treating me when they heard of my loss.

As I was trying to hitch out of Eilat, the man from the rent-a-car drove by after I had been standing in the broiling shade of a gas station for an hour and a half. "You haven't found your wallet?" He told me to wait a bit. Some Swedish girls had rented a car from him and were driving to Masada. He would ask them to give me a ride. Half an hour later, they pulled up and, in the spirit of the land, drove me all the way, sharing drinks.

At the bank, when I wailed without the exact numbers of the lost traveler's checks, since I couldn't read my own illegible handwriting, they helped me out gruffly as one would a very foolish son. Wherever I reported my loss, I had to endure not only sympathy but the kind of head-shaking look that one gives to one's children: When, Maishe, at last, will you grow up?

At Chanoch Bartov's for supper, the phone rings and one of

the members of Parliament calls to thank him for a column in that day's paper. Yoram Kaniuk talks about his conversations with the then ambassador to the U.S., Rabin, a former commander. It is a country where the prime minister calls you up to praise or bawl you out like an aunt or uncle.

At Abba Kovner's reading, afterward, they tell jokes from the era of the British Mandate. A pompous English judge is sitting on the case of a Jewish horse thief. "Did you steal the horse?" demands the judge.

"No, your Honor."

"What do you do for a living?"

"I walk around."

"What do you mean, 'walk around'?"

The old man weaves about the judge's bench as he illustrates. "I'll walk around you. And you'll walk around me. And we'll both make a living."

Someone tells the tale of the irascible Hebrew poet, in Paris after the War of Independence, who was approached by French intellectuals and reproved. "You Jews have always had such a great 'spiritual heritage.' How can you give this up for a material gain like a land, farms, buildings, factories, like everyone else?"

"We'll give you half of our 'spiritual heritage,'" says the poet. "And you give us half of your material gain. And in ten years, we'll see who is doing better."

Relatives, friends, keep asking me in the last weeks of my stay, "When are you coming back?"

And in Haifa, two days before I leave, as I spill out my tale to A. B. Yehoshua, a writer who has retreated to the north in order to escape the merry-go-round of Tel Aviv and Jerusalem, he leans over the table and pats my arm. "You know," he says. "It's easier to be a Jew in America."

After Yom Kippur

\/\/\/\/\/

ISRAEL IS SO CHANGED since the summer I visited it! "All changed, utterly changed," Irish lines of Yeats. After the Yom Kippur War, I heard about the Holy Land as the Jews of Alexandria, Rome, Marseilles, must have heard about the fall of the Second Temple, not from newspapers but in the faces and voices of friends from Israel, in letters: a terrible sadness reborn. And one catches in the resonance of world opinion (hollow phrase, hollow globe) the onset of that old disgust at us, a troublesome, arrogant people.

"News of the Yom Kippur War," bannered headlines as I passed a newsstand on my way to a free seat at an uptown Orthodox Temple on the Day of Atonement, walking from my apartment, fifty blocks away, the other side of Manhattan, my stomach empty, the big black letters like a dish of acid. Sitting in the synagogue fasting, the attack was a nightmare eating inside one as the cries of guilt streamed from the prayer book. "We have trespassed, we have dealt treacherously. . . ." What had we done to deserve this?

"What are you people doing?" a friend, not a Jew, cries to

me, half annoyed, as I meet him unexpectedly, walking in Central Park during the late afternoon break in the service.

"What are we doing?" I answer. "I thought Israel was attacked."

Yet I am arguing with myself, the same question. "What is strange," an Armenian-Irish lawyer says, putting down the manuscript pages of my Israeli journal, "is that you assume that I *know* that you Jews are all involved in this continuous self-examination and guilt." The lawyer talks about Golda Meir on TV after the Yom Kippur War, the wincing as she spoke—a moment of self-scrutiny before she opened her mouth.

The old itch to argue. "Though he slay me, I will argue with him." Job's exclamation. And if not with God, then with oneself. What had we, the Jews, done? And sitting, faint, dizzy with thirst since I am a poor faster, at the end of the service, the faces around me shaking not only with personal atonement, guilt, but the sadness of a whole people, since everyone in the hall knew what was happening at the instant across the sea; the story of the ten martyrs and the demands of an insidious judge, next to the opening Kol Nidre perhaps the most awesome moment in the holiday liturgy, now had a silent commentary appended. It is a fable of justice not for an actual crime but a crime committed in our mythology, an outsider stepping in to judge us for an act of sin in our own family. "Oh, the anguish of my soul," exclaims the narrator in tears as he begins. The Roman emperor summons ten great rabbis of Palestine, puts the question to them, "What is the judgment against a man who sells his brother into slavery?"

"Death," they reply.

"Who has paid for the crime of Jacob's sons, who sold their brother Joseph into captivity? If they were alive I would have avenged it on them, but now you must answer the sentence."

The rabbis accept the sentence. One has his flesh torn off by iron rakes, another is burned to death. Yet they accept, and as we weep and tear at our chests through the prayer shawls, we too accept the crimes of our mythology, crimes to which no other people would submit.

We have not sinned against Egypt, Syria, Jordan, but the Palestinians are our brothers. We Jews cannot rest easy until we have brought them back out of their misery. We can argue the injustice of the Arabs toward the Moroccan, Yemenite, Iraqi Jews, and perhaps the scales will balance in a human measure. But ours is a far stricter account. It is not to found another tedious state but to bring the dream of our prophets, of a messianic age, closer that we, not only the Israelis, but all Jews, are rooting themselves in the land of Israel, of Jacob. And I dream that we will fall upon the Palestinians' necks with kisses and show the world how really crazy we are. At the end of the week, the Jew and Arab pull agreements out of the coals. *Vey iz mir*, what are we to think?

The Spanish kabbala, the Zohar, looked suspiciously on Jacob and Esau's act. "And they wept," yes, as Genesis says, "And Esau ran to meet [Jacob] and embraced him, and fell on his neck and kissed him, and they wept." But why? Jacob is weeping because he's afraid of his brother. And Esau is weeping because their father is alive and he can't do any harm to Jacob. "There is a tradition," the Zohar footnotes, describing the two brothers locked on each other's necks, "that Esau's teeth were suddenly lengthened to keep him from biting."

Rabbinical paranoia?

For weeks after Yom Kippur the whole Jewish population of New York was delirious. I walked around like a Puerto Rican delinquent with a transistor radio against my ear until the cease-fire, trying to stay with the news minute by minute as if a moment's inattention would cause God to forget us and the Red Sea to come in over our heads. What can I do? Write speeches, give money? A few years ago in a fight with my Israeli cousins when I shouted at them for their chauvinism, they cut in with, "What's Israel to you?"

"I care about it."

"Yeah, what did you ever do for it?"

"I . . . I . . ."

"Right."

So now when the secretary for the local temple sees me in the bank, I rush over to her. "I'm giving. I'm making out a check. Hold on. Don't leave. Who do I make it out to?"

"Make it out to the Israel Emergency. Wait a minute. Why shouldn't you make something? *Nu*, make it out to the Israeli Bond, this way, you'll get back interest, etc."

Down in Washington, I meet an Arab, a US senator. After a bout of initial sparring, we start to agree, both of us upset. I volunteer to write a speech for him, start calling friends about my ideas. In New York everyone has turned around 180 degrees. The secret Jews are suddenly militant, those bastards, kill them all, while the *Commentary* conservatives are full of charity. We expected it. You could smell. What do you expect? So try, you never know.

Meanwhile, I'm trying to find out what happened to my cousin. I reach a friend of his in the consulate. It's okay. He was on the Golan but only suffered diarrhea.

But now the reports are coming back from Israel itself and we are getting the taste of a sadness as thick as cabbage soup. Yoram Kaniuk, the Israeli novelist, writes:

Dear sad crazy Mirsky man from the land of stolen wallets. I was very glad to hear from you. All letters start that way, but this one of course is different. The war was terrible. I'm still somehow in it. About six of my closest friends lost their sons in this mad war. So much grief and soul searching everywhere. . . . I wish I could write you a nice funny letter but I am in a dark sober mood. Life here now is a rage and we fight for sanity. Politics takes most of my time.

An Israeli who teaches at City College tells me that the whole population is walking around in shell shock asking, "Why do they want to kill us?"

A reporter who has seen Yoram just after the war tells me he hears the same question from the same faces in the identical room, the exact duplicate of the Miró print on the wall among Palestinian intellectuals in Beirut, Jewish in Tel Aviv. And a photographer (Jewish) who has been a friendly witness to Castro's Cuba cries, "They're hypocrites, that Israeli left. In the United States the peace movement had the courage to refuse to pick up guns and go to war. Here we don't answer the draft."

Baffled rage twists my larynx. I try to answer politely. I wonder, as Yoram must have, while furiously quarreling with his government, if surrounded by anxious grandfathers, grandmothers, one's children, wife, friends, the border a few miles away, one could really sit at home and hope that peace would come through passivity.

Stories of cruelties, castrations, and mutilations on the Golan: and I find it difficult to write to Moroccan friends whose troops may have committed these horrors, acts committed not out of malice but because that's the way the Moroccan soldiers received the tradition of war, demented children. Yet I made no secret of my Judaism deep in the deserts of Rissani, Ksar el Souk, and was our common delight, brotherhood, now annulled. "If only the Israelis would give them their pride. That's what they want," a Lebanese friend says to me.

If it's only that? Only all that bad-mouthing, that hysterical Jewish aggression which overkills, overmocks, overteases, in an effort to hide the terror: the insecurity of the boast—we are a holy people—flung out, and then dread shakes us. How easy. Simple. "Give it to them," I cry out. "We'll give it to them."

Only who? Who'll give it? Who'll take it?

"We died among your chairs," an Israeli poet calls to the government, and the papers are spilling over with a bitterness that I am told was unthinkable before Yom Kippur. Articles questioning the existence of a Jewish state. "Why should we stay here to die?" a columnist quotes a young soldier, writing into *Yedioth Ahronoth*, one of the mass-circulation newspapers. "I am 24 years old and my friends and I have spent a life in the reserves."

"I have no answer," the journalist replies.

We are a ghetto in the Middle East, Israelis at my home complain. Only in Europe we could get out of the ghetto. In the Middle East it's impossible. Such self-hatred, I think, such scathing breast-baring, how can I not love such a family? This is the real thing, holiness. How many states question their existence?

As the Palestinian Liberation Organization strides the halls of the United Nations, oil money in their pockets, and the Israelis are slowly pushed into the corner, we Jews find ourselves in the traditional role again, the underdog. Bitter as it is to see the countries of the world deserting us, ready to sell us into bondage for the sake of a few more years of wasting gas and oil. A sense of old tribal allegiance becomes manifest. Jewish intellectuals who feel no religious intuition animating their bones and to whom the bourgeois preoccupations of the American synagogues and sentimentality of its "official Jewish" culture is obnoxious, discover that strange love of Zion, of Jews as family, and of Israel as a homeland of Jews. Their tie to Israel is far deeper than they suspected, and through Israel to the mysterious identification and tradition of Judaism, those long volumes collected through centuries of agonizing moral questions and messianic hopes.

The problems of Israel are our problems. We all, Jew and sympathetic Gentile, have a share in its dream. "In dreams begin responsibilities," says Delmore Schwartz.

A few weeks after the Yom Kippur War, interweaving ancient and modern Israel in a lecture on how to recognize God, Rabbi Soloveitchik rises behind his table, on the tips of his shoes, at the Maimonides Institute in Brookline before the assembly of students, old men, fuzz-cheeked adolescents, the end of the Saturday night lesson.

"To recognize God is important for a people as well as individuals—how?—by having an excellent ear which is sensitive to the footsteps of God as he walks in the Garden of Eden. . . . And interpret them properly. We are now, the Jewish people, in the center of history . . . to understand what God wills us to do.

"In 1967 his footsteps were eastward towards Sunrise. . . . Now it is in doubt whether God is walking east or west. Such an absurd situation has never occurred in Jewish history—why should three thousand young boys die, and the best? It is the duty of every Jew to listen and to respond. If God is walking in the Garden and his footsteps are audible—it's apparent—he's lonely—he wants man to join him."

At Maalot. At Ein al Helweh.

4
Jewish
Trips

Architecture and Holiness

WWWW

IT IS THE CURSE and the blessing of being Jewish that one imagines oneself at the center of the universe, the fate of the Jews and the fate of the world at one. If Israel seems the powderkeg in the Middle East, and the Middle East the powderkeg in the midst of the nations, it is not entirely an unwelcome position for a people that has been dreaming of Apocalypse and its unique responsibility for it. The very deprecation with which the Israelis speak of the land, Jerusalem, "that pile of rocks," is a kind of rude joking with our own arrogance.

Do we Americans dare to address our country as "The Holy Land?" Even the addled among us who flap the flag most fiercely would be ashamed at such presumption. Hitler, a madman, came closest to such protestations, but God was absent from his pledges of allegiance. No wonder Charles De Gaulle, no slouch at the sentimental, found Jews objectionable. Not individual Jews but the Jewish position as such. It mingles God, patriotism, fetishism, and metaphysics in such a way that its demands must always seem unreasonable. The individual solipsists who take the helm of their countries must always find irritating this whole quarrelsome tribe of pretenders to the throne.

As obnoxious as Jews seemed through the centuries to the new Jews, Christians, with our catcalls that their Messiah was a hoax, as a dispossessed people it was always possible to condescend to us. Now, seated again, despite improbable odds on a good two-thirds of our former territory, the spectacle of this tribe, whose only reason for not disbanding has been the expectation of a messianic voice, ought to be vaguely disquieting. "God put you in your mother's womb so that you could be the instrument to bring about the rebirth of Israel after two thousand years," the chief rabbi of the Holy Land is supposed to have said to Harry Truman, whereupon great tears rolled down the president's face. If not magic, the understanding of what magic the Jewish myth exercises over the minds of Christain Europe and America is never far from the Jewish *kopp*, intelligence. Arabs are not immune to it. The Koran states that the Jews must be back in their place before the Day of Judgment. Yet how about the Jews' relationship to their own myth, the landscape of holiness?

Oh, horror.

In the Holy Land, the Jews just dump their garbage and offal wherever they please. Littering seems to be a national pastime. At times one suspects that it is almost a studied contempt for the earth they tread as if they were taking vengeance upon it for the troubles its claims of sacredness have brought them.

This paradoxical contempt on the part of the "man in the street" carries over to the planners. If use determines ownership, then one cannot quarrel with the Israelis' right to this land. Jerry-built, yes, but still a modern industrial state, its buildings rising out of the shacks and shanties of a half-deserted Arab backyard. Yet one shakes one's head over this modern Israel, dejected. What were we promised, Miami Beach, Dayton, Ohio? Only in Arab or Druse Israel, on the West Bank enclave, is the land of the Bible visible among the people, do I feel that I am in my geographical homeland. It is the dream of the ancient Hebrews that brought us here, and will nothing be left of the landscape of that dream but a biblical Disneyland? Air-conditioned restaurants at the foot of Masada, a basketball court in front of the Wailing Wall within a circle of modern bungalows and comfort stations? Outside Shechem I see the tents of Bedouins encamped on the hillside and a thrill creeps down my back as our car speeds by. Like our father, Jacob, they are still following the mountain ridges and valleys out of the desert to the cities of the far north, breaking through fences, bruising the crops of the town-dwellers, wandering, wandering.

The Israelis smile. They'll put a stop to this nonsense. Settle these vagabonds down in air-conditioned garages with barbed wire to bind their flocks in and schools to erase the past. Rage rises in my throat at a people who have always lived out of history in love with an ancient tale, suddenly sick with a fever for the most superficial progress. In Jerusalem, over the brow of the Mount of Olives into the Valley of Kidron where the dead will rise on the day of resurrection, creeps the Hotel International* upon the graves of the pious who have come like elephants to die in the holiest charnel field of the Hebrews, over the joints of my great-great-great-grandfather Reuben. And the anger thickens in my throat and I sing darkly, the land will cast us out.

Soloveitchik said the land does not belong to any one generation of Jews. It belongs to the Jewish people. No matter how badly one generation may act or abuse the Holy Land, it does not matter. For it is not in the possession of individuals but of a people, and it is held in trust for the past as well as the future.

For thousands of years, Jewish ethics and Jewish poetry have been homeless, landless, and even its contemporary architects, Freud, Marx, Einstein, have wrought their wonders in an abstract, spiritual world, divorced from insular nationalistic bonds.

---

* In fairness to the Israelis one must state that this particular piece of sacrilege was built under Jordanian auspices.

Now the Jew is tied again to Eretz, the land, and perhaps none too soon. The geographers of Man come back horrified by the landscape, their gaze distracted from the beast by the ravages to his grazing ground. Returning from India, the anthropologist Lévi-Strauss is shaken by the way human beings have overwhelmed their habitat. "In America what I saw in the first place was the physical universe, whereas in India, I saw only human beings. A sociological order worn away over hundreds of centuries was collapsing."

The implications of man not coming to terms, not in balance with the natural world, are frightening. In *Tristes Tropiques* Lévi-Strauss warns,

Freedom is neither a legal invention nor a philosophical conquest, the cherished possession of civilizations more valid than others because they alone have been able to create or preserve it. It is the outcome of an objective relationship between the individual and the space he occupies, between the consumer and the resources at his disposal. And it is far from certain that abundance of resources can make up for a lack of space, and that a rich but over-populated society is not in danger of being poisoned by its own density, like those flour parasites which manage to kill each other at a distance by their toxins before their food supply runs out.*

Even radicals begin to resent the notion of progress as engineered by our architects and city planners, surburban developers; it is in this context that the Israelis with the backing of the other Jews of the world have begun to build a state. Can Israel in its cramped borders afford to repeat the inanities of urban sprawl afflicting the rest of this globe?

Yet can we afford to experiment? Israel is hemmed about by hostile neighbors, threatened by a growing native Arab population from within. Again, either we are Jews or we are not Jews. We exist to do it better than others. When we were out of the land, Eretz, we could ignore our surroundings, though at bitter cost. Like the Jewish child in Isaac Babel's

* New York: Atheneum, 1974.

story "Awakening," many of us were brought up in a world of human root and limb so dense and entangled, we were ignorant of trees, leaves, the names and knowledge of the earth under us. We carried, like our grandfathers, our landscape intact, from country to country. Now, the responsibility to land, the Holy Land, cannot be evaded. But what and how shall we build? Can we build so as to assuage even the jealousy of the Syrians, Egyptians, Palestinians?

For hundreds of years our ancestors roamed up and down the length of Canaan with an ark in a tent. Jerusalem was not taken decisively from the Jebusites until under David, when the land was "ours." Now again, Jerusalem returns to the Jews, not only the Temple Mount but much of the historic kingdom. Our hands may still not be clean enough to put up the Temple, temples. David was not allowed to build a house for God; that was reserved to his son, Solomon. David's hands were bloody from warfare. Even that gladhander, the present mayor of Jerusalem, always plumping for a new building, suggests that we await the Messiah for the next Temple. How about the other temples? We don't have to wait for the Messiah, but we have to pause and ask if we have architects who have a sense of responsibility to a "Holy Land" and do not simply pour concrete. If not, then perhaps like King David it is better to do nothing and wait for successors who are pious, blessed with the intuitions of mystery, who speak, however briefly, like Solomon, "the tongue of the birds."

After an article of mine which began, "Architects are the mass murderers of the Twentieth Century," in which I pleaded for a return to past sanities and simplicities, the elegance of the cathedrals, the fine lines of colonial houses, the Shirley home in Roxbury, Boston, I received a biting letter from the writer Cynthia Ozick.

You are angry at the concrete garage, at the sewer pipe playground, because you are angry at the moral nature of our age.
    Yes.

But now let us speak of the moral age of the cathedral, or to take the Roxbury example I have no comprehension of whatever, of the age of the Shirley Mansion. Or of the age of the winding alleys . . . weathered fronts . . . cornices floating on the warehouse tops. . . .

Or of the moral nature of any age. Pyramid. Cave. Pantheon.

In Cynthia's protest, in Lévi-Strauss's warning, I find one of the dilemmas of today's architecture. Morality without religion is a very bleak prospect to me. We have become more conscious morally, but our inferiority in religious sensibility before past ages is conspicuous. To build without a sense of holiness is to court disaster. Halldor Laxness, the Nobel Prize-winning novelist of Iceland, said, after I finished railing in his living room against the concrete condominiums that were defacing the volcanic vistas of Reykjavik, "Modern architects are the only sect who have taught us to curse the sun."

Why was I stung by Ozick's letter? Because underlying it is the ancient antagonism of Jewish thought based on moral considerations, for the aesthetics of the Greeks. It is a struggle which goes back to the days of the Maccabees. So they build pretty temples? Yeah? How do they behave? Never mind is it *beautiful*, is it *good*? In today's ecology these questions cannot be kept separate. Man's life is made indecent when house is piled onto house and the land is obliterated. Aesthetics are not foreign to the Bible. Far from it: the Song of Solomon is a song of a city. All through the Prophets, the Psalms, injunctions sound as to the land, from building codes to poetry praising its hills and valleys. (It is the principal sadness of Diaspora Judaism, a Judaism in exile, to have excluded so much of aesthetics for the sake of a movable landscape.)

It will be a generation before we shake off the sad habit of Diaspora. If this is a bad age for architects (I believe it is) let us give the land of Israel a sabbatical, a decade of rest. The whole world might follow our example and stop their pell-mell rush to build skyscrapers, "piles of black bile," as Edward

Dahlberg calls them. The most striking architecture I saw in Israel, although its intention had not been completely fulfilled, was the University of Haifa, buried in a hillside. Would that it had been invisible in the hill, so that one could walk above on the paths of Elijah and burrow below into the fall of man from those blessings. The best architecture is no architecture at all! Give us the landscape to dream in. Give us the Bible as literal as we may make it, not Disneyland papier maché, but simply the terrain.

What discipline, what vision it would take to live thus, to construct an inner architecture; to withdraw, in exile from the modern world, that absolute Diaspora of the soul.

The horror that separates Jew and Palestinian today is the notion of a modern state with all its vulgar trivia, its immorality in which the buildings of socialism, communism, are no less ugly than the mushrooms of capitalism. Let us seek instead an ancient state. Our dream moved through empires, mightier than the shepherds shifting between the water holes of Judea and Samaria could have conceived of, shaking apart temples, cities.

It was the dream of an earthly paradise. We have remained Jews because we deny the heresy that the kingdom will come in the hereafter. "If not now, when?" Hillel cries, not so different from his descendant Rabbi Levi Isaac of Berditshev who shouted at the end of his prayer *until there was a finish, an end of the exile*, a better deal for Israel, he, Levi Isaac, wasn't budging from his place. The first scouts who came back from Canaan were punished because they saw only the real land full of dangers, hostile towns, and in their own eyes they became "grasshoppers." It was Caleb and Joshua who grasped the earth itself, a land of milk and honey, who heralded the readiness of Jacob's children to enter the Promised Land. And those who think that one can simply withdraw into the architecture of the mind, indifferent to physical circumstances, are not pious but simply spiteful to God's creation.

The laws, the halakhah, are enough for a good life, cry the Orthodox.* No, it's not so. This is the Judaism of the Diaspora. The failure of Orthodox Jewry to protest the shoddy living arrangements of modern Israel, its silence on the subject of environment, ecology, points up a dangerous deficiency in their development of traditional law. One of the most formidable rabbis in this century, Abraham Heschl, sounds a warning that has ominous echoes when it comes to Orthodoxy and the landscape.

A Judaism confined to the limits of Halakhah, with all due respect be it said, is not exactly one of the happiest products of the Diaspora. Such condensation and parochialism has little of the sweep and power of the prophets. He who would restrict Judaism to Halakhah will distort its image and deprive it of its grandeur. Those who cite the words of our sage: "Since the days of the destruction of the Temple, God had no more than four cubits of the Halakhah in His world," forget that these words are not an expression of triumph but, on the contrary, an expression of pain and sorrow that the Shechinah was expelled from the wide world of history and nature.

We were enjoined as men not to cut the corner of our beards. To leave ourselves in a state of nature. At the hem of our garments to wear a fringe so that the commandments of holiness be before us. How then can we shear the terrain of Israel until bald, unlovely, an asphalt patch, its paths, towns, concrete blocks disfigure our lives?

What? You nut! Maishe, I'm supposed to live in a tent, with kids? What am I? A refugee? A Palestinian?

What are we about if not such craziness? We are a whole people trembling like priests before God. For the sake of bare

---

* Despite the inherited Jewish disdain for environment, part of our inheritance from those thousands of years when no soil was truly ours and the only landscape of the Jewish soul was internal, behavior, two extraordinary cities in terms of "siting" or physical location were founded by Jews. Granada in Spain and Sifre in Morocco are examples, perhaps, in their fountains and diadem of hills, of the persistent memory among Jews of our mountain capital, Jerusalem.

Judaean hills, I will sleep in a two-by-ten coffin. (I would almost do the same for a green Manhattan and an unobstructed river view.) If I can walk out into field and forest while the sun shines, or sit in fine public halls, academies, the universe of private space for sleeping and eating becomes less pressing.

Oh, let us not live, build, like the other nations of the earth. Let us be different. This land which the talmudists have personified just short of idolatry, so that it senses misdeeds and sickens over them—beware, dreams are sifted through its soil.

Simeon Ben Yohai, that strange sage of the first century, said, "He who looks upon a tree, deserves death." But this is the song of a permanent subterranean hidden in a cave for years on end with Roman soldiers overhead. It is time for the Jews to come up from the cisterns into the sunlight. What is the alternative? A tin state from Dan to Beersheba, one split-level Holiday Inn? With a splinter of Palestinian nationals across the borderline trying to overshadow it, two levels, three, four, five? This is nightmare.

I'm not suggesting that the Israelis turn away from technology. Far from it. I'm saying that it is up to us as Jews to make the technology of the twentieth century human. To dismantle the Golem, clay man, which is taking from us the ground of the Holy Land, ready to strangle its creators in its clogged, deadly arteries, subdivisions, skyscrapers, the asphalt corridors of its thickening artificial grid. Where we build towns, let us put a circumference to them so that there is no one in their towers who cannot look far out into a mysterious countryside. Restore the biblical landscape as far as we can, removing the trace of our footsteps above the earth. Look within ourselves and the soil for solutions to traffic, transportation. How sweet the Sunday Sabbath was for me in the streets of Florence, Palermo, when all automobiles were silent. Instead of confining such intuitions to the narrow-minded in Mea Sheariim who stone the peace-breakers, we could build a land of Sabbath where one would walk within the circle of desire each day. A friend told me that he heard Romans breaking into song again in the new quiet of those Sundays of the energy crisis. To walk the circuit of the town walls, from crowds to solitude, how human we will discover we are, how precious!

The kibbutz brought to fruition the dreams of the Essenes, the Fourierists, the Marxists without force or bloodshed. Only the kibbutz itself is in danger from the technology of the century, the clay man. It is not the green fields, pastures, but the ugly clusters of houses, factories, that are crowding in on our vision. Human arrogance imagines that human beings are the end of man and that the rest of creation is irrelevant to God's plans. Woe to them who lay the foundations to this new Babel. It is not a common language we will be deprived of this time, but any language. It has already brought forth a mute, stunned generation.

Only imagine an Eretz in which the ibex, the hind, even the leopard roamed from end to end, in which the ancient Jerusalem stood against the Palestinian hills as the new Jerusalem rose slowly, circumspectly, in awe and trembling; a coast on which the sea beat without villas or condominiums and bands of desert held sacred, inviolable, forests, a great international preserve of dreams, a park in which Jews, Christians, Moslems could come and worship. If we Jews gave up more and more of the land to this use, I think we could quicken the Palestinians to our dreams. Nothing pleased me as much as those West Bank *fellahin* tilling the soil in the garments of our ancestors, their cottages haunted by biblical shadows. If we could keep this and restore more! This would be a piety to shame those old Bedouin thieves in Mecca and summon the pope to sandals and a pilgrim's staff. Let us set ourselves against this age!

Women

VVVVV

WITH THE ORTHODOX I pray in the morning, "Blessed art thou, O Lord our God, King of the Universe who has not made me a woman." But who can say that without irony? Seeing that my mother ran our house, our lives, my father (who was no easy character to keep the reins on), my sister and me (until we ran away from home). And her mother kicked my maternal grandfather out of the house, according to the family stories, and sent him on trips to Israel and other parts unknown, back in the chauvinistic dawn of the century, anywhere, so he would stay out of her hair, the children's, the business which she ran and in which he only made a mess when she let him finagle for a few months. Twelve children my grandmother had, and every one a classic of the same: my mother's brothers all deferring to their wives, my mother's sisters dictating policy to their husbands. My own mother ran an orphanage, went out alone as a disaster worker after her marriage, was the commissioner of industrial accidents in Massachusetts in which capacity she was known to eject fresh mouths of the brawny legal profession from her courtroom and give the ex-governor, appearing before her bench, a piece of her mind.

"Willy, can't you ask her?" my father's cronies would beg, hoping for a favor.

"She's her own boss," Dad would sigh. "It would only hurt you."

And on my father's side, never mind my aunts today who are all tough cookies with their own jobs, careers, my great-great-grandmother back in the Neanderthal ages of Poland who lay on her couch in Pinsk, collecting store rents, awarding favorite rabbis donations, making up dowries for poor girls: and it's her biography that is featured in the book of the city my father's cousins preserve, not that of my great-great-grand-father Baruch, who was sent out to stumble about in the gutters in old age, collecting bottles, while his children ran about on errands doing Mumma's bidding. And my Tante Tsirrel in Montreal who terrorized the family strung out across Canada, her husband, Aaron, who used to be a big barge captain in Pinsk, now sunk to a mere stevedore on the St. Lawrence docks, and once the economic basis for equality had collapsed, the poor man who mocked to death at his own table; Tsirrel's tongue that everyone was in fear of, brother, father, children. So what are we talking about?

I thank God for not making me a woman. I don't want to be the oppressor.

Where I grew up, from kindergarten the girls were all brighter, and let you know it. I was the weaker sex. Hit a girl in Dorchester, the mother would come out and beat you with a rolling pin. Adolescence? You couldn't get near a girl of your own age. They would talk faster, smarter, and they looked at you like an infant. As for sex, a neighborhood hero occasionally might be allowed to graze the breasts of his "steady" or fiancée-to-be, but most of us simply sat, miserable, and tried to garner some satisfaction out of holding hands, pecking, staring.

When I left the circle of middle-class Jewish girls in Dorchester, things changed slowly for me. My paralysis in front of women relaxed. Girls who listened, who let me abuse them, this was something new. Only these women, often Gentile, and I, misunderstood each other's intentions so that it led to frequent bouts of anger, bitterness, and dramas of estrangement that verged on the comic. How could they or I know that my cutting banter, sour irritation, pretense of boredom was actually a mark of my deep affection? Between my mother and father there was a loyalty so absolute that at moments when the bond was threatened, the energy radiating from the stress was as frightening as a nuclear reaction. "Why did you marry Dad?" my sister and I kept asking my mother almost from infancy.

"I was tired . . . he seemed okay. He kept pestering me." My mother would make fun of our romantic quest. A veil of amused condescension hid the privacies of their love. Then, during my sister's days at Smith College, when she was having difficulties in school and in her personal life, unsettling my parents, I remember in our kitchen pantry, drying dishes together, my mother turning on my sister as the latter tried to joke about Dad's reaction to her problems at Smith: my mother's voice trembling so I almost dropped the plate, "You leave your *father* alone!" In the moment of danger, it was to her husband, not to us children, that she clove. My mother, Ruth, always shy of showing physical affection, rarely hugging or kissing us, I turned my gaze away from the ferocity of her grip upon my father in the last months of her life, dying. Saw the sinews of a marriage so strong, they, rather than her bones, carried her flesh into death.

A man who has lost his wife is only half a man, according to the rabbis. The liturgy of the Jewish mystics, which has often been accused of hostility to the rights of women, on the contrary bases its metaphysics of balance, justice, ecstasy on the marriage of male and female principles. The portraits of family life which the Jew has held up as pastoral idyll, Sarah and Abraham, Rebecca and Isaac, Rachel, Leah and Jacob, are all of strong women. Sarah is Abraham's sister, Rebecca towers over Isaac, Rachel defies her father, the house radical, she makes off with his golden idols. Jacob has to toil fourteen years for her. *Nu?**

On the other hand, to assert that the Jewish tradition is in favor of unisex would be a gross distortion. Judaism is about separation, setting oneself apart, and it is an inescapable part

---

* In the Midrash, that sea of Jewish legends surrounding the events of the Bible, Rachel alone knows how to shake common sense into the Almighty. When Jerusalem was destroyed for the sins of Israel and the Holy One, Blessed Be He, determined to drive the Jews out of the Promised Land forever, the Patriarchs came begging, one more chance for their progeny.

Abraham, Isaac, Jacob and Moses too pleaded and wept. No, God was adamant. The Children of Israel had whored their one last time with foreign idols. Too much. Enough. The love affair was over.

Suddenly Rachel appeared. . . . "Lord of the Universe," she said. "You are well aware of the great love with which Jacob loved me and for which he served my father seven years. But when the time came for our marriage, my father plotted to have my sister take my place. I found out the plan and gave Jacob some signals to recognize me. But then I thought better of it, swallowed my desire and took pity on my sister. That evening, when she was given to Jacob in my place, I disclosed all the signals to her. More: I stayed that night under the bed upon which Jacob lay with my sister: when he spoke to her, she kept quiet, and I answered, so her voice wouldn't give her away. I did right by my sister: I wasn't jealous of her, and I didn't cause her shame. And what am I? Flesh and blood, dust and ashes. And what are you? A great, living, merciful God. If I wasn't jealous of my sister when she caused me grief, how could you be so jealous over some meaningless idol-worship that you would exile all my children and hand them over to the enemy?"

At this the mercies of the Holy One were stirred. "For your sake, Rachel," he said, "I shall return Israel to their land."

For it is written

> Thus saith the Lord
> A voice is heard in Ramah
> Lamentation and bitter weeping
> Rachel is weeping for her children
> And refuses to be comforted.

(This arrangement and translation of the Midrash is by Neal Kozodoy, from "Jerusalem Destroyed, God Rebuked," *Midstream* 9, no. 4 [December 1963]: 81–87.)

of the inheritance that one begins with a commitment to an identity, male or female, as you were created. "Evil comes into the world because one person tries to do the work of another," say the rabbis. Is it inconceivable that, as a man, one is in awe before the childbearing of the woman, the possibility of life and the fear of death as the child grows in the woman's body? A man may well thank God for absolving him of this responsibility. And a woman who feels the craving for a child within her? Does she not submit to it? "I thank God for having formed me according to my needs." It didn't prevent Deborah from being a judge, or my mother a commissioner. I don't thank God for giving me a penis. That would be male chauvinism.

Searching the differences as they are legislated in Judaism further, however, we discover that there are rabbinic precedents for the admission of women to full legal prerogatives as members of the *minyan*, the group of ten Jews which constitutes a congregation. On the basis of these, the Conservative Jewish movement in America has voted to call women to the Torah and count them as part of the ten. The question of equal rights in many American synagogues is now moot, and this has been introduced not as an *innovation* but as a *restoration* of ancient privileges.

I admire the decision and I welcome women to the *minyan*, but I must admit that I believe, as the Orthodox do, in separate seating arrangements. To assert the equality of women is not to agree that they are the same.

I must as a man speak for myself. The prayer of men together has to do with old and barely understood animal sensations. In the Air Force, marching with a company of men, coming down on one foot, chanting, one felt part of a herd, a drove of men moving in the rhythm of hunters over the earth, and despite the heat, sweat, ache in our bones, a kind of exaltation of body and well-being went up from us as we wheeled and reversed, back and forth, at the sergeant's commands.

Or as an adolescent, crowded into a car cruising the streets

of Roxbury, Columbus Avenue, giggling, looking at women:
are these the more primitive manifestations of instinct which
the male section of the synagogue perpetuates, transforming
the bestial laughter of Esau into the prayer of Jacob? Prayer,
which must come out of the roots of a body to have meaning
until we wail, transport ourselves into the awe and wonder of
the Unknown, is a form of love-making. In the company of
others it is group love-making. And it is no surprise that a
Tsaddik, a Chassidic prince, explaining the noisy prayers,
flailing, howling, the crazy gestures of his followers, should
compare it to that act. "When you don't know God, you
thrash about trying to get familiar. A little later, you don't
have to grope but can come easily into the Holy One's embrace. And when you really *know* Him, ah, the slightest touch
will set you off." (This says as much about Eastern European
love-making as praying.) If one will admit, and the rabbis for
thousands of years in the context of the Song of Songs have
insisted upon it, the frank sexual nature of prayer, that division
of men and women in the synagogue will be intelligible. I was
grateful at the Wailing Wall for the separation. I could give
myself up to prayer. When there are pretty women in the
vicinity, the distraction is too much.

The modern confusion over the roles of rabbi and priest
confuses too often the just efforts of those who are trying to
redress the injuries that traditional Judaism has offered in past
centuries to women. Insofar as a rabbi is a teacher there is no
bar to full participation and leadership by women. Can it be
an accident that Golda Meir was the premier of Israel (and
not by inheritance, as in the case of her colleague, Mrs.
Gandhi)? Neither in ancient nor modern Judaism have we
hesitated to put our people under a woman's leadership.

When we come to prayer, however, we encounter priest
not rabbi, the mystery of transformation from sexual to
spiritual desire.* The separation of sexes in the synagogue

---

* Judaism in its classical period chose a hierarchy of men at the First
and Second Temples for the task of purifying itself, but not one that had

preserves for me this mystery, the awareness of the stamp in our bodies of amazing differences, of the double nature needed in the task of creation. (It is, after all, not of separation but of union, a cleaving, that Judaism dreams of.) The women danced at the celebrations of our ancestors. At Biskra, Gide records the movements of their descendants, North African women, Jews and Arabs, swaying together in a courtyard, possessed. It is a rite of exorcism, and also of ecstasy, women,

wild eyed, seeking to lose consciousness of their flesh, or better to lose all feeling, were reaching the crisis in which, their bodies escaping all control of the mind, the exorcism can operate effectively. After that instant exhaustion, sweating, dying, in the prostration that follows the crisis, they were to find the calm of deliverance.

Just now they are kneeling before the basin: their hands clutching the rim, and their bodies beating from right to left and foreward and backward, like a furious pendulum, their hair whips in the water, then spatters their shoulders; each time they jerk forward they utter a low cry like that of a woodman chopping, then suddenly tumble backward as if they had an epileptic fit, frothing at the mouth and their hands twisted. . . .

Some Jewesses danced too. They sprang in disorder like delirious teetotums. They made only one leap and fell back immediately, dazed. Others held out longer . . . their madness communicated itself to us: we fled, unable to stand it any longer.

That is the prayer of women locked in ecstasy. Where do we have it in America? I don't regard division as segregation. I quarrel with Chassidism because it has denigrated the prayer of women. Still, the Chassidim understand the prayer of men together. Perhaps the effort of the synagogues ought to be to restore the balance, rather than merely mixing inhibited couples. If in separation we can cry out in ecstasy, think then of union. Messianics!

---

to give up sexual relations. Other rites have other institutions, vestal virgins, celibate Nazarites, but for the Jew, celibacy is an aberration. Even the sterile couple is enjoined to live together, make love.

Some time ago, I got into a wrangle about an essay I had written on Simone Weil, the brilliant French essayist who came from a Jewish family. Like so many daughters of assimilated parents, Simone had heard only nay-saying in the vinegar and pessimism of her ancestors' texts. She turned to Christian, Greek, Egyptian myths to find a language of nakedness, of sexual union with God. Nakedness to Simone Weil, however, was absolute. It ended in her starving herself to death in London, ostensibly as an act of sympathy for the sufferings of the French under the Nazi Occupation. It ended in an imitation of Jesus that Jews have always found a dangerous example, tinged with cruelty and the unnatural. God finally does not exact human sacrifice. Between Jesus and Abraham the quarrel is absolute—Isaac is not abandoned, dying, to cry out, "Father, father, why hast thou forsaken me?" Ecstatic nakedness as self-torture does not appeal to the Hebrew.

And what had nakedness meant to the Egyptians whom Weil admired? It wasn't ecstasy but slavery they forced upon the Jews, using them like breeding stock, finally forbidding male children, as if the penis were the public property of the state, pharoah's prerogative. Used thus, the Jews came out of Egypt, I theorized, in a state of shock where they had been yoked like oxen, their organs in trauma.

I argued with correspondents who insisted that the men weren't in such bad shape, sexually, in the Exodus. No, I insisted, the rabbis indicate that male Jews came out of Egypt in a debased state, craven, cowed by years of slavery. They showed themselves to be impure, unworthy to enter the Holy Land. And searching about for proof of the wounding of the male genitalia,* I came again to the story of Zipporah and Moses. "A bridegroom of blood, you are to me," she cries,

---

* Exodus begins as a story of strong women, the mother of Moses, Miriam, Pharoah's daughter. The men are slaves, anonymous. It is the women who are defending the family. What are the men doing? Fighting in the street. It sounds suspiciously like the contemporary sociology of the black ghetto.

throwing the foreskin of their eldest male child in the dust before the prophet's feet. In his haste to bring freedom to the Jews in Egypt, Moses has forgotten to mark the sanctity of his own heir. (Their are many commentaries on this incident, beware, mine is only one.) It is Zipporah, his wife, who is concerned with the holiness of the covenant. Again, it is Deborah, the prophetess, who according to the Zohar supervised a "general uncovering of flesh," a renewal of the act of circumcision among the Jewish tribes before they were firmly established in the land of Israel. Women are the guardians of purity among Jews. More important than even the priestly heritage, they antedate the priesthood. They are older, more sacred are these tasks.

To be blunt, the covenant is in the women's hands. That is why Jewish identity depends on descent on the maternal line. She decides if it's kosher, what goes in and out. And only the woman knows where the seed within her came from. This is why, I believe, Deborah and Zipporah are concerned about circumcision. Women guard the sanctuary and are the sanctuary. And this is what conditions the attitude of Judaism toward its female half.

In the buried life of the Jewish tradition, the weight of sexual authority is all on the woman's side. According to the Talmud and its commentators, a woman's pleasure in bed is a man's duty. He must forget his own to satisfy hers. This obligation supersedes even pregnancy. A man may not divorce a woman on the grounds of barrenness, but a woman may leave her husband if he refuses to give her sexual pleasure. One pities the poor masturbator who fell into the clutches of a sixteenth-century rabbinical court.

The following happened right here in Safed in the year 1548 in the presence of R. Joseph Karo, R. Isaac Masoud, R. Abraham Shalon, my teacher R. Joseph Sagis and several others: a wife appeared before them and reported that her husband had been indulging in such a practice. The Rabbis thereupon excommunicated him and wanted to "burn him with fire." In the end they "ran him out" of Palestine. May God protect the remnant of Israel from sin and guilt.*

At the heart of Judaism, as Rabbi David Feldman points out in *Marital Relations, Birth Control and Abortion in Jewish Law,* is a truly radical assumption. A man has a legal obligation to give his wife sexual pleasure.

"Before setting out on a journey," or "when he notices her desire," or "by her manner of dress or of action"—these and similar circumstances . . . add to his minimal obligation. . . . Indeed the legalistic obligation itself is based on an estimate of her sexual needs; if these exceed the estimate, so does his duty. Other significant provisions of the law—such as that forbidding the husband to force his attentions on his wife—will be discussed anon. What it all adds up to is a concept of marital relations as the duty of the husband and the privilege of the wife. This is in contradistinction, for better or worse, to the Christian egalitarian view (I Cor. 7:4) and, for better, stands in neat contrast to the

* Sefer Haredim, Part III, Ch. 2. Quoted by Rabbi David M. Feldman in *Marital Relations, Birth Control and Abortion in Jewish Law* (New York: Schocken, 1968), p. 158. I have taken the liberty of assuming that the "unnatural act," since it appears in the context of a discussion of onanism, refers to masturbation. Regardless of specifics, however, what is significant is the presumption by both court and wife of her rights in bed. (I also assume, in response to an editor's query, that the lady came into court because she wasn't "satisfied," and wanted absolute sexual attention.) There is an absolute gulf between traditional Christian attitudes toward sex as a necessary evil and the Orthodox Jewish celebration of it as a joyous and mysterious gift of God. Sex in some of the rabbinical accounts precedes the sin of eating the forbidden fruit (it's a disputed point, centering on whether Cain and Abel were begotten within or outside the Garden of Eden) but it can in no way be attributed to a commission of evil or an unfortunate act. We have seen Harry Wolfson tease Saint Augustine for the latter's mistranslation of Greek and Latin, taking the word "continens" ("wise") for "continent" (footnote, p. 66), a schoolboy error that led the Church further away from the Jewish point of view. However, it's not fair to lay the blame entirely on the saint. Jesus, after all, set an example for his saints, and Jesus was celibate. The founders of Judaism, Abraham, Isaac, Jacob, Moses, were all lusty, and doing without a wife or girl friend was considered anathema, not an act of holiness.

attitude deplored by modern writers, according to which sex is seen as the man's right and the woman's duty.

Given these sexual prerogatives as hallowed by Jewish practice, one cannot come with any easy clichés to the discussion of the degrading of women in the Orthodox tradition. It was my mother, not my father, with his classical Hebrew background and talmudic training, who was most disturbed by my gentile girl friends and my sister's marriage to a non-Jew. On the day of their wedding, Mother crashed the family car trying to park it. It was with a responsibility of priesthood ancient as Rebecca that she shook at the wheel. As the day of Jacob's marriage approaches, the matriarch Rebecca wants her favorite married into the covenantal family, the children of Abraham's father, Terah, not into the family of the Canaanite daughters of the land, Heth's brood. "And Rebecca said to Isaac, 'I am weary of my life because of the daughters of Heth, such as these, of the daughters of the land, what good shall my life do me?'" Judaism cannot survive merely on Jacob's piety. He has to marry within a clan of women who will safeguard the covenant. Who will accept the rite of circumcision (a rite which I believe is a substitute for human sacrifice)? If you understand women as actors in a priestly drama, as performing ritual purification in the house, the prohibitions about contact during menstruation begin to assume religious overtones. According to Jewish law, a man is also unclean when he has an emission. If you can't accept the conception of the home as a theater for the ceremonies of the temple, the period of separation makes no sense. However, enter the logic of anxiety, which gives all religious ceremony its strength, and far from degrading the woman, ritual purity is an indication of the seriousness of her part in fulfilling the injunction to become a nation of priests.

At a crucial moment in *The Lonely Man of Faith*, Rabbi Soloveitchik, pointing out the difference between the Adam of the first account of creation and the Adam of the second, the "lonely man of faith," talks about the latter's union of equality with Eve. It is not a union of convenience; "the two are better than one" of Ecclesiastes, but a religious union "to cleanse, redeem and hallow their existence."

Under the issue of purity is sex. Jews are all Freudians; or rather, Freud was just another Jewish commentator. For mystics and rationalists alike, holiness on earth is bound up with real physical love between man and woman. It has always seemed to me that the stronger partner in the division of sexual powers is woman. (I can remember my awe window-shopping in the streets of Amsterdam's red-light district. How long could I sit in one of those windows? Guarantee satisfaction? I was overwhelmed with my weakness as a male.) There is an overt recognition of this in the Orthodox house. It's not housekeeping but sex that the Jewish home is all about, and the woman is clearly the superior here. The rabbinical texts ring with warnings to the unwise man who crosses his wife. "Great is the cause of peace," says the Talmud, "for even God deviated from strict truth in the interests of peace. Sarah had said, 'Can I, then, give birth, seeing that my husband is old?' —whereas God, in reporting this to Abraham, asked, 'Why did Sarah laugh,' saying, 'How can I give birth, seeing that I am old?'" Rabbi Feldman quotes this, saying "To preserve domestic peace between Abraham and Sarah, God had 'modified' her statement so as not to offend Abraham." It seems to me that God is afraid that Sarah's laughter will inhibit poor Abraham.

Seeing that there are no bans to women becoming teachers, that there are traditional arguments for them joining the *minyan*, that in ancient and modern Israel they have been leaders of the nation, we come to a question that you must seriously argue and make a choice upon. Is it good to be separate, to have different roles, to come together from different tasks? If your answer is no, the same—we part company. My Judaism is about a marriage, under an Orthodox canopy striped with heresies.

In Jewish mysticism, philosophy, where men have been the major theoreticians, their thoughts drift back to women, inevitably. They place the oath of Jacob, the covenant sworn by his sons between his legs, in the thighs of their wives. What made us Hebrews was our refusal to give the blood sacrifice,* our first born, to the thirsty furrow gods of Canaan or the smoking altar of Baal of the other West Semitic tribes. When Abraham takes Isaac for that sacrifice, the patriarch had to smuggle the boy away from his wife, Sarah, under false pretenses. (Legend adds that Sarah was so angry when she found out, she separated from Abraham.) Judaism is Sarah's religion.† The foreskin is that piece of flesh which substitutes for the horror of human sacrifice. We owe our lives, we male Jews, to Sarah, her indignation. She and her daughters are the guardians of Jewish anxiety, religion, practice, before God. They demand the rite of circumcision as a token that their male children will not be slain. And that God who at the last moment, out of Sarah's sight, trembled to take Isaac's life—has the Almighty not changed under Sarah's influence these many years? We will come to our strange Unknown and Jewish dreams, last chapter.

* This sacrifice persisted among the Jews to the days of Isaiah. Buber records the drama in his chapter on the prophet in *The Prophetic Faith*. Ahaz, King of Judah from 735 to 720 B.C., subjected his eldest to the horror. "But he [Ahaz] walked in the way of the kings of Israel, yea, and made his son to pass through the fire, according to the abominations of the heathen whom the Lord cast out from before the children of Israel" (Second Kings, XVI: 3).

† The Zohar says that Sarah's righteousness redeemed Noah's drunkenness and won eternal life for her descendants, herself, and Abraham. Indeed, Sarah was so pious that the serpent who is responsible for death had no power over her.

Hebrew-American Literature

VVVVVV

"WHY DON'T YOU write a non-Jewish novel?" my first editor begged me, and leapt on the pages of a draft of my third—which was about American politics—in his haste to leave the smell of Blue Hill Avenue, my home thoroughfare, behind. "You're such a nice boy," Dwight MacDonald sputtered at me when I first came to New York, "but what is it with this Jewish stuff?"

A terror of nostalgia, of the immigrant joke posing as a serious novel, bathos of the postghetto generation, dogs the intelligentsia here. And we have to ask, Is there really an American Jewish literature? Have we as Jewish writers struck root in English so that the echoes of its past, as in Melville, Hawthorne, Faulkner, give timbre to our work?

Critics like Irving Howe warn that even their favorites, Bellow, Roth, Malamud, may belong to no more than a minor genre. But I no longer find my kinship in those pages. I think there is another tradition, secret, bastard, like the Moabitess, Ruth, a foreign marriage that so enriches the native stock it begins to bring forth fruit of Eden. Hebrew has influenced

America. William Bradford, the governor of Plymouth, whom we can call our first American stylist, possessed a large Hebrew vocabulary. The Old Testament ribs his prose as it does that of his successor, Cotton Mather. These rhythms reassert themselves in the middle of the nineteenth century, and the Bible, that Jewish Testament, haunts the decks of the *Pequod*, the maples of Walden Pond, the *House of Seven Gables*. These are Hebrew documents, a stern prophetic voice ringing in them. Hebraic survives among some of the most powerful of the gentile writers, William Faulkner, Flannery O'Connor, even to the present day.

So a Jewish writer in the United States is not as friendless as one might suppose. The Bible (without the rabbinical commentaries, granted) has been at the center of the American literary family and one may borrow the long sentences of Faulkner, the gothics of Hawthorne, Thoreau's sober wonder, with a clear sense of inheritance. The King James is the standard text for Jew, Protestant, Catholic alike, and since for almost three hundred years in this country it was the only text against which to ring the slang of the American street and barnyard, the American Jew shares with his gentile brethren a common literary stock.

Rooted in the Bible, one is also rooted in mysticism, in commentary. Those American Jewish writers who deftly produce upon the English models and manners, the picaresque, seem to me hopelessly distant from their birthright in literature both as Jews and Americans, shadowy sentimentalists, as Disraeli was to Victorian England.

So I find myself contradicting friends who quote the standard authors, Bellow, Malamud, Roth (Philip and Henry) as the important Jewish writers in the United States with Abraham Cahan as their spiritual grandfather. I don't seem to descend from this line.

I admit that there is perversity in this attitude. I read Malamud and Roth carefully when I first began to write, and in rejecting them I can be accused of turning against teachers. I am too close to them to say whether I agree with Howe's judgment that they are minor. Irving Howe must stand to judgment too, alas. Yet it is true that they appear old-fashioned to me, in a way that Faulkner, Melville, do not. And weighed in the balance of influence beside the South American writers, Marquez, Borges, Manuel Puig, and my Jewish masters, Isaac Babel, Osip Mandelstam, who worked in Russian, they are light indeed. Against the great inheritance of rabbinic literature, the Babylonian Talmud, the Zohar, that "mystical novel," as Gershom Scholem notes, their pages are thin. You can't cannibalize their work as Unamuno did Cervantes', and then Borges, preying on Unamuno's Cervantes: or Melville on Shakespeare and then Edward Dahlberg on Melville's Shakespeare. A good writer has digested several predecessors (the classic example of this is James Joyce's *Ulysses* where he shows off his appetite, a window into his stomach, in the hospital chapter), and teething, one has to bite into novelists whose prose is juicy, bred out of ancient stock and bloodlines. Language is palpable. "Cut these words and they would bleed!" Emerson exclaims. A writer who has not indulged in necrophilia has no secrets. You cannot create a hidden text, fraught with irony, unless the ghosts of past repasts are upsetting you. All great books are haunted.

How can you be a Jewish writer and ignore rabbinics? One is staggered when Gide declares, "Why, Jewish literature hardly goes back more than twenty years, or at most, fifty." Gide, who retells the fable of the prodigal son—where does he think that story comes from? The whole world of western literature has been inextricably involved in Jewish writing for two thousand years. In some ways, the holy triad, Bellow, Roth, Malamud, and their critics, reflect this willful ignorance. Their Jews are not traditional, nor do they want to know from the traditional, yet still they are the "Jewish" writers. And the absolutely assimilated talents—Edward Dahlberg, Nathaniel West—who are never thought of as "Jewish" because their subjects are not self-consciously so, but to whom language is paramount: I find them more nourishing, *nu*! In their poetry I can feel anger, prophetic horror, aye, Hebrew devils in America.

Philip Roth's work is a textbook not of anger but confusion. The indictment of American culture which Nathaniel West can draw, spare, savage, mocking the Christian ethic of self-sacrifice, ringing the clichés and poetry of Protestant America against a cartoon Betty Boop and a male/female *Miss Lonely-hearts*, oh, the ironies of that book, what a Jesus; this is impossible for Roth. *Goodbye, Columbus, Portnoy's Complaint*, his major works, don't strike against the vulgarity of evil, suicidal love, but against mockups of the same. The heroes, villains, are not crazy but confused, almost sweet. And Roth's voice, his famous laughter, is not "black" or frightening—okay, he jerks off on Mamma, Pa, the aunts, but come on, isn't it cute? There is a shadow of genuine sadness in Roth. I'll come back to it in the final chapter, but I'm not at all sure it's intentional. I admire the real talent in the writing of *When She Was Good*, but this is *total* confusion. A Jew writing the all-American, all-gentile novel. Fine, West did it, but did it absolutely, *totally*, so that it was finally a Jewish tale. In Roth, it's a ventriloquist's act, very clever, but the language is saw-dust, the book pulp for the ages. One feels the sadness of sociology rather than literature.

Sociology of course is what journalists are most comfortable with. So, Bellow bears away the prize. *Augie March* is a mouth-ful of the same, for heroic appetites of this gruel. *The Victim* is a fascinating text, love and hate of Gentile for Jew neatly balanced by reversal, making the goy, the non-Jew, the in-sider, into the outsider. But once that is grasped, there is no more to say, the voice is shallow. Without language to sustain them, the turns of plot, character, begin to look like gimmicks.

But Maishe, the *intelligence*, they tell me. This man Bellow is an intellectual. He scares the critics. I remember Irving Howe lecturing at Stanford on Faulkner, what a dope the latter was. When the southerner stepped into the narrative and tried to explain his own text, he made a mess. No authorial intrusions, please Mr. Billy. William Dean Howells, on the other hand, could come right into the middle of his novel, give you a lecture, explain, so smooth you never even noticed. Who was the great writer? asked Irving. Intelligence is not necessarily a novelist's gift. The nightmares of Bellow are flimsy, easy, the fast reader's delight, but they don't return the next night to haunt you. *Augie March* is good sociology. *Dangling Man*, a nice existential text. Only what shall we say of *Mr. Sammler's Planet*, groaning with ideas, so constipated that it seems as if all of the novelist's library had impacted in his bowels? The black man shows the Viennese doctor his prick. Embarrassing? What to do? Like the old lady in the Jewish joke, shout from the balcony to the darkie doctor of Sammler's soul, "Give 'im an enema."

I haven't mentioned *Herzog*. *Herzog* almost redeems Bellow. Not for any of the obvious reasons, the funny letters, the fashionable breakdown in the Berkshires, but those scenes in the ghetto of Montreal. If only we could have had a book of these tied more closely to the aging, desperate Jewish intellectual whose sweat bath in a tropical New York City sheds the tears of the Diaspora. . . . Sift the political science, psychology, sociology out of *Herzog* and you have a book to chew on.

So that brings us to the last in the triad who ruled over the land of Jewish literature in my infancy. Bernard Malamud. And I am inhibited, since he is the only one I actually have met. We smile at one another at New York literary gatherings. I wave timidly. He threw me out of his study thirteen years ago in the midst of an interview.

Why?

I kept pressing a question, angrily, obnoxiously. "Why do you write about Jews?"

"Because they're rich in culture and . . ."

I look up from my pad. I'm a pipsqueak, a *pishekeh*. Still, something smells bad here.

"I can't accept that."

The stern-faced, middle-aged writer whose exterior is like a vice-president of Gimbel's, the principal of a Reform Jewish synagogue, smart, snappy, stares at me, annoyed.

"Why?"

"You use Judaism as a solution, a talisman. In *The Lady of the Lake*, the floorwalker loses the lady because he won't admit that he's Jewish.* The character in *The Assistant* is compelled to commit circumcision. You're telling me now they do it for the sake of rich cultural associations?"

Malamud's eyes glazed. He stood up from his seat. "Send me these questions in a letter. I have to go."

So, of course, I sent them in a letter to which I received a single one-line reply. "The answers are all in my books."

---

* When I told Malmud I was writing about him, he exclaimed, "I just gave an interview to *Paris Review*. I tell a lot." I rushed out to get a copy and had to laugh, the same business.

INTERVIEWER: Are you a Jewish writer?

MALAMUD: What is the question asking?

INTERVIEWER: One hears various definitions and insistences, for instance, that one is primarily a writer and any subject matter is secondary: or that one is an American Jewish writer. There are qualifications, by Bellow, Roth, others.

MALAMUD: I'm an American, I'm a Jew, and I write for all men. A novelist has to or he's built a cage. I write about Jews, when I write about Jews, because they set my imagination going. I know something about their history, the quality of their experience and belief, and of their literature, though not as much as I would like. Like many writers, I'm influenced by the Bible, both Testaments. I respond in particular to the East European immigrants of my father's and mother's generation: many of them were Jews of the Pale as described by the classic Yiddish writers. And of course I've been deeply moved by the Jews of the concentration camps, and the refugees wandering from nowhere to nowhere. I'm concerned about Israel. Nevertheless Jews like Rabbis Kahane and Korff set my teeth on edge. Sometimes I make characters Jewish because I think I will understand them better as people, not because I am out to prove anything. . . . but the point I'm making is that I was born in America and respond, in American life, to more than Jewish experience. I wrote for those who read.

INTERVIEWER: Thus S. Levin is Jewish and not much is made of it?

MALAMUD: He was a gent who interested me in a place that interested me. He was out to be educated.

Bernie, Bernie. I love you. Only who's kidding who? Malamud's Judaism is tortured, unhappy. In those stories where
his embarrassment is drawn cruel and vivid, it's *Art*. In some
of the work, however, the embarrassment is glossed over with
sentimentality, cleverness. Ecumenical birds circling Frank's
head at the end of *The Assistant*, last-line jokes that trumpet
the finale of the Fidelman stories, too easy pornography and
empty gymnastics of academia in *The New Life*. Even that
marvelous prose style marred in a work like *The Fixer*, hollow,
imageless, repeating his own lines.

Yet the Malamud of *The Magic Barrel*, *Idiot's First* meant
so much to me, clipped, sweet idiom, Yiddish running under
the English. A friend of mine attended his classes that summer
of the interview, and I sat in. Malamud spoke with a passion
about writing that dissolved his polite exterior. Afterwards I
looked at the stories my friend had submitted to him for cor-
rection, and noted Malamud's red pencil, cutting through
flabby prose, drawing the lines taut until they hummed with
his own music.

How painful it is for me to speak any ill of Malamud, or
even Roth and Bellow. Yes, there is anger, but their nakedness
is the nakedness of fathers. One rages but wants to keep it
quiet, in the family.

The persistent danger to the Jew writing in America is to
forget that he is a minority writer, that the will to be Jewish
is to remain a nay-sayer, stubborn, arrogant, more often than
not alone. Especially alone in one's own community. In the
brief flowering of Yiddish literature, the writers were in the
enviable position of being at one with their audience. After all,
they were naming the world in print. Almost like the Israeli
poets, whom businessmen had to come to for words. They and
the masses shared a secret language, Yiddish, a language without
kings, scholars, grammarians, its royalty the writers. In fiction,
Yiddish did not attempt those complexities of narrative that
require an aristocracy of skilled readers. In Hebrew, where
such a genius, Agnon, did appear, his audience was small, and

none of the golden mass adoration that clings to Sholom Aleichem's cloak attended his career.

What happens to the American Jew who forgets that he must set himself apart? He begins to sentimentalize. The curse of Jewish writing in the English-speaking countries is sentimentality, easy tears, empty laughter, facile jokes about Jewish life, caricature that is asking for the same, or worse, that fatal attitude, "I can write the American novel just as well as the Jewish one"; hence such sad counterfeits as Bellow's *Henderson the Rain King*, Roth's *When She Was Good*. (Malamud does a switch on this by writing *The Fixer*, the great Yiddish novel in English, an imitation of a genre that was bad even practiced by its master, I. J. Singer.)

The temptation to commit these horrors is perhaps the fault of another tribe of American Jews, the critics. Here, the very position of outsider, Jew, has sharpened the faculties of the eye, nose, for what is specifically American, with just that touch of cosmopolitan, so one has a sense of European horizon, breadth, tradition.

It also creates a disposition to applaud the efforts of their "lantsmen" in fiction in order to be emancipated alongside them. What better than a Hemingway adventurer who talks like a Jewish drugstore captain (if only Henderson had been from the Bronx, his adventures might have made sense); but this fraud on language goes undetected because it neatly fulfills the dream life of the critics. While impeccable in their understanding of Henry James, William Faulkner, Mark Twain, their own language too often remains flat. They cannot give themselves to a work the way D. H. Lawrence or Dahlberg, Charles Olson, can; cry out in words that bleed. And so a peculiar deafness, almost anger, overwhelms them as they hear the voices of American Jews to whom the tradition is alive, frightening, and whose language is vascular. What—that damned Jewish embarrassment again? Please, it's been done. It's over with. I myself just wrote the last word.

At their best those older Jewish critics bring the psalms of morality to American literature. They make the claims of decency, righteousness, goodness on its authors. But their sobriety infects their judgment. It is sadness, shame, confusion that is their inheritance in Israel. They are insensible to new songs of joy. They can't understand the music. Are they not the last of the tribe? Passed over from the death throes of the European ghetto to America on the streets of Brownsville, Williamsburg, into a brave American world? This must be some family of fakers, halfwits, the retarded. "You are dead! Jewish writing is already over. There are no more miracles."

Hear them. Irving Howe:

Whatever the hopeful future of individual writers, the "school" of American Jewish writing is now in an advanced state of decomposition: how else explain the attention it has lately enjoyed? Or the appearance of a generation of younger Jewish writers who, without authentic experience or memory to draw upon, manufacture fantasies about the lives of their grandfathers. . . . Just as there appear today young Jewish intellectuals who no longer know what it is that as Jews they do not know, so in fiction the fading immigrant world offers a thinner and thinner yield to writers of fiction.

Ted Solotoroff:

I think that the vogue of Jewish fiction, with its heavy component of an outgrown and overvalued past, has begun to be as much of a drag on talent as it is a glut on the market. Perhaps it's time to be up and going again, to carry the search for roots and continuity into the present.

While Irving Howe mercifully withholds names, Ted Solotoroff, in *The Red Hot Vacuum*, attacks Jerome Charyn's *Once Upon a Drohzky* and Seymour Simckes' *Seven Days of Mourning:*

Jewish camp . . . the essential impulse of both . . . an impersonation act.

Though Simckes is said to have come "from a long line of

rabbis," I doubt if he knows much more about Broome Street than I do or that Charyn knows about the recondite culture of the Café Royal and the plays of Jacob Gordis.

The joke is that Simckes does know more about Broome Street than Ted (both gentlemen are friends of mine), and Charyn spoke Yiddish before he learned English.

Certainly there were weaknesses in Charyn's and Simckes' books (and my own first novel, *Thou Worm Jacob*, which received a review in this vein in the *New York Times* from Martin Levin), but the critics don't want to discuss plot, characters. It's the Judaism of the writers which is under attack, their "authenticity."

Solotoroff again:

No Zionist of the old school railing against the pathology of the ghetto would begin to conceive of the grotesque Shimanskys locked up together in this flat and their dementia. In a race with nausea, I shall try to be quick. . . . Folk material has a way of taking its revenge upon the writer who is exploiting it . . . in the case of Simckes it quickly sickens, dies and rots in his hands."

This isn't criticism, it's cursing. Only half-buried in the lines is a curse upon seed, the seed of a generation to come.

Literature has another dimension which eludes the social historian, not only what is said but how it is said. It is language that is the barrier between the old generation and the new.

"Style is the absolute limit of a man's character and bad writing shows a lack of love," Edward Dahlberg proclaims, excoriating Herman Melville for his mechanical moments in prose. But you cannot impress lyrics on ears tuned to mechanics. Even the discovery of the novel *Call It Sleep* (neglected when it was published in the 1930's) by which the Jewish critics believed they redeemed themselves has a streak of tin in its musical echo. Certainly *Call It Sleep* is precocious, talented, a wonderful first novel whose final pages burn with the promise of James Joyce on the trolley tracks. Yet Henry

Roth's book is flawed. The attempt* to give the pure Yiddish speakers a slightly elevated stage English while saddling the children with cartoon lingo, eccentric spelling of the East Side gutter slang, only shortchanges the book. It leaves behind neither real Yiddish rhythms in English (as Malamud, Roth, and Bellow do) nor Hebraic echoes in an American voice. Dahlberg's *Because I Was Flesh*, despite confusions, repetitions, bizarre lapses, rings with seventeenth-century strains, milk and honey sipped through the cups of Elizabethan and Stuart England on "hot horsefly afternoons" by the Missouri.

Kansas City is a vast inland city, and its marvelous river, the Missouri, heats the senses; the maples, alder, elm and cherry trees with which the town abounds are songs of desire, and only the almonds of ancient Palestine can awaken the hungry pores more deeply. It is a wild, concupiscent city and few there are troubled about death until they age or are sick. Only those who know the ocean ponder death as they behold it, whereas those bound closely to the ground are more sensual.

There is an aesthetic of dreams which must elude the critic who comes with preconceived notions of right and wrong, form, content, instead of being borne along by the power and sincerity of the images. The great works of Judaism, the Bible, the Talmud, Zohar, have always towered above their later codifiers, explainers, redactors. Intelligence may be a burden when the reader is being asked to sink into the text and be carried off by it.

Yea, I will judge myself. My generation is stunted. My contemporaries flounder about in novels too big for them or

---

* Jerome Charyn disputes me on this. He says that despite "the forced naturalism" of *Call It Sleep*, the lyricism and ease of the English in which the Yiddish-speaking mother and aunt talk between themselves (in what we presume to be a translation of their native languages) creates a heartbreaking sadness when contrasted with their clumsy attempts to speak English. And of course it is the very confusion of the child in his efforts to understand the tongues around him that leads to the near tragedy and poetry of the book.

cannot suit the language to the story. American Jewish literature is still mostly promise. The roots are there, although not
in the conventional talents, but the trunks have yet to rise.

Sentimentality is the dread curse of the Jewish writers. So
many tears have been shed that it is too easy to invoke their
memory. The critics are frightened. Are these real tears? they
want to know. The holocaust is taboo unless you have the
stamp of Buchenwald on your arm. Don't you dare! Were you
there?

But the tears of the holocaust do belong to me, as absence,
terrible dry tears for hundreds of cousins I am never to know.
We have shed these tears, our older brothers cry, enough!

Only it is precisely those tears that I find sentimental, in-
adequate. Of such horror only jokesters like Jakov Lind in
Soul of Wood can make sense. It is the serious works like
André Schwarz-Bart's *The Last of the Just* that I find weepy,
too easy. The imagery is simply not adequate. I have the same
problem with Elie Wiesel when he moves into fiction. The
fable is not equal to the experience. On the contrary, when he
speaks as a journalist, as in all the firsthand accounts of the
death camps, fiction begins to overwhelm the lines and we
are truly reading a parable we dare not comprehend. I sympathize with the severity of the older Jewish critics, their desire
to be guardians of the holocaust, the memory of the generation
before it: their fear that it will be banalized by easy tears, cheap
laughter, but I don't think they realize that their very close-
ness to the thunderclap which obliterated Eastern European
Judaism has left them shell-shocked. For some the holocaust
is the end of Diaspora Jewish culture. Others who go on to
mourn the slow death of Yiddish, its ethos and community in
America, have no taste for the green shoots from the ashes.
Acid tears they shed.

Sentimentality?

Irving Howe is willing to allow the sentimental to Eastern
European storytellers as a condition of their harried environment. In his introduction to *A Treasury of Yiddish Stories* he

excuses sentimentality in Yiddish fiction, "emotion in excess of the occasion." But it's not emotion in excess of the occasion but a dream in excess of the occasion, object, situation, that is the heartbeat or bugaboo of much of Yiddish fiction and which ties it to the American Jewish world, the dream that despite the poverty, bad behavior, ignorance, the Messiah is in the family, *nu*, maybe, even . . . I, Thou?

At the root of the Jewish writer's difficulties, whether he works in German, Yiddish, English, French, Russian, Hebrew, is Judaism. Even a master like Isaac Bashevis Singer becomes clumsy when he tries to extend his story lyrics to the epic rhythms of the novel. Under the strain of the longer form, the concealed sentimentality begins to sound. Why shouldn't the peasant woman in *The Slave* stay a good Gentile or the protagonist of *Enemies* be happy with his Polish wife, Yadwiga? Why not have Frank in *The Assistant* remain a pious non-Jew?

That marriage outside Judaism matters and that this is irrational is the problem that these writers have evaded. Their longer texts are mesmerized by that central terror of the male Jew, the loss of his secret marriage to the Shekhinah, the female presence of God, the Jewish Bride, but the writers' own problems with Judaism banalize it. I'll come to a fuller discussion of this in my final chapter because it's bound up with Messianics, but I can't help note that the less traditional writers, Philip Roth, Saul Bellow, by facing the question squarely, are able in *Portnoy's Complaint* and *Herzog* respectively to plot their novels to an honest and satisfactory end. *The Slave, Enemies, The Assistant*, smack to me in their final chapters of shmaltz, sugary fat; "I cried at the end of *The Assistant*," I told Malamud, walking across the Harvard Yard after his class, "but I resented my tears."

"I hope you get some laughs from my next one," he snapped.

Symbolism and religion, as Dante and his critics understood, are one and the same. Poetry is the first language of theology. You cannot ask your reader to believe if your own beliefs are not deep in the text. If you cannot believe, that must be the strain of your psalm. The language of the generation before me is too often cute, counterfeit, like Salinger's pious falsehoods in *Frannie and Zooey*, pretending to perform for the fat lady in the audience.

What condescension! It is you who are the fat lady, *vous hypocrite lecteur, mon semblable, mon frère*, it is my Judaism, my sin, I who must be circumcised. "Woe is me," the Jewish poet sings, "I am a man of unclean lips." Until that cry goes up, we must endure very thin work from the formal "Jewish writers." For it is a put-on, an act, their subconscious, the nightmare world which only comes up in real dreams will not surface. Better to search among the totally assimilated, Kafka, West, Dahlberg, or as the scribes of old did, admit a pious Gentile's scroll, Job, to the canon.

The Jewish Traveler

VVVVVV

It was said of Rabbi Eleazar ben Dordia that he did not leave out any harlot in the world without coming to her. Once, on hearing that there was a certain harlot in one of the towns by the sea who accepted a purse of denarii for her hire, he took a purse of denarii and crossed seven rivers for her sake.

As he was with her, she broke wind and said, "As this broken wind will not return to its place, so will Eleazar ben Dordia never be received in repentance."

He thereupon went, sat between two hills and exclaimed. "O ye hills and mountains, plead ye for mercy for me!"

"How shall we pray for ye?" they replied. "We stand in need of it ourselves, for it is said, *For the mountains shall depart and the hills be moved.*"*

So he exclaimed, "Heaven and earth plead ye for mercy for me!"

They too replied, "How shall we pray for thee? We stand in need of it ourselves, for it is said, *For the heavens shall vanish away like smoke, and the earth shall wax old like a garment.*"†

He then exclaimed, "Sun and moon, plead ye for mercy for me!"

* Is., 10
† Ibid. LI, 6

228

But they also replied: "How shall we pray for thee? We stand in need of it ourselves, for it is said, *Then the moon shall be confounded and the sun ashamed.*"*

He exclaimed, "Ye stars and constellations, plead ye for mercy for me!"

Said they, "How shall we pray for thee? We stand in need of it ourselves, for it is said, *And all the hosts of heaven shall moulder away.*"†

Said he, the matter then depends upon me alone! Having placed his head between his knees, he wept aloud until his soul departed. Then a *bath kol* [heavenly voice] was heard proclaiming, "Rabbi Eleazar ben Dordia is destined for the life of the world to come." . . .

Rabbi [on hearing of it] wept, and said: "One may acquire eternal life after many years, another in one hour." Rabbi also said: "Repentants are not alone accepted, they are even called Rabbi!"‡

I TRAVEL NOT BECAUSE I want to but because the dreams are too awful, staling whatever place I'm in with promises of something else and slowly sickening the comfort of my circumstances until I'm forced to set out if only to set the fantasies to rest. I am missing it, I know, my *life*. There is a girl strolling now down Saint Germain, O'Connell Street, King George in Jerusalem, who'll change my life; a view, a taste, a smell that will turn all to good, set off the dazzling colors, make me one with my adventures. The tenor of my voyages is despair, more active and aware than usual. Bitter melancholy in strange streets by day, the taste of sweeter fantasies at night, sad knowledge at the trip's end that reality is poorer than imagination, and only later, months, years, recalling all; these moments were my most intense. The dreams after all had not faulted me, for I trod Paris, London, Bogotá, Tel Aviv, with such hunger that hallucination became actual—experience had to come, did,

* Ibid. XXIV, 23
† Ibid. XXXIV, 4
‡ Babylonian Talmud, Abodah Zarah, 17a.

was magic, even if the banal expectation of it lasting hour to hour, day to day, poisoned my pleasure in those moments.

Drivel? The traveler outside appointments, tour groups, moving from one unfamiliar language to another, talks to himself. And talking finds a peculiar pleasure in himself, the thief, stealing against time. At eleven years old, it was literal, I was thrown out of the White House for trying to cut off the tassle of a blue velvet drape. Thirty still found me tugging at doorknobs at Bloom's house on Eccles Street, but the apocryphal thing, solid brass, would not break off.

The worst was Amsterdam, years ago, the dreams real in every window of the red light district, those tiny eighteenth-century alleys where the going narrowed to a shoulder's width, elbowing among the crowds of somber men, sailors, laborers, in dark suits, eyeing the windows where all the girls of adolescent wet sheets, all the untouchable creatures who were always too old, sophisticated, sharp-tongued, "grown-up"-looking like my Long Island cousins or the cool Nordic blonds of cigarette ads, the teenage motorcycle queens of Dorchester, even a few of the lost, damned souls always beyond reach, the crazy dropouts of Radcliffe and Wellesley, their eyes brushing you from these windows, reaching out. I sickened at the possibilities, exhausted by enthusiasm that rose and fell as one imagined possession of toy after toy, images, images, the sin and joy of idolatry so palpable one could shatter the glass. I left the alleys reeling, a cloying horror—I could have one, maybe two, but only in my imagination possess them all.

One night in Barcelona, I saw the goddess of love, Aphrodite, black hair, red lipstick sticky on her lips, "love" cut in crude hand-etched letters in her leather belt, painted out in pinks and greens, full blown and beautiful, staring into a shop window. I wheeled on the Ramblas, looked sideways in the doorway, buried myself in the shirts and velvet suits of the case next door to breathe, and looking up saw her flanks disappear into the crowd to the right or left; dazed, I could not tell

which, but in a moment, recovering, I ran one way, then the
other—in vain, vanished, clear gone.

Beside me at the pool in Palma de Mallorca out of its cup
the nipple of a blonde Swedish princess floats.

Do such secular thoughts befit the Jewish traveler? Twisted
and tormented by my *yetzer*, my evil urge, the son of Wolf
(my father's Hebrew name) wanders the streets torn between
sex and sanctity. Is eroticism a curse or a blessing?

The morning after my trip through the rose-colored zone of
Amsterdam, I am standing in the Rijksmuseum, in front of
Rembrandt's *The Jewish Bride*, weeping with unexpended
seed. I enter the painting.

In the red of the man's nose, the dark stubble shadow of his
chin, the deep crease of his cheek; and in the tongue and
puckered-in cheek of his wife (as if she were tasting something), his hand on her breast, her jeweled hands over her
private parts in the rich red folds of her dress, almost an
explosion of that flesh; and in the chunks of golden paint
erupting in the sleeve of the man's arm leading to the bound-
in bosom of his wife, we can eat of the fruit of the wedding
night. Now I understand the pout of the bride. It is heat, her
fingers over the cleft far below in the folds of her girdle as if
to rip the veil of mystery away, his sad but sensual look of
patience, very Jewish. I have seen this couple in a pawnshop
in old Monterey, California.

Motorcycle helmet in hand, I was rifling through some Army
surplus when the wife, who ran the shop, caught my eye,
smiled. I smiled back. "Are you Jewish?" she asked.

I nodded. Tribal recognition. They wanted to know if I
had a place to stay the night, eat supper, twenty years past
their bridal night, but still some hidden wisdom in their amused
expressions.

My Jewishness clings to me, speaks to me, cries out upon
me. In Tangier, dazed by the press of tourists bent upon
illicit sex, of the little boys of the street clawing over me,

offering themselves, I fled to the synagogues. At the hotel when I'm asked by the Arab waiter what I am, it's not "American" that comes to my lips, but "Jewish."

"The owner here is Jewish," he replies.

Two old people sweep into the dining room, take me into their back parlor, direct me to the Rue des Synagogues where among tarnished silver hangings I find the children of Don Quixote who seat me at a service that is more a family meeting; eleven "men" ranging from thirteen to ninety and I perch on a bench like the last of the lost tribes coming home, eyed with appreciative twinkles. Why am I here, stumbling through incomprehensible Sephardic Hebrew? Or later, at the synagogue in Fez where the *shammus* makes me his special charge, a balding young man who takes me around town, offers me half of his shabby bed, scolds me for eating *traife* so that I have to show up at the kosher restaurant? In the bustle of dishes, shouting, handshakes, it's not so different from the old New Yorker Cafeteria on Blue Hill Avenue, but the women, ah, they are the originals from which the Dorchester girls were struck. Saucy, imperious, sparkling with jewelry, these are not Arab ladies. Is She here?

Who?

Whether it is Bogotá, Toledo, Amsterdam, Copenhagen, I seek out synagogues, the long table of grumbling elders, as if they were wizards, concealing in the dusty tiles, the faded hangings of the ark, tarnished silver boxes, the secret door to Paradise. Once, in Marrakesh, it almost came true; a young girl, her breasts outlined under a white jersey, about fourteen, shows me her grandfather's synagogue, a large granite room just beyond the family kitchen. She speaks a bit of English, laughs, and smiles, dancing on her toes as I draw her out, and I dream that night in my hotel, still feverish from the heat, of carrying her off to America.

Is it Naamah, that sister of Tubal Cain, whose name means "pleasantness," and who in Rabbi Joseph Soloveitchik's words is "the incarnation of unhallowed and unsublimated beauty"?

Am I seeking "overpowering beauty," which in the Agada is synonymous with the queen of the demons, Naamah, that seductress "who lieth in wait at every corner" in the warning of Proverbs, against whom the wisest of men is helpless?

No, as I lean against the wall of the Sephardic synagogue in Bogotà, wondering if the *shammus* who is talking to me has a daughter, or as I search with dizzy eyes in the byways of the camel market for the Jewish Berbers I was told still inhabit the sands of the Sahara, looking among the shy black faces strung with silver coins, half-hidden behind veils, for sisters, it is a more mysterious queen I have come for.

Rembrandt has painted his wife's features into the face of *The Jewish Bride.* Living among Jews, he understood the secret which is often unspoken, intangible gnosis among us. "As a little bit of musk fills an entire house, so the least influence of Judaism overflows all of one's life."

It is the perfume of the Bride, not an abstract bride, like Sophia, wisdom, nor an institutional bride, like the Church or Temple or the pin-up bride of secular beauty, no matter how alluring her artificial scents. That last one is a terrible temptation to the Jew, male and female, for Judaism is an erotic religion. It is a religion of action, and more than once the books have fallen from the scholar's lap as he seeks its consummation in the arms of beauty.

The sweetness of that musk is melancholy. There are tears distilled in it. Heady, erotic, yet sad, Rachel weeping for her children in the eyes of the bride. But if you reach through the musk, you will hear the laughter. It is that final sweetness which is denied the Unbeliever who will not come fully into the arms of bride or groom.

"Jewish piety and Jewish wit dwell in the same organ, namely the Jewish heart: there is no road thither from alien minds and hearts," said Franz Rosenzsweig.

Frustrated by their inability to come to an earthly paradise, Messiah, a messianic age, the imagination of the Spanish Jews, their French and Italian brethren too take refuge in gnostics, secret knowledge, Kabbala. The most striking plan of these fictional gardens unrolls in the Zohar, "a mystical novel." In the chapters of this vast geography of Jewish dreams and nightmares, a leap of the Hebrew imagination took place. The Messiah is portrayed as a woman, the Shekinah, the brooding face of God upon earth, a female presence which will come to every male Jew who seeks Him. You come to Him through Her.* Anyone familiar with Dante's *Divine Comedy* (composed within the same half-century) will recognize a similar intuition in the portrait of Beatrice, who leads the Catholic poet upwards into Paradise. Only because Judaism is always concerned about its monotheism, the Shekinah is a very different female from the personalized Beatrice, a real sweetheart (an adolescent love of Dante's) metamorphosed into a divine one. The Shekinah is not, and never was, a person. It is an aspect of God, the Holy One, Blessed Be He, which in the infinite recessions of light that the Zohar posits as the process of creation can only be called beyond sex, male or female, *Ayn Sof*, Without Limit.

The Divine Comedy is known as one of the major influences on western literature. The Zohar had an equally powerful hold on many of the codifiers of Jewish law, although it is largely unread outside the world of Judaism. The contrast between Dante's Beatrice and the Shekinah of Moses de Leon (according to Scholem, the secret author of the Zohar) is revealing. Beatrice scolds Dante for having forgotten her, for abandoning her spiritual beauty and pursuing earthly women. The Zohar on the other hand warns the Jew that She, the Shekinah, cannot be encountered in purely spiritual realms. Where is the Shekinah to be found? The answer might give the uninitiated a start.

* The Philonic God and the God of the Prophets comes as a male presence but requires that the Jew wed Him by becoming female. The language of male, female, and religious ecstasy turns over and over in Jewish history.

There is a twofold reason for cohabitation. First, this pleasure is religious, one that gives joy to the Shekinah, and second, an instrument of peace. As it is written, "And thou shalt know that thy tent is in peace, and thou shalt visit thy habitation and not sin" (Job, 5:24). You ask, is it a sin if he does not visit his wife? Yes! For he thereby takes away from the honor of the celestial partner who was joined to him because of his wife. Second, if his wife should conceive, the celestial partner bestows upon the child a holy soul, for this covenant is called the covenant of the Holy One, Blessed Be He.

Therefore a man should be as zealous to enjoy this pleasure as to procure the pleasure of the Sabbath, at which time the union of the sages with their wives is consummated. Thus, "Thou shalt know that thy tent is in peace," since the Shekinah comes with you and abides in your house and therefore "Thou shalt visit thy house and not sin," by performing with pleasure the religious duty of conjugal intercourse in the presence of the Shekinah.

Thus the students of the Torah, who separate from their wives six days a week in order to study, are accompanied by a heavenly partner so that they remain "male and female." When the Sabbath arrives, it is incumbent upon them to give pleasure to their wives for the sake of the celestial partner's honor and to perform their Master's will.*

On the holiest night of the week, the Shekinah is at home between one's wife's thighs. Imagine Dante's wife listening in on Beatrice's nasty words. (According to history Dante and his actual bride were separated for most of their lives.) Such hokey-pokey couldn't go on in Jewish homes. The spiritual bride was firmly anchored to the earthly one.

Of course this introduces a certain strain into Jewish marital relations. The Hebrew bride assumed for her mate an almost impossible role. She became his Messiah, Savior, a door into a spiritual paradise. This theme is latent, buried in the Judaism

* I have mingled two translations here, the standard text of the Soncino Zohar, Vol. 1, pp. 158–159, and an alternative in Gershom G. Scholem's *Zohar, the Book of Splendor, Basic Readings from the Kaballah* (New York: Schocken Books), pp. 35 and 36.

of later centuries, but it explains some of the extremities of sexual decorousness ritualized in the rules of mystical Orthodoxy. It may account for the frightening expectations of marriage even among secularized Jews who are serious. In this light, one can understand Kafka crying,

Marrying, founding a family, accepting all the children that come, supporting them in this insecure world and perhaps even guiding them a little, is, I am convinced, the utmost a human being can succeed in doing at all. That so many seem to succeed in this is no evidence to the contrary; first of all, there are not many who do succeed, and secondly, these not-many usually don't "do" it, it merely "happens" to them: although this is not that Utmost it is still very great and very honorable (particularly since "doing" and "happening" cannot be kept clearly distinct). And finally, it is not a matter of this Utmost at all, anyway, but only of some distant but decent approximation: it is, after all, not necessary to fly right into the middle of the sun, but it is necessary to crawl to a clean little spot on earth where the sun sometimes shines and one can warm oneself a little.

The capitalization of "Utmost," the concealed image of Daedalus' son, Icarus, who flies too close to the sun in his overweening imitation of the gods, the appearance in the last breath of the telltale caterpillar of the *Metamorphosis* all betray the presence of more than secular anxieties. So at the end of Philip Roth's *Portnoy's Complaint*, the tragedy that taints its comedy is the search for a wife. For "Shicksa America," the dream of the blonde ice-skating girl in the frozen blue American sky, her eyes glinting off the ice, that image which blinded us fig-eyed Semites, making us sick with nostalgia for the childhood of *Life, The Bobbsey Twins*, has been shattered, forever. That America has been abandoned and the goddess whose eyes were empty lies in a heap in the courtyard. Who will we worship? One recalls in Portnoy's frantic last-moment flailings in the land of Israel, his marriage proposals, impotence, the rabbinic dictum, "A man without children is only an image, a *golem*." A *tsellum*—shadow. Worse of course is the man without a bride. There is a serious question of whether he will merit the Hereafter. And what is he losing now? The presence of the Shekinah? The light of God upon his face. When Roth recalls, in a loving parody of Hemingway, the baseball games among the men in his childhood, it is the present he is grieving, the peace of marriage blessings. It is not any wife who can bring them to him, however. He has gotten mixed up with mysteries, although neither hero nor author realize it. So it is in Malamud's *Lady of the Lake*, this early story in which the language of Sir Walter Scott and Arthurian romance brilliantly cloak the spiritual wife of the assimilated New York floorwalker. The Shekinah appears in gentile disguise asking the Jew to be true to himself, to find his poetry therein. Using the horror of the death camps to give a realistic pathos to the Bride of Israel, the Lady glimmers and disappears before the inability of the Jew to claim his own identity, sad and shabby though it may seem to eyes of the outsider and to his assimilated self. Even in the text of Nathaniel West, who is never overtly involved in a Jewish context, one may detect the tug of that strange woman. The vacuous, comfortable girl friend, healthy, sweet, but lacking that touch of divinity that can dower peace on Miss Lonelyhearts: Betty, nicknamed in mockery "Betty the Buddha," fulfills his erotic notions but remains a spiritual cartoon.

Perhaps this explains the Jewish obsession with the Mother who is the foretaste of the Bride. Edward Dahlberg raises the cry: "In almost a hundred years of American literature we do not have one feeding, breeding, sexual male, not one suffering, bed-pining Manon Lescaut or a Shulamite. There are no ripe women here." It is the Jewish spirit bursting like new wine in his throat. Not Faulkner, Hawthorne, Melville, Thoreau, but something unique, compulsive, mystical to the Jew, and when we are only "whacking off" to rhythms that were holy and conscious in our ancestors, it is sour comedy. It is our curse, our blessing, to be born into a nation of priests, prophets, madmen. Dahlberg, that Jewish orphan cries:

Had Jesus married the illuminated prostitute, Magdalene, he would have forsaken the Acts, the overthrowing of the tables of the pigeon and money-vendors, and the Bleeding Cross and given man as inheritance an imperishable generation of gentle little children or Galilean verse.

But there is no Magdalene, not even a Mary or Martha, in the Puritan Testament, woman does not exist in these literary master-pieces, in *Moby Dick* or in *Walden.* . . . Christ as healing "feminine" image has always taken the place of the Virgin Mary.

Sir Philip Sidney sings, "Leave me, O Love, which reachest but to dust; / And thou, my mind, aspire to higher things."

No, no.

We Jews will have our cake and eat a bit of it too. We are not, as Soloveitchik says, "afraid of contradictions." For us men, woman, a real woman, is the Messiah, the foretaste.

And in this, that madcap, Miguel de Unamuno, agrees with me and for a solitary moment has intoned a Hebrew psalm, "The longing for immortality is rooted in the love of a woman, for it is there that the instinct for self-perpetuation triumphs over the instinct for mere self-preservation, substance thus triumphing over appearance."

Jacob Frank, false Messiah, anarchist, madman, and poet of Judaism, dreamed that the third and final Messiah would come, no longer as an aspect of God, a feminine Presence, but as a woman, flesh, blood, and spirit.

Who knows? Meanwhile.

In my thirty-sixth year now, naïve, unhappy. ("Who is happy?" asked Soloveitchik at a recent lecture. "I wasn't happy when I was in my twenties. I wasn't happy when I was fifty. Now in my seventies, I'm not happy. Let no one tell you he leads a successful life. He is either an idiot or a liar. Because he [man] is out to find the Almighty and he's frustrated.") What a relief to know that unhappiness is a metaphysical truth! So, ladies and gentlemen, no answers, not from me, not in my thirty-sixth year. No secrets of Jewish success.

Eroticism and death are bound up, though. I know that.

Because the doors to the kingdom of death have swung open for moments when I understood how alone I was after partners I lived with had broken off and once, twice, in the arms of a woman I loved, I also floated away, into oblivion.

Visionary animals, we recognize each other by our dreams. When the chimpanzee begins, not to count, but to speak to us of his nightmares, then we will embrace him as a fellow soul. And our human dream is a vision of judgment. It will matter, what we did. We are, were, unique. The circular universe of the philosopher, that horror which Borges in this century has detailed, a constant, eternal repetition, or the absolute chaos of Epicurus, these are the ancient alternatives to judgment. They deny our uniqueness and in doing that, perhaps, they deny the very faculty which allows us to entertain them. We Jews want to be unique, not only as individuals but as a nation. Harry Wolfson points out in *Religious Philosophy* that Jesus shed the same tears on Golgotha as Rabbi Johanan did fifty years later in a village thirty miles away.

When Rabban Johanan, the son of Zakka, fell ill and was about to die, his disciples came to visit him. Upon seeing them, he began to weep. His disciples said to him: "Light of Israel, right pillar, mighty hammer, wherefore weepest thou?" In his answer he explained that he wept because his soul, which would survive his body, would have to face the inscrutable judgment of the supreme King of Kings, the Holy One, Blessed Be He.

This . . . is exactly the reason why Jesus awaited death amazedly, sorrowfully, and "with strong crying and tears." It is because he believed his soul was immortal and would have to face the inscrutable judgment of the Lord his God, the Most High: for even though, as we are told, "In him is no sin," certainly there was not in him the sin of being righteous in his own eyes.

It is not a far-fetched old Hebrew myth—the judgment. It is the constant question of each man and woman. Does it have meaning, my life, any life? Thousands of years have brought us no closer to an answer. I chose the judgment and choosing it, why not shed tears of joy, erotic tears?

There has to be a reason for our sexual craziness, if reason, if judgment, inheres in this universe. Hosea saw the likeness of Israel in an unfaithful wife. Isaiah raged at Jerusalem whoring herself to the nations. They cursed, then blessed the harlot of their desire, holding her dear at last. The rabbis puzzled over how to bring real man, not ideal man and woman, together in lasting union, and rather than trying to reason the itch away, they reasoned with it. My forefathers, the sages, in the Talmud married the prostitute Rahab to the judge Joshua, drew from this marriage a line of kings, and prophets. King David descended out of the loins of Moab, an incestuous union between father and daughter. This is the messianic line. Messianism is not a self-righteous vision. Let us not cluck over mixed marriages and impossible rules of *kashruth*. Let us instead get to know the tradition and admit our own evil, cry over it, make it public—judge it. Rabbi Simeon ben Elezar said:

I shall speak to you in a parable—to what can we compare the evil urge? To iron that one has put into the glowing fire: while it is in the glowing fire, one can make utensils from it, anything you like.

And just so it is with the evil urge: there is no way to shape it aright, save through the words of the Torah, which is like fire.

So, the Jewish traveler, searching not for Holy Grail, Virgin, Mother, but, with his erotic madness, his glowing "utensil," for a wife, bride, as she for him, the open doors of judgment, the door, "Come in, come in," the gates of our vision swing open.

Who shall come in?

"He that hath clean hands and a pure heart."

Into a mystical Universe.